Praise for the Book

"McCleneghan and Moses have composed a beautiful book of stories and reflections on motherhood and ministry. From the blissful days of becoming pregnant to the harrowing nights of sleeplessness, these two gifted pastors invite us into a view of parenting through the lens of faith. No other parenting book will explore Paul Tillich's notion of God as the 'ground of being' in a chapter about structuring baby's bedtime, and certainly not with so much humility, honesty, and humor. McCleneghan and Moses have written a jewel of a book to be shared with new parents everywhere."
—Verity Jones, executive director, Center for Pastoral Excellence at Christian Theological Seminary

"*Hopes and Fear*s injects some much-needed spiritual wisdom into the sometimes wild, always messy world of baby boot camp—and beyond. Amid the diapers, day care, and discipline, McCleneghan and Moses assure us that God is present in surprising ways. The result is a book that both comforts and challenges. *Hopes and Fear*s is warmly accessible even as it takes us to remarkable new places."
—MaryAnn McKibben Dana, author of *Sabbath in the Suburbs: A Family's Experiment with Holy Time*

"This is a book you can pick up when you are sleep–deprived and emerge laughing with recognition and buoyed by grace. The authors are honest and generous in sharing their parental struggles,

joys, hopes, and fears. They welcome us into their sticky-floor kitchens and surprise us with moving reflections on faith."
—Heidi Neumark, pastor and author of *Breathing Space: A Spiritual Journey in the South Bronx*

"When looking at the broad landscape of Christianity, we recognize that we stand in an amazing time. Women, who juggle the worries of pregnancy, the thrill of babies, and the exhaustion of breastfeeding, also proclaim the Word of God, pour the waters of baptism, and break the bread of life. In *Hopes and Fears,* Bromleigh McCleneghan and Lee Hull Moses acknowledge this revolutionary moment through showing us how ordinary it is. By cultivating the rich ground of motherhood and ministry they present us with an abundance of messy, beautiful, and human theology."
—Carol Howard Merritt, author of *Tribal Church* and *Reframing Hope*

"Moses and McCleneghan have crafted a theology of family that is smart, faithful, and wonderfully expansive. There's a place for the how-to guides that cover the logistics of parenting. But there's also a place for *Hopes and Fears*, which reflects on the soul of parenting: the top of the bedside stack."
—Katherine Willis Pershey, author of *Any Day a Beautiful Change*

HOPES
AND
FEARS

HOPES
AND
FEARS

~

Everyday Theology for New Parents and Other Tired, Anxious People

Bromleigh McCleneghan and Lee Hull Moses

The Alban Institute
Herndon, Virginia

The Alban Institute
2121 Cooperative Way, Suite 100
Herndon, VA 20171

All Scripture quotations are from the New Revised Standard Version of the Bible, copyright © 1989, Division of Christian Education of the National Council of the Churches of Christ in the United States of America, and are used by permission.

Library of Congress Cataloging-in-Publication Data

McCleneghan, Bromleigh.
  Hopes and fears : everyday theology for new parents and other tired, anxious people / Bromleigh McCleneghan and Lee Hull Moses.
    p. cm.
  Includes bibliographical references.
  ISBN 978-1-56699-431-6
  1. Parents--Religious life. 2. Parenting--Religious aspects--Christianity. 3. Child rearing--Religious aspects--Christianity. I. Moses, Lee Hull. II. Title.
  BV4529.M375 2012
  248.8'45--dc23
                        2012029491

12   13   14   15   16   VP   5   4   3   2   1

To Fiona and Harper, who started it all,
and to Calliope and Jonathan, who came along
at just the right time.

Contents

Foreword

KINCAID, THE YOUNG NARRATOR IN *THE BROTHERS K*, DIDN'T REALIZE the power of his dad's table grace until Papa Chance vacated the house to spend dinnertime in his homemade baseball shed perfecting his pitching. His "three-and-a half-second masterpiece"—"*Giveus gratefulheartsourFatherandmakeusevermindfuloftheneeedsofothersthrough-ChristourLordAmen*"—was the "indispensible block," the "rustic but reliable footbridge" that led the family over a crevasse of conflict into a shared meal.[1] Learned from his own father (and *The Book of Common Prayer*) and uttered in lightning speed with the demeanor of a bashful auctioneer more than supplicant, it left no opening for clowning, fidgeting, genuflecting, or apostatizing, appeasing both the atheistic belligerence of an older brother and the pushy piety of Mama Chance. And it pretty much covered the basics of faithful living.

Hopes and Fears is chock full of such building blocks and foot-bridges. In beautifully candid prose, Bromleigh McCleneghan and Lee Hull Moses depict the rich but mundane moments that hold families together—or have the power to tear them apart. Indeed, honesty about the tensions and hardships, the personal foibles and gaffes is one of the most appealing qualities of this book. The deep friendship between Bromleigh and Lee—I use their given names here because they speak with us on such a first name basis—is key to making this book work. They have been open with each other (even if Bromleigh initially hid her first pregnancy for all sorts of understandable reasons) and they share this intimacy with readers. You feel as if you are there in the bed or kitchen or car with children crying, vomiting, crowding you out, *and of course*, cuddling, smiling, and spouting wisdoms to break your heart.

Bromleigh and Lee take turns writing chapters, first one, then the other, but they stand united in grappling with the dilemmas that face partners whose love leads to the conception of children. Their lives have been so closely intertwined since the pursuit of ministerial education together that their first children were born within a week of one another. By now, they live miles apart and only see each other on visits scheduled around busy lives as married couples with jobs. But one feels their connection and conversation as they try to answer fundamental questions about the abundant life in Christ, now framed, as the book itself, by the birth of four children between them.

Writing in a blogging style of personal memoir, Bromleigh and Lee name challenges with which most middle-class parents will immediately identify. Books on how to parent abound for just this educated elite and some of this burgeoning literature makes its way into their footnotes. Yet few authors recognize as Bromleigh and Lee do how the plethora of middle-class resources—home pregnancy tests, prenatal care, ultrasound, breast pumps, baby books, parenting best-sellers, kid birthday extravaganzas—offer choices unheard of among the world's less advantaged and yet also trouble and distort their lives. They question the privileges that narrow their compassion and the cultural lies that lead parents to seek perfection, encourage competition over cooperation, and buy the Disney Princess line.

This book also stands out for its pastoral and theological wisdom. Although the focus is on the home and not the parish, Bromleigh and Lee are both congregational ministers. "Being a pastor is a wonderful calling, for a lot of reasons," Bromleigh remarks early on. "One of those reasons is…a growing familiarity with Scripture and the hymns of the church over the years of doing this work, a familiarity that increasingly allows me to engage with the ancient stories of faith and to hear echoes of my own story within them." This engagement echoes throughout the book. They want readers to know that parenting is profoundly theological and faith-laden. In a later chapter, Lee tells us she began to memorize hymns and sing them as lullabies when walking a fussy baby. This itself is just one example of helpful practices this book inspires. Memorize hymns, sing them as lullabies. Bromleigh and Lee show how theology happens in just this way, in our very midst as we name our children, work out who washes diapers, deal with anger, and move over to make room for new family members. Granted, Christianity and other religions are ambiguous. They cause real strife and harm. But they also foster gratitude and grace, two of the most essential ingredients for healthy family life that percolate throughout this book. With intellectual savvy and a progressive approach, Bromleigh and Lee engage scripture and theology anew, showing how the Psalms or creation stories or mandates about women's roles might be reinterpreted to empower parents and children and uphold shared love and domestic justice.

Kincaid "never thought about" his dad's dinner grace. He "had scarcely listened to it, really" until the prayer was gone and all hell broke loose. Sometimes we don't notice the ordinary practices that shape family life. But how we structure our coming in and going out, our rising up and falling asleep, our bedrooms and dinner tables and laundry rooms matters. In such mundane details and decisions, our basic convictions lie. Small practices—a prayer before eating, a goodnight ritual, a kiss at the door—form us even more than we dare imagine. So an "anemic little grace" becomes a linchpin of family faith. Noticed or not, seemingly anemic words and deeds add grace to our lives.

With a grace all their own, Bromleigh and Lee help us stand up and take notice of God's activity in our midst. From the very beginning of a love relationship to the scary potential of birthing a child to the messy diaper changing and crowded noisy joy of a shared bedroom, they cover the basics of faithful Christian living: grateful hearts for all our blessings and compassion for the needs of others, children and adults alike. Renewed gratitude and a return to compassion for those with whom we live most closely—these two practices alone seem more than sufficient for a faithful family life.

Bonnie J. Miller-McLemore
Author of *In the Midst of Chaos: Care of Children as a Spiritual Practice* and *Also a Mother: Work and Family as Theological Dilemma*

Acknowledgments

FOUR CONGREGATIONS PLAYED A SIGNIFICANT ROLE IN THE DEVELOP-
ment of this book, though they often fade to the background of
these pages. To the people of Riverside United Methodist Church,
Baker Memorial United Methodist Church, First Christian Church
(Disciples of Christ) of Falls Church, and First Christian Church
(Disciples of Christ) of Greensboro, thank you for inspiring us and
being kind with shared early drafts, for giving us time to write, and,
especially, for loving our children.

Many thanks, also:

To a number of friends and colleagues who read these drafts
and offered feedback: Kevin Boyd, Ben Dueholm, Sari Fordham,
Marti Hazelrigg, Alex Hendrickson, Deborah Suess, Laura Jean
Torgerson, Elizabeth Varner, and The Reverent Writers: Jenn
Moland-Kovash, Erica Schemper, and Katherine Willis Pershey,
who knew and loved this book before it was born.

To the Editorial Board of the Young Clergy Women Project,
who cheered us on along the way.

To Beth Gaede, our editor, whose encouragement and wisdom
made this a much better book than we could ever have hoped to
write on our own, who never balked at missed deadlines, and who
even managed to turn our failed attempts into cause for praise.
("I'm really quite impressed that you spotted the problem with this
draft! Self-editing is so hard! You make my job so much easier!")

To Doug Davidson, our copyeditor, who let us keep far more
"ands" than he would have liked.

To the folks at the Collegeville Institute, where we dreamed up this book in the first place, and to our fellow writers, who convinced us we could do it.

To the people at *The Christian Century,* who put Bromleigh on the blog, which led to her connection with Alban, which led to a wonderful correspondence with Richard Bass, which led us here.

To Bonnie Miller-McLemore, who was kind enough to read and offer feedback, and whose book *In the Midst of Chaos: Caring for Children as Spiritual Practice* was formative for us and in many ways, inspired us to write our own. Many of the themes she raised are reflected here.

To Kris Culp, professor, dean, and friend, who let us stay at her house and work at her kitchen table and fed us amazing paneer-and-cauliflower curry. This book is smarter simply by being worked on in her presence.

To Cynthia Lindner, professor, mentor, and friend, who told us over and over again that we belonged in the parish, and that we ought to be writing for the church.

To our parents, Brett and Lauri McCleneghan and Richard and Linda Hull, who taught us more about parenting and faith than we could ever put into words, and our sisters—Lynn, Whitney, and Taylor—who shared our childhoods and shaped our motherhood, the dearest of friends and most beloved of aunties.

To John Hammond, father-in-law extraordinaire, who, among other loving things, occupied his grandchildren for countless hours so Bromleigh could write when the day care was closed and the kids were sick.

To Josh and Rob, who read draft after draft, allowed us to tell their stories, encouraged us to write and made time for us to do so, but mostly, for being good dads to our kids and partners to us. We love you.

And finally, to Fiona, Harper, Calliope, and Jonathan, who will read this someday: Thank you. We hope we haven't embarrassed you too much. We are so grateful to be your mothers.

Cast of Characters

LEE, A THIRTY SOMETHING PASTOR IN THE CHRISTIAN CHURCH (DISCIPLES OF CHRIST) AND MOTHER OF TWO. Lee is a pastor's kid who grew up to be a pastor. She arrived at seminary not entirely clear if she should pursue ministry or be a high school history teacher. Once upon a time, she wanted to be a documentary film-maker, but now she tells stories in other ways. She loves to cook, and to run (on occasion), and to eat ice cream (often). She has dark, wavy hair and freckles. She grew up with her mom, dad, and younger sister, Lynn.

BROMLEIGH, A THIRTY SOMETHING PASTOR IN THE UNITED METHODIST CHURCH AND MOTHER OF TWO. Bromleigh is not the same person as Lee. That said, she's also a pastor's kid who grew up to be a pastor. She also arrived at seminary not entirely sure she should be in pastoral ministry, thinking about something more along the lines of doing faith-based justice work. She has dark, wavy hair and freckles, and loves to read. She grew up with her dad, her mom, and her two younger sisters, Whitney and Taylor. When she grows up she wants to host a show on religion and politics for NPR.

ROB MOSES, A THIRTY SOMETHING IT PROFESSIONAL AND FATHER OF TWO. Rob and Lee met in college. They're both Midwesterners who have landed in North Carolina, which they've come to love, although Rob misses the winters of his native Minnesota. He's a geek, but that's a good thing: He works for an Internet hosting company and takes care of all the technology needs of the Moses household. He sings in the choir at church, reads voraciously, and likes to watch old *Doctor Who* episodes. (Somebody said to Lee recently, "When you write about Rob, he sounds like a really good guy." It's true: he is.)

JOSH HAMMOND, A THIRTY SOMETHING TEACHER AND FATHER OF TWO. Josh and Bromleigh met while she was in grad school: Bromleigh shared an apartment with another student, who happened to be Josh's childhood best friend. Josh was teaching at an inner-city school blocks from the university. Josh grew up in both Portland and Upstate New York, and from these he carries a loathing for snow and a love of the San Francisco 49ers (whose reign of greatness when Josh was a child overshadowed more local teams). Josh is a middle school math teacher, with equal passions for fantasy football, politics, and computer programming. He wasn't raised in the church, but he teaches the three-year-old Sunday school class, because he is a good person and he loves his wife, who asked him to do it.

FIONA LOUISE HAMMOND, A PRESCHOOLER. Neither Bromleigh nor Josh is a "big" person, and both went through their growth spurts in their late teens. Their firstborn is thus a tiny kid. But, oh, does Miss Fee have a lot to say. She loves art and stories and singing along to her favorite bands and musicals. She loves dresses and tights, and being silly, especially with her dad and her grandpas, John and Brett.

HARPER LYNN MOSES, A PRESCHOOLER. Harper is a talkative, social kid, with just the right amount of spunk for a four-year-old. She has good friends at preschool and church and just about everywhere else she goes, but her very best friend is a blue elephant who sleeps tucked under her chin every night.

CALLIOPE JANE HAMMOND, A TODDLER. Calliope sports what her father calls "a Ben Franklin 'do"—very little hair in the front, and lots in the back. She is, somehow, blonde in a family of brunettes. She is a bit of a daredevil, who loves to play, give her baby doll a bottle, and read stories. Favorites include *Hop on Pop, The Cat in the Hat,* and *No, No, Yes, Yes.* She also throws (toys, food, pilfered picture frames from the side table) overhand and with surprising force for someone her size. Her parents are anticipating a career in major league baseball.

JONATHAN BRUCE MOSES, A BABY. Well, we're still getting to know Jonathan. So far, he's pretty easy to please with a clean diaper, some milk, or a snuggle. He's got dark hair, like Harper's, and a grin like his dad's. He's just recently figured out the use of his hands. He adores his big sister and the feeling is mutual; she loves to make him laugh.

The Hopes and Fears

On friendships, and babies, and telling the truth

> You will know the truth, and the truth will make you free.
> —John 8:32

I CANNOT TELL A LIE. CALL ME GEORGE WASHINGTON.

I offer this tidbit of information not as evidence of some great virtue but more as a confession. I should say that I cannot lie *well*. I cannot tell an *effective* lie. While this is probably something in which my parishioners might take comfort, there are times when I experience my lack of a poker face as a frustrating limitation.

An example:

One night in late 2006, Josh and I were supposed to meet up with Lee and Rob at a brewpub in Arlington, Virginia. Lee and I had gone to grad school together and had gotten to be friends as we finished our ministry degrees at the University of Chicago. We'd managed to stay somewhat close since graduation, despite the fact that I'd settled in Illinois and she'd taken a job at a church in Virginia. That Thanksgiving weekend, Josh and I were in town visiting my grandparents. We'd found out not three days before that I was pregnant.

It's not that I had any good reason to keep this information from Lee and her wonderful husband. In fact, I was so excited and terrified that I wanted to do what I always want to do when my head and heart feel so very full: I wanted to tell everyone—friends and family and the checkout lady and the waitress.

There we were, at this awesome and funky bar, reminiscing about old times, sharing gossip, and catching up. Given the fact that Lee and I were building our respective lives a thousand miles apart, we were surprised at how they seemed to parallel each other. As we'd started our careers and grew into being married and found our way through our late twenties, we'd both often felt as if we were forging a new path, seeking out new life and new civilization, going where no one—much less our friends from grad school—had gone before. Back when we'd first started seminary, there were those who struggled to tell us apart, a bemusing thing for two young, independent women who were both used to standing out. That night, receiving further confirmation of our similarities was funny, if still a bit unexpected.

Despite how close-knit our foursome was that night, I attempted to keep the news of my pregnancy under wraps for a couple of reasons. The first was a matter of propriety. I had gotten pregnant almost immediately after Josh and I started "trying." Many folks try for months and months, but the secret to our quick success was, I think, simply a matter of luck and an extremely regular cycle. We knew our "target dates" with relative certainty and aimed for, um, multiple opportunities for conception during that five-day period. The announcement of a new pregnancy these days seems always to prompt a set of questions, which includes, *How long were you trying?* Divulging our experience seemed like just the tiniest bit of an overshare.

Then there was my great and abiding fear of somehow jinxing this new and fairly tentative pregnancy. Whereas my beloved husband had looked at the positive result on the little stick and had almost immediately begun to consider legally changing his name to Joshua "Viable Seed" Hammond, I was nervous. At least 10 to 20 percent of known pregnancies spontaneously abort, or end in miscarriage, within the first twelve or thirteen weeks, and an even higher percentage end in the very early weeks. I didn't want to tell anyone in case something happened, in case we didn't make it out of those first biologically tumultuous weeks.

Finally, I was reluctant to speak about the pregnancy because I suspected I was about to enter a whole new way of life. During the coming nine months, my work and interests and the fullness of my identity were about to be subsumed in this pregnancy and in becoming a mother. This was without a doubt an incredibly exciting prospect—one for which I had planned and hoped. I wondered, though: Once I was a mom, would I still be me?

Out of this combination of jumbled emotions and half-baked reflections, Josh and I decided we were going to play it cool and keep the news to ourselves. We sat in this trendy microbrewery together, good friends, over a holiday vacation. We were a group joined by many things, not the least of which is a shared appreciation and love for excellent beer. I exclaimed about the clever names for the different lagers and ales and *weissbiers* and tried to decide which one I would most like to sample. I wasn't kidding—I hated to be denied, and would have happily tried any of the offerings. But I ordered a decaf coffee.

Subtle, right?

My order may have raised eyebrows as I bungled my lie of omission (if not commission). I think I made some lame excuse about coming down with a cold—I can't really remember now. I remember only how futile and silly it was, because a few months later, I heard that Lee was pregnant, too. And she probably had been pregnant on the night we were together in Arlington, though only just, and not even far enough along to have known (hence her one beer).

Fiona and Harper were born the next summer, a week apart.

⁓

It is no reflection on my religious upbringing, I hope, to suggest that the first and most powerful lessons I learned about truth and lies were gleaned not from the Bible or the teachings of the church,

but from the now-cancelled soap opera *All My Children*, which I
watched regularly during my elementary-school lunch breaks. The
fictional residents of Pine Valley, Pennsylvania, were forever caught
up in compromising moral dilemmas. They engaged in activities
that were ridiculous and sinful, if not downright criminal (hostile
takeovers, infidelities, attempted murders, kidnappings, and imper-
sonation), and then exacerbated the havoc they had wreaked by
lying about their actions: "Why, no, of course I didn't sleep with
your brother. Of course our child couldn't possibly belong to him.
What, he needs a life-saving transplant? Uh, . . ."

It's pretty obvious that Erica Kane and her cohort weren't
exactly living in the word of Christ and thus as his disciples. Most
of us, I imagine, are not nearly so involved in the complications of
truth and lies as that bunch. The untruths and falsehoods we deal in
are likely pretty mundane in comparison. Nonetheless, I considered
this soap opera education useful, though it did color my understanding of the nature of sin: I was convinced for a long time that
as long as I never tried to, say, throw my twin sister in a well and
assume her life, I could avoid straying off the narrow path. And that
seemed easy enough, since I didn't even *have* a twin sister!

Still, I think there is a more pervasive lie in our culture (and
believe me, it pains me to mention this, because I love culture). This
lie influences how we relate to one another and how we understand ourselves. It goes like this: There are two kinds of people
in the world, those who are pretty much holding it together and
those who have so much crazy that it comes pouring out of them
on reality television. We faithful people, presumably, would like to
believe we belong in the first category.

But we're often afraid, despite our trust in God, to admit we
are not actually keeping it together all that well. Some of us worry
that if we let the little things start to slip, we're edging one step
closer to the edge of crazy—and if we're not careful, we'll fall into
the crevasse. Worse, if we start to fall, someone will notice. And they
will despise us.

Glennon Melton, whose blog *Momastery* is the next big thing, described this cultural myth a bit in a post that began with this story:

> A few years ago, strange things started happening to me at church. I'd find myself in the middle of a lighthearted conversation with a woman I'd just met, and the woman would make a joke that didn't sound like a joke suggesting that our family was "perfect," and that this "perfection" made her feel bad about her family. This happened three of four times over a two week period. Once a woman said, "You are so PULLED TOGETHER. It just makes me feel so APART."[1]

Glennon and her husband were totally bemused by this, because while they are thin and beautiful and have nice clothes, they are also sort of a disaster. She also felt bad because she in no way wants to make other people feel bad about their lives. So she started her blog and decided her thing would be "openness." She was going to tell her story, warts and all, in hopes of building bridges for people, especially moms.

I appreciated her blog post, although I must assure you that no one has *ever* told me how intimidated she feels because of how perfect my life is. I am not pulled together. I joke that my office, my home, and my general appearance are all specifically designed to help other people feel good about themselves in comparison. But at the same time, I do try to keep it together. I loved the book *Bad Mother,* and I get a kick out of all the cynical and humorous parenting books on the market—but I do not want to be a bad mother myself, ironically or otherwise. I don't want to raise cynical kids. I want to come at parenting with faith and hope. I want to have a happy and healthy marriage, and I want to have happy, faithful kids. But I reject the pervasive cultural lie that a happy marriage and the faithful kids are somehow the byproducts of some rigorous and largely unattainable personal or moral perfection.

Lies have power only if no one is willing to tell the truth. The Bible reminds us that the truth can set us free. But I can count on one hand the women and men I know who, in the first days and weeks of parenthood, when they were bewildered and tired and afraid, turned to the Bible or got down on their knees to pray for guidance. It doesn't really occur to many of us. It didn't occur to me, and I'm a pastor. But then again, I was raised on soap operas.

At any rate, the Spirit of truth, the Spirit that liberates, is present in a lot of places, and many of us might miss it if we're not careful. In the days and weeks and months after Fiona was born, I experienced grace, and the Word of truth—that sustaining hope, the relief of laughter and shared pain—in conversation and relationship with friends, particularly others who were asking the same questions and looking for the same courage in parenting that I was. The lie that everyone else had it together, had their babies on a schedule, and had no doubts or fears was banished by the comforting knowledge that I was not alone. In the parlance of my Wesleyan tradition, these relationships that brought such knowledge could be called Christian conferencing, or holy conversation—and they're a means of grace.

There are other, critical, means of grace in Christian life, even for those in the first years of parenting, though some of these means may require hiring a sitter. Kids can share in Holy Communion and hang out while parents read the Bible and pray. The very young and unvaccinated may not want to accompany mom and dad when they're visiting the sick and imprisoned and working with the poor.

Lee and I have been friends for a long time now, and, I believe, we've been useful in helping each other find an anchor, or some solid ground, in the turbulent first years of pregnancy and parenting. Lee has been a means of grace in my life. In the weeks when our daughters were both so new, I know how much better I felt when I called her and found she was as hungry for adult conversation as I was, as excited and exhausted. When I talked to Lee, I was no longer the only new mother in the world. We could manage it, maybe, if we stuck together.

We've been nervous, as we've told people about this book and tried to find the words to describe it, that we were portraying ourselves as "having it all figured out." We'd really rather not contribute to the big cultural lie. Instead, we're hopeful that as we share our lives—the trials and tribulations and incredible joys— other parents will feel inspired to reflect on their own experiences, and perhaps even to consider new ways in which their own faith is relevant to their identities as parents. We hope that, to borrow a phrase, others might gain "eyes to see" the means and very real presence of God's grace already at work in their lives.

Being a pastor is a wonderful calling, for a lot of reasons. One of those reasons is, for me, that I have developed over the years of doing this work a growing familiarity with Scripture and the hymns of the church, a familiarity that increasingly allows me to engage with the ancient stories of faith and to hear echoes of my own story within them. I was pregnant with Fiona over the Advent and Christmas season, and whenever our congregation sang "O Little Town of Bethlehem," with its line about "the hopes and fears of all the years are met in thee tonight," the phrase captured my imagination. That's what pregnancy and parenthood felt like to me, even in those first weeks: *the hopes and fears of all the years.* All those hopes and all those fears might have proved significantly more daunting, however, if I hadn't had the reminder that a lot of women, a lot of people, have faced hopes and fears, bound up together, since the beginning of time.

Even with that comfort, it cannot be denied that parenting in this country is hard work. There is not nearly enough parental leave, and childcare is exorbitantly expensive, but most families can't afford to live on one salary. And that's just the economic dimension of raising kids. There are decisions to be made about everything. But then again, it's also among the greatest and most

wondrous things ever, for those called to it, for those lucky enough
to become parents. Having children (no matter how one comes by
them, whether through adoption or reproductive technology or
remarriage or old-fashioned sexual reproduction) can reveal God's
presence and grace in the world. It's an endeavor that takes on "the
hopes and fears of all the years" and claims them as part of this very,
very good and holy work.

Leap of Faith

On if, and when, and the will of God

I REMEMBER THAT NIGHT AT THE BREWPUB WITH BROMLEIGH AND Josh, the week of Thanksgiving, on the cusp of our adventure as parents. It was just the four of us, back in the days when it was still relatively normal to meet up with friends for a drink at nine o'clock at night. I noticed the decaf coffee Bromleigh ordered while the rest of us had beer. I didn't say anything, but I noticed.

I also remember the first time our daughters met. They were two months old, and I was in Chicago for my sister's wedding. I wasn't sure when I'd get back to Chicago next or when Bromleigh would be coming east again, and I had that new-mama pride thing that made me think everybody in town needed to meet my new daughter. I'm pretty sure Bromleigh felt the same way, so she invited me out to her house for lunch. I strapped Harper in the car seat, packed up the diaper bag, and braved the Eisenhower Expressway out from the city to her house in Riverside.

This is how I remember it: Harper screamed in the car all the way there, peed on the dining room table while I tried to change her diaper right after we arrived (why, I wonder now, didn't I use the changing table Bromleigh surely had nearby?), and wailed through our entire lunch until I finally gave in and went to nurse her on the couch. Sweet little Fiona, on the other hand, slept politely in the living room through all this drama and only let out one pleasant little yelp to let her mother know she was hungry.

I left with the feeling that they weren't sorry to see us go (though Bromleigh graciously tells me now that this wasn't the case). But I also left feeling somehow reassured that I wasn't in this alone. Here we were, both of us enmeshed in this brand new world, one in which we couldn't complete a full sentence, couldn't finish lunch without being interrupted by a wailing baby, and could hardly, try as we might, talk about anything other than this new reality.

I pulled out of the driveway thinking—not for the first or last time—*what have I gotten myself into?*

When I was in middle school, a good friend and I spent a delightfully spooky afternoon pretending we were characters in a story being written by a man living in the sky, who was, at that very moment, narrating every action we took. "Look!" we'd say as we waved our hands above our heads. "He just wrote that I waved my hands!"

"Do you want to go get a Coke?" we'd ask, and then gasp in wonder because he—the man with the book in the sky—knew we were going to ask.

It was an exercise in existential wondering, playacting the question of our place in the universe. I'm sure we were not the first preadolescents to have had this conversation; it's the stuff of slumber parties and late-night coffee shop conversations, science fiction and movies. (Remember the movie *Stranger than Fiction*? My childhood friend might well have sold Will Ferrell the idea.)

It's also the stuff of theological debate. Without having the language for it, my friend and I were asking questions about God, about destiny, about fate and providence. We were wondering who was in charge of our lives. We were asking questions about free will and the will of God. We were trying to figure out if there was a plan for our lives, if God was the designer of that plan, and if we had any say in the matter.

These are among the trickiest questions in the Christian tradition, and there's no end to the discussion of them. Some Christian

traditions have settled the matter; others leave things open for interpretation. They are the questions—whether we articulate them or
not—that lie behind most of the big decisions we make in our lives:
Should I take that job on the West Coast? Should I marry my high
school sweetheart? Should we sell our house?

Should we have a baby?

As with most major decisions in my life, I approached the decision about whether to have a child with as much deliberation as
I could muster, with lots of conversation and reading. It seems I
thought that arming myself with as much information as possible
could ward off the panic caused by standing on the brink of such
a life-changing and irrevocable decision. To that point, none of my
life choices had been irreversible. I could always find a new job,
move to a different city, sell our condo. The hard truth is—even
though I hate to think it—even marriage can be undone. But there
is no going back from having a baby.

Several months before we finally decided to start trying to get
pregnant, a friend from out of town visited me for the weekend.
She is the kind of old and dear friend who can ask direct questions
without being nosy. "So," she asked one afternoon as we went for
a walk through our neighborhood, "when are you two going to
have a baby?" It was a question I'm sure lots of people were asking.
Even I was aware of how predictably my life was shaping up. Grad
school? Check. Wedding? Check. Job? Check. House purchased?
Check.

Next up? Baby.

"I don't know," I said to my friend. "I kind of like just the two of
us. We're happy. It's quiet. We've got a pretty good thing going on."
But I knew that didn't really explain my hesitation. Rob and I had
always assumed we'd have kids. Children—in the abstract—were
always a part of the family I imagined when I thought of our future.
It was making the shift from the abstract to the concrete that was
the hard part. Far-off-into-the-future children were okay. Actually
having a baby—me, us, my body, here and now—that was scary.

I discovered I was not alone in my uncertainty. I can't remember how I happened upon *Maybe Baby,* a collection of essays by writers struggling with the questions of when and if to have children. It may have been Bromleigh, or another friend, who suggested it to me, and the title alone was enough to convince me to order it right away. I devoured the essays, so perfectly did they capture my own uncertainty: Did I want to change my life so completely and so dramatically? Was I ready to give my body over to an alien life form growing inside? Could my body even do that? I read with heart-ache the stories of women (and men) who wanted to be parents but found that their bodies couldn't make a baby. I read with some longing the tales of women who were perfectly content in their childless lives, enjoying lazy weekend mornings and clean kitchen floors. I read with a sort of curious delight the stories of parents whose lives had been forever altered by the arrival of a baby. I read, and I tried to imagine which of those stories my life was headed toward.

As if the reading and talking weren't enough, Rob and I attended a workshop offered at our local hospital. We met for two hours one Tuesday night in a classroom on the second floor of the hospital, led by a nurse who told us all the things we ought to consider when deciding whether to have a child. I remember nothing about the other participants in the class and very little about the content—except the section in which the nurse told us just how much it would cost to have a baby: *a lot.* I do remember feeling just the slightest bit ridiculous; sure, it's a big decision, but since the dawn of time, women have been having babies without the benefit of hospital education classes to help them decide if the time was right. Still, I was glad for the chance to think, learn, and study the question some more.

My father happened to be visiting that week. On the way home from the class, we stopped at the grocery store to pick up a carton of ice cream to take home and share with him. "Well?" he prompted when we arrived. "What did you learn?" And despite

the oddity of talking about reproductive plans with one's father, we
told him.

"Our bodies are built to have babies at nineteen," I said, over a
bowl of mint chocolate chip. "I'm already ten years past my prime."

We laughed at that, but it got me thinking: in this culture, we
spend a lot time trying to keep young women from getting pregnant at seventeen, eighteen, or nineteen years old, when that is
exactly what their bodies are ready to do. Then, women in their
thirties, and now even forties and fifties, go to great expense (finan-
cially, physically, emotionally) trying to get their aging bodies to
be fertile again. It was a luxury for me, at twenty-nine, even to be
contemplating this choice.

The truth is that all this intentionality is relatively new to the
whole parenting experience. When and if to have a baby hasn't
always been a choice—and it still isn't for many women around the
world. With the help of birth control and fertility treatments, the
questions of if, when, why, and how to have children create—in
the words of *Maybe Baby* editor Lori Leibovich—a "wilderness
of choices" for us to navigate on the way to becoming, or not
becoming, parents.[1]

I wondered if Rob and I were thinking of having a baby just
because it was expected of us. Were we doing it just because babies
are cute? Was I letting my hormones—and there's no denying that
my uterus was a major participant in all these conversations—take
precedence over my brain? Were we considering children just so
we'd have someone to care for us in our old age, and someone who
would clean out our attic after we are gone and decide what to do
with the dishes? Was choosing to parent a child an act of selfless-
ness or did it reflect a selfishness bordering on narcissism? I wanted
answers to all these questions before we went any further. I wanted
to *know* this was the right thing to do.

There were also questions about timing. I'd been invited to
travel internationally that summer, something I couldn't do if I
was pregnant, and there were mission trips and youth group events

to attend. My sister had recently gotten engaged and was planning a wedding next fall—halfway across the country. I did the
math: If we got pregnant this month or next, I'd probably be able
to make it to the wedding. If it took much longer than that, there
was a pretty good chance I'd be stranded at home while the rest of
the family watched her walk down the aisle. (Happily, the timing
on this worked out fine: Rob juggled the stroller and diaper bag
throughout the reception; I figured out how to nurse in a brides-
maid dress.) The question wasn't just "Should we have a baby?" It
was also "Should we have a baby *now?*"

But even that wasn't the end of the questions in this "wilderness of choices." Should we, I wondered, look into adoption instead
of trying to get pregnant? I really struggled with this one—and still
do. I know there are so many children who need parents to love
them. I know overpopulation is a major problem. I talk and preach
and teach about living in community with our neighbors, about
taking into consideration the needs of others, about the incredible,
interconnected web of life that God formed on this planet . . . and
then I want to add more people to the mix? More bodies to use up
the precious resources of this earth? Isn't there something incredibly selfish about all this?

I can't say I'm fully comfortable with our decision not to adopt.
I look at families with adopted kids, and I'm so full of gratitude for
what they're doing. I know, of course, that adopting a child is not an
act of charity; it's not mission work or service. Adoption is another
way of creating family. I know I could love another child as much
as one I gave birth to. All I can say is that at the time, I wanted to
get pregnant if I could. I wanted the experience of growing a baby,
of giving birth, of participating in the procreative capabilities of this
body God gave me. "Because I want to" is not the well-reasoned
justification I was going for, but that's where I ended up.

In the end no amount of information could make the decision
any easier. No conversation would make the difference. No list of
pros and cons would settle the thing. This decision wasn't—as I

probably knew from the beginning—something I could sort out logically, some equation I could solve.

In the end we just made the leap.

When I got some perspective on all this, several years later, I realized that what I was doing through all those conversations, books, and classes was the practice of discernment. It sounds like a fancy word for "deciding," but there's more to it than that. In a particularly helpful book called *Practicing Our Faith*, religious education professor Frank Rogers Jr. describes discernment as "the intentional practice by which a community or an individual seeks, recognizes, and intentionally takes part in the activity of God in concrete situations."[2] That's what I was trying to do—making the move from those abstract children-of-my-future to the concrete have-a-baby-now. I was—perhaps subconsciously—asking how I could "take part in the activity of God."

"You're taking this decision very seriously," my father noted, that night after Rob and I attended the hospital workshop.

"It seems to be how I do things," I agreed. "It's worked out so far."

He shouldn't have been surprised, actually. I learned this from him. My dad has a saying that is particularly famous in my family: *Make the best decision you can, and make the best of the decision you made.* This advice is just under the surface of just about every major decision my sister and I have made in our adult lives—college admissions, new jobs, cross-country moves, home purchases. "You know what Dad would say," one of us will say to the other as we're weighing pros and cons. "Make the best decision you can, and make the best of the decision you made."

It's good advice in part because it eases the pressure of trying to figure out the right answer. It's a reminder that there is life beyond the moment of decision, that the universe will not implode if we make the wrong choice. It's also good advice because it acknowledges that there isn't a particular preexisting plan for our lives, one that's already mapped out for us. Rather, there are simply the

choices we make and the choices we don't, and the way we live
with what we decided.

Last summer, just before Harper turned four, she attended a
vacation Bible school program at the church where she goes to
preschool. It's a big church, and they used one of the popular
published VBS programs, the kind with a catchy name, a cute
mascot, and a collection of synthesizer-music songs that are repeated
so often that you are numb to them by the end of the week. I was
glad she had that experience, especially since our church hadn't
done a traditional VBS program for a few years. I was not, however,
particularly excited when she brought home the CD.

She insisted on listening to it at bedtime for at least a month.
Sometimes it takes her a couple of hours to fall asleep, and she
kept the CD player set to repeat, the pseudo-dance-club techno-
beat music reverberating out into the hallway, the lyrics leaving
their indelible mark on my brain. One song in particular, called
"God Is Watching Over You"—with lines like "Twenty-four seven,
watching over you!" and "Your life is in his hands"—kept pulsing
through my mind.

I couldn't help thinking there was something a little creepy
about the song. Maybe it was the dark disco backbeat. Something
about it reminded me of the way I felt as a preteen, imagining that
writer-in-the-sky who was narrating my life, entirely controlling
everything I did. But even so, I'll grant that this is not terrible
theology for preschoolers. For the most part, I agree—and it's good
for kids to know—that our lives are in God's hands. It was that next
line that wouldn't leave me alone (literally, as I heard it over and
over, every night at bedtime): "He's got great big plans!"

This song had apparently been pulsing through Harper's head,
too, because she asked me about it over breakfast one morning.
"What are plans?" she wanted to know. "Does God have plans?"

Ah, good question, child. Good question. "I think God imagines what you're going to do with your life," I said. "I think God has

big dreams for you." I tried to explain to Harper (ignoring my high school English teacher's admonition not to define a word by using that same word) that plans are, "like the plans we have to go to the swimming pool tomorrow." Talking about the will and purpose of God is something entirely different.

I'm wary of thinking of God's plans as some sort of agenda for our lives, a calendar of activities already lined up for us, as if we have any idea how the mind of God works. To presume that God has a plan seems as presumptuous as to suggest that we know what that plan might be. A better question, I think—instead of "What is God's plan for my life?"—is, to borrow Rogers's phrase, "How can I take part in the activity of God?"

My faith tells me God is at work in the world, in all kinds of predictable and unexpected ways, and invites us to join in and be a part of the action. So rather than trying to figure out what God has in mind (an impossible, if not idolatrous, task), it makes more sense to me to think about accepting the invitation to join in the work God is already doing. Rogers puts it this way:

> What are we to do in the midst of this vertigo of uncertain insights and conflicting impulses? It is enough to leave one utterly confused. Christians believe that we are not alone during such times. God is present, hoping and urging, in the midst of all the situations of life. As Christians, we believe that God is passionately involved in human affairs and intimately invested in all our questioning. Moreover, we believe that God's involvement in our lives has purpose and direction. God is seeking to bring healing and wholeness and reconciliation, transforming this broken world into that New Creation where there will be no more sadness or injustice or pain. Our decisions and our search for guidance take place in the active presence of a God who intimately cares about our life situations and who invites us to participate in the divine activities of healing and transformation.[3]

Folks in the Quaker tradition have a helpful way of thinking about making decisions, about participating in the "divine activities" of God's work in the world. Discernment, for Quakers, involves trusting that "way will open"—that is, the direction in which to proceed will become clear through prayer and trust in the Holy Spirit.[4] Several years after Harper was born, I asked a Quaker friend of mine about all this, and she introduced me to the idea of a "clearness committee," a process by which an individual facing a difficult decision surrounds him- or herself with a small group of people who will provide support and prayer throughout the discernment process. The committee doesn't make the decision— only the individual can discern the way opening, but the group provides a place for the individual to sense the presence of God, the nudging of the Spirit, by asking questions that help make the way become clear. I laughed to myself at the idea of having a committee to talk things over back when I was deciding whether or not to get pregnant. But then I realized that in a way, I did: my husband, my parents, my sister, my friends, books written by strangers contemplating the same questions, classes offered by those who had some expertise. Without knowing it, I had assembled my own sort of committee to help me see the way opening ahead.

In retrospect, I think we'd already decided by the time we took that Tuesday night class. And when I say "we," I really mean "I." Rob by no means rushes into things. We dated for three years and were engaged for two more before we got married; neither of us could be called impulsive. But he makes up his mind sooner and then sits back and waits patiently for me to work it out.

I have always been grateful for his sense of certainty—his assurance that things will work out all right, and that even if things don't go the way we want them to, that we'll be able to figure out a way through them. Case in point: We recently ordered a set of chairs for our dining room, and because we'd gotten the table elsewhere, we hemmed and hawed about the color of the chairs, not at all sure we could find a perfect match. After several days of watching me agonize over the color, he said, "Look, worst case scenario: they don't match, and we have to have them stripped down and restained." I didn't want to hear it—so sure was I that it would be the end of the world if they didn't match. But he was right.

Babies are not chairs, of course, and the decision to have a baby is not a reversible one. But Rob's certainty that having a child was the right thing for us assured me. His confidence was more than certainty, actually; it was trust. It was trust that whatever happened, we'd figure it out. It was trust that we'd make the best decision we could, and we'd make the best of the decision we'd made. It was trust that—in the words of Romans 8:28—"all things work together for good for those who love God."

This is different from saying that God has a plan for our lives. Our lives are in God's hands, to be sure. There is the way that opens in front of us and the way that closes behind us. This is not to suggest that there are no bad choices; clearly, we humans sometimes make a royal mess of things. And there are also times when we make good decisions, and things still do not go well. But even then, God figures out how to work for good. After all, for the whole of history, God has worked through the lives of perfectly human, deeply flawed people to move the story of grace and hope along. This is good news.

I'm not so interested in finding the right path or discovering God's plan. I am, however, compelled and called to be part of this world that God created and keeps re-creating. I think I could have done that by adopting a child, creating a home for a kid who needed one. I think I would have found ways to do it even if we hadn't had kids at all. But I also think that I'm doing it by creating a child, sharing my body with a baby for a while, rejoicing in my body's ability to create and nurture life. I hope I'm doing that by raising this child to be the best, most fully human person that God imagines, realizing everything God dreams for her, helping her participate in God's creative work as well.

It was the best decision I could have made.

My Body, My Fault

On pregnancy, and anxiety, and hope

THESE ARE THE STAGES OF PREGNANCY:

1. Hope
2. Fear
3. Joy
4. Disbelief
5. Nausea
6. Belief
7. Anxiety
8. Love
9. Responsibility
10. Realism
11. Anticipation
12. Discomfort
13. (Momentary) Relief

Stage 1: Hope

I had been in love several times before I met my husband, Josh. And, to my chagrin, with the benefit of hindsight I have discovered that I have a type. Brown eyes, good with words, funny, smart. Looks good with a five o'clock shadow. Kind, committed to the Good Society. Skeptical of religion, but willing to be in conversation.

It is not my intention to suggest that Josh is indistinguishable from his predecessors in my heart, but rather to say that despite the similarities and my apparent lack of romantic imagination, it was clear almost from our first date that he was the one with whom I wanted to make my life. In previous relationships, when questions of the next stage arose, something deep within me hesitated. No. With Josh, the opposite was true. As soon as an idea was on the table, I knew. Exclusivity? Yes. Sex? Yes. Cohabitation? Yes. Marriage? Yes. Kids? Yes.

Josh has always wanted to have kids. He's good with kids; he likes kids. I could say the same for me. An early bonding point as we dated was discovering that we'd both spent college summers working as camp counselors at our local YMCAs. As much as I loved his quick wit, his latent idealism, his refusal to show partiality (James 2:1–10), and his equal propensities for silliness and social justice, what drew me to Josh so quickly and so deeply was the sense that he would be a fantastic dad—and, not to put too fine a point on it, the way my heart, stomach, mind, and (ahem) *loins,* seemed to be begging me to let him impregnate me.

We got married first, got settled a bit. And then, one sunny Columbus Day, we walked to the zoo right near our house and spent the day trying to be unobtrusive as we ogled the families ogling the animals. We saw dads carrying kids on their shoulders, moms pushing strollers, siblings holding hands, and toddlers dripping ice cream down their chins and trying to catch the errant streams in their increasingly sticky hands. We wanted to be them; we coveted a family.

We were in luck: We had the means to make one.

Or so I hoped.

Stage 2: Fear

I was afraid. Superstition is unattractive and counter to faith in God, but nonetheless, as soon as we knew we wanted to make a baby,

I began to fear that any and all past sins would keep me from this dream, that somehow they had been tallied against me, that I would be found underqualified to offer the sort of love a baby required.

There are plenty of voices in both theology and culture that urge people—especially women—to experience extreme guilt regarding just about everything related to sexual thought or practice, an unreasonable guilt I'm mostly able to avoid. But the degree to which I wanted to make a baby with this man, my beloved husband, caused my reason to falter. There was so much at stake, it seemed, in our ability (or inability) to conceive. I wondered. I feared. For example: pastorally, theologically, sociologically (pick a discipline), I am not convinced that consensual premarital sex between young adults is among the top sins, if it is sinful at all. I'm a preacher's kid, but the adolescent sex talks in our house were more instructive than prohibitive: my mother warned me that sex complicates and escalates relationships, and thus ought to be postponed. But our broader cultural narrative, peddled in my youth at young Christians and young women through *Dawson's Creek, 7th Heaven,* and a vast swath of conservative Christian publishing, contends that there are punishments awaiting women who stray from stringent notions of purity. It's a powerful narrative.

Now, in my early adulthood, I started to count up the times I'd counseled a friend to trust her better instincts (instead of what her church told her) or locate a prescription for the morning-after-pill. I feared that in the divine arithmetic they would add up to infertility. I fretted that the routine STI tests I'd had before my marriage had been too infrequent, despite a longstanding practice of taking many precautions and a (very) limited number of partners. (As my sisters and I got older, sex advice from my mother focused on public health concerns: "Don't let him touch you without a doctor's note attesting to his freedom from infection. I knew this girl in college who got herpes from her first boyfriend, and she's had to deal with it for twenty-five years.") I was sure I would be unable to conceive due to an infection I'd never detected. Fear is often irrational, I knew. But it is real.

Stage 3: Joy

When those double pink lines appeared on the stick, I couldn't believe it. I don't think I stopped grinning for a week. I wanted to hug Josh and tell everyone we knew, all at once, right this minute! Joy. Wonder. I was embarrassed by what felt like our unbelievably good fortune. All that fear for nothing! We were surely the only couple in the world who had ever been so blessed. (My mother wasn't the least bit surprised by our quick success. When I told her the news, she said, "Yeah, we're fertile. Your father didn't have to do anything more than hang his pants up in the same room as me, and I'd be pregnant.")

Stage 4: Disbelief

Many ob-gyn practices don't want to see you right away. The at-home pregnancy tests are considered trustworthy, so there's no need for an immediate visit to confirm the pregnancy. As long as you're having no troubling symptoms and have access to prenatal vitamins, they record the date of the first day of your last menstrual period (I couldn't remember and swore I could feel the intake nurse's incredulity and judgment through the phone) and make an appointment for week eight, nine, or ten. You hang up, and your expectant partner looks at you, and you have to report that you will have no further information for at least two months.

In the weeks that follow, the reality of the pregnancy begins to fade. We can leave the pregnancy test that revealed this monumental news perched ceremonially on the bathroom counter for a few days, but, honestly, it's a piece of plastic we peed on, not a keepsake, and it becomes the first in a long series of child-related items that we previously would have junked without question but now must debate the significance of.

The first weeks of my pregnancy passed by with very few symptoms at all. Life returned to normal. I would worry intermittently, wondering if everything was all right. (The baby books said we should be concerned if symptoms decreased . . . but how could something decrease from nothing?) With no evidence of pregnancy and no way to get my head around the idea that our lives were about to change so dramatically, that there was a blastocyst/zygote/embryo/fetus getting comfortable and making a home in my body, I stopped believing I was really pregnant. "I'll believe it when I see it," I thought.

Stage 5: Nausea

For many women the reality of a pregnancy is driven home not by a blissed-out glimpse of a pulsing kidney bean on a sonogram screen or the frantic swashbuckling of a fetal heartbeat emerging from the static, but by the onset of nausea. Or fatigue. Or vomiting while exhausted, which exacerbates the exhaustion. Sometimes, for lucky women, the first symptom is bigger breasts. But most women I know would trade a porn-star figure for the ability to keep a meal down. Pregnancy makes us practical; it's a biological imperative, I think. My first symptom was not nausea, but a gnawing hunger and frequent lightheadedness that would lead to a dead faint if I didn't eat breakfast quickly enough.

Stage 6: Belief

I could not get up in the morning, could not wait to get to bed at night, could not skip my afternoon nap. The dust bunnies in our living room and under the beds outpaced the fetus's growth. Josh would periodically dare to inquire as to whether I'd done any thinking about dinner or ventured to the grocery store. If he was lucky, I would simply snore in response. There was now no doubt in anyone's mind that I was pregnant—or hugely depressed, with a coincidental need for a larger cup size.

Stage 7: Anxiety

As the reality of my pregnancy belatedly set in, the paranoia I had experienced prior to conception returned. I was reading *What to Expect When You're Expecting;* Josh was reading *The Expectant Father.* Both of these popular books, along with frequently released news stories, advised us to examine the whole of our lives for practices that could endanger the pregnancy. How much coffee was safe to drink? How much could I lift? Was I too stressed out? Was I getting enough folic acid? Suddenly, there were soft cheeses and hot tubs everywhere, hiding on sandwiches and lurking around corners. The whole world began to look dangerous.

To be fair to all those pregnancy books, I should mention that I was predisposed to anxiety. The wonderful thing about professional ministry is that the pastor is invited to walk with people through their most joyful and devastating moments and milestones; the terrible thing about pastoral ministry is that you see, up close and personally, just how much suffering people have to bear. When I was a student chaplain years earlier, I visited with a mom who had delivered a baby at twenty weeks. I remember the baby's too-tiny, alien-skinny body. The form that looks so huge, that fills the ultrasound screen, is astoundingly tiny and fragile in the outside world. The mother was grieving, and rightly, but she did not doubt that this tiny being was not ready and would not survive.

I am far enough into the childbearing years now that many of my friends have had babies or been pregnant. It devastates me to know how many of them have experienced a loss. Once upon a time, I told myself that as long as I was young, as long as I could try to follow most of the "rules," all would be well. But it's simply not true. My friends and peers were doing everything "right." They wanted their pregnancies. They were in their twenties or mid-thirties. They didn't eat deli meat or sushi or too much tuna. They went to prenatal yoga and low-impact water aerobics but postponed running the half-marathon. They loved their spouses. They got excited, but not too excited. They prayed and went to church. And their water broke months too early. Or their babies' intestines grew outside their bodies. Or the babies died in labor. Or they were born with genetic diseases with potentially fatal outcomes.

Worse? The two women I know who drank during their pregnancies—not routinely, but who allowed themselves a drink or two late in the third trimester—each had two remarkably healthy children. The ones who ate soft cheeses? No listeria, no problems.

The crazy-making thing about pregnancies, of course, is that although many, many of them lead to the birth of healthy babies, many others end in miscarriage early on. And even when the child is carried full-term, sometimes things can go *terribly* wrong. And we have no real way of knowing why and no way of preventing these disastrous developments. Good, solid medical research suggests there are things women can do that may contribute to "better outcomes": we can avoid alcohol and try not to gain too much weight (even though the only thing we can routinely keep down are fast food breakfast sandwiches and chocolate milkshakes) and stop playing fast-pitch softball to reduce the risk of taking a line drive to the abdomen. Good prenatal care is key. We can quit smoking and, if our partner smokes, we can make him smoke outside the house. Maybe he'll get so irritated by having to be exposed to the elements whenever he smokes that he'll quit, and then we'll have more money to spend on the baby! Everybody wins!

Well-meaning partners (and a host of less involved bystanders) often join in our attempts to eliminate all threats to our future children. Josh would watch me carting my overstuffed computer bag off to work and gently suggest that I take out just one or two extraneous books. He would, with significantly less subtlety, give me the evil eye on those (frequent) mornings when I went to pour myself a second cup of coffee. "Do you want our baby to have heart defects?" He was kidding, mostly; but it was clear he was unwilling to tempt fate with even the smallest risk . . . especially if that risk was on my part. (*He* didn't give up coffee.)

I would not begrudge a woman crumbled blue cheese on her salad; it is neither Christian nor humane to wish another ill or to take joy in one's comeuppance, especially for the great sin of taking a hot bath after a long day. But when we're afraid of something—especially something so dire as a risk to a much-wanted pregnancy—we do everything in our cognitive power to figure out the rules. Much of the pregnancy literature aids and abets this grasping for control. As much as I loved reading all the updates each month in *What to Expect*, I began to despair when I realized how far my food intake varied from the "Best Odds Diet." We want to know the system. Whether the rules are from God or the Fates or the laws of nature, we are indifferent. We are prepared to obey—at least to a point. A second cup of coffee seemed to me a reasonable risk, but it did feel like a risk. Many folks are also prepared to blame others when things go wrong. "Well, she wanted her precious sushi." "God needed another angel." "It's my fault: I didn't do the kick counts frequently enough, and I slept on my back!" Feeling culpable, knowing who's at fault—whether the "fault" is our beloved Creator senselessly turning the divine back on a friend, or our very own selves—is far better than facing the frightening truth that there's no one at fault, there's no one in control, and our rules are merely talismans against the unthinkable.

Rabbi Harold Kushner, in *When Bad Things Happen to Good People*, writes about our human need to make sense of tragedy, and reflects on this need in light of his theology.[1] The way Kushner walks readers through this philosophical reflection is really useful. Here's my summary of his reasoning (cast in terms of pregnancy):

1. Judaism and Christianity believe God is good. If God weren't good, why would we worship? Why would we long

for connection? So, if God is good, God won't kill babies—even if their bad, mean mommies eat shellfish.

2. Some things are neither good nor bad, they just are: gravity, the existence of bacteria, our mortality. They are simply realities of life on earth.

3. God has made us free. Free to choose God, free to choose love over fear, free to choose whether we're going to shower now or later on a lazy Saturday, free to choose to read this book over that. There are limits to that freedom: Josh and I can try to make a baby, but we can't guarantee a pregnancy or that the pregnancy will "take." But God doesn't have a hand in that. The Lord of All Life might well long for those who experience infertility to know an end to their grief, but God has covenanted not to force our hands, either in messing with our reproductive capabilities or forcing us to adopt; that's what the doctrine of free will is all about.

Reading Kushner's reflection, I was startled to encounter this entirely germane example, straight from the good rabbi's pen:

> When a man and a woman join in making love, the man's ejaculate swarms with tens of millions of sperm cells, each one carrying a slightly different set of biologically inherited characteristics. No moral intelligence decides which one of those teeming millions will fertilize a waiting egg. Some of the sperm cells will cause a child to be born with a physical handicap, perhaps a fatal malady. Others will give him not only good health, but superior athletic or musical ability, or creative intelligence. A child's life will be wholly shaped, the lives of parents and relatives will be deeply affected, by the random determination of that race.[2]

We know, too, that countless other variables are at work in making a baby and the unfolding of a human life. Some work to the good; some lead to hardship and grief; sometimes the self-same variables lead to both good and ill. My uncle Mark was

born with Down Syndrome, a condition that has a host of manifestations and that, at his birth, caused my grandparents to question what they had done wrong. Their theological wrestling and
their love, care, and dedication of resources to Mark, in a time
when many people encouraged institutionalizing and forgetting
handicapped children, played no small part in my father's life of
faith and strengthened his commitment to care for the vulnerable. Mark is one of the reasons my dad entered the ministry and
has spent his life serving Christ in others. My dad's witness over
the years is certainly one of the reasons I'm in ministry. And yet,
all things are not to the good. Mark struggles as a man in his
late forties who has many of the cognitive and emotional limitations and frustrations one would expect of a sexually mature
six-year-old. He is lucky not to have the heart problems many
other folks with Down syndrome experience, but his health is a
concern. My grandparents worked hard to make sure there would
always be resources to care for Mark, even now that they are
gone, but many, many other disabled folks' lives are jeopardized
by a lack of funding for such care.

Anxiety differs from fear by definition; fear has an object. The
anxiety of pregnancy for me was total and without any clear cause
or object. As I tried to make sense of my unease during those
middle months, I thought of that staple of middle school language
art classes, the typology of conflicts: man versus man; man versus
environment; man versus society; man versus the unknown. Other
than the fact that I am rather obviously not technically included in
that gendered language, all of those seemed to describe my feelings. The terrible things I knew were possible seemed impossible to
bear; the lack of certainty and the randomness Kushner describes
were equally fearsome.

Stage 8: Love

If we're lucky, nausea may begin to abate with the ending of the
first trimester. The same cannot be said of the anxiety I, and many

of my friends, experienced. Whether we believe we're locked in an endless pursuit of God's favor or protection, or we've resolved that sometimes awful things happen for no good reason, these myriad fears are often worsened by an otherwise wonderful development in the middle of the second trimester: quickening.

I lived for the monthly doctor visits when I'd get to hear my sweet child's heartbeat, and I was greedy for more reassurance of her presence and her growth. But she took her sweet time offering it up. And then, one day, she did. A little flutter. Then a twinge. As weeks passed, her movements became more obvious, as she'd punch my bladder. As she grew larger, I would press Josh's hand to my belly and, finally, he could feel her, too. It was magic. We were smitten, in love with each other, with this unknown life, with the world.

Teenagers and young adults are often criticized for their sense of immortality, their fearlessness and rumored irresponsibility. Every now and again I recall one of the incredibly stupid things I did in college and marvel that I am alive and healthy. Some folks manage to mature all on their own, but it took the constraints and realizations of love to get me to be a grown-up. Understanding that losing me would break Josh's heart, just as the loss of him would destroy me, helped me appreciate the weight of mortality.

Falling in love with this new life, sight unseen, impressed upon me once more just how much emotional stake I had in this baby's well-being. The idea that her continued development, her chance at life, my chance to know and love her was neither something I could guarantee or control nor something I could bargain with God for in exchange for my submission or obedience or reverence left me unmoored. Kushner reminds us that tragedy is rare, however. This is part of our hope—and it is why we are so shaken when it befalls someone in our community, our families, or ourselves. It is because things go right so very often. This, he writes, is a miracle in itself, evidence of the Divine in our remarkable bodies.

Reading the good rabbi's description, I couldn't help but think of an episode of *Family Guy* from a few years back, parodying *American Beauty*. The doofus dad, Peter, is watching a plastic bag blowing in the wind, marveling: "Look! It's dancing with me! It's like there's this incredibly benevolent force that wants me to know there's no reason to be afraid. Sometimes there's so much beauty in the world it makes my heart burst." God, pictured as a balding man with a long white beard, standing on a cloud, yells down, "It's just some trash blowing in the wind! Do you have any idea how complicated your circulatory system is?"

In my anxiety, with my focus on the possibility of tragedy and my attempts to exert control over unknowable forces, I was missing the miracle. Loving someone you've never met: there's a miracle. Sharing in the creation of that future person: there's a miracle.

Stage 9: Responsibility

The most difficult thing about pregnancy for me—and for many of the incredible women I know—is that growing a new human being is hard work, work that taxes and tires a body. We women who are used to pushing ourselves simply can't do so during our pregnancies—at least not to the same degree. We have to take care of ourselves.

One evening at my parents' house, I reminded myself aloud to take an extra chocolate calcium chew when I got home that night. Josh joined in offering some good-natured nagging: "You have to have enough calcium!" My mother, notorious in her enduring refusal to drink milk, busted out with, "I was afraid Bromleigh would be born with no bones!" Clearly, this did not happen.

"Of course, she was fine," my mom added. "But I do have to take a ton of calcium now and that osteoporosis-preventing medication."

Most women would do just about anything for their babies, to give these new lives the best shot possible. We are in love, after all, and our love wants to give all it can to its object. But we're lousy at taking care of ourselves. Christians are quick to spout off the greatest commandment—to love our neighbor—but too many women are lousy at recalling and living out the second critical step. We're called to love our neighbors *as ourselves.* That means we have to love ourselves. And not just in a warm, fuzzy, Oprah-self-esteem sort of way. We have to take care of ourselves in a love-with-justice sort of way.

The Gospel writers require this mutuality in love because they know our lives—those of our neighbors and ourselves (and in Luke's Gospel, our enemies)—are all bound up in one another. We're all connected. This is never more true than in pregnancy. The fetal life needs its mother to eat enough, rest enough, and relax enough; the mother must be healthy so that the baby can grow healthy.

The twentieth-century Christian theologian Reinhold Niebuhr defined the primary human sin as pride. But feminist theologians, with some indignation, look at the oppression of women around the world and suggest that more frequently women are prone to "self-abnegation." That is, we try to negate ourselves. We try to make ourselves disappear. We act as though we are nothing.

I always hesitate when I get too close to gender stereotypes, but I think there's something to this critique. I don't mean to suggest that if things go wrong in a pregnancy, the mother is to blame for failing to care for herself. But I believe we women need to give ourselves permission to get what we need. We must provide for our children by providing for ourselves. So much rhetoric in this country pits the desires of selfish women against the vulnerable needs of in-utero innocents. But that's what we in the theology business call a false dichotomy. We cannot separate ourselves from these babies; we are not separate. They are dependent on us for life.

And they'll steal all our calcium if we're not careful, leaving us brittle and bent before our time. They're trickier than you'd think.

So, I chewed my calcium and continued to wrestle with the tension between my growing sense (both hope-filled and despairing) that I could not ensure the birth of a healthy baby and the dawning realization that I had responsibility to properly care for *both* of us. My wrestling had theological implications. Christian theology has traditionally suggested that the primary tension experienced by human beings is that we are sinners in need of, and recipients of, grace. But theologian and ethicist H. Richard Niebuhr (brother of Reinhold!) suggests there's more to life than that tension. He notes that humans are responsive creatures: responsive to God and to other people and to the events and actions that affect us. In some theological models, human beings are just supposed to submit to the will of God and repent when we fail to do so. But H. Richard describes our task here on earth as one of interpretation: his emphasis is on *how* we discern God's presence in what is going on around us and what we do in response. We are called to act "fittingly," which means we're supposed to look around us and first ask, "What is going on here?" Then, we're supposed to respond in ways that reflect our commitment to and faith in the knowledge that all creation is being saved by Christ, right now, and forever.[3]

What in the world does that mean? It means that in all things we're supposed to choose life. Now, the word *life* in the American context of pregnancy can be pretty political, so I turn to the Bible, which has a helpful habit of complicating matters. In the Hebrew Scriptures, when the Lord tells Moses to make a covenant with the people on the divine behalf, Moses ends the lengthy discourse with these words:

> I call heaven and earth to witness against you today that I have set before you life and death, blessings and curses. Choose life so that you and your descendants may live, loving the LORD your God, obeying him, and holding fast to him; for that means life to you and length of days, so that you may live in the land that

the LORD swore to give to your ancestors, to Abraham, to Isaac, and to Jacob.

Deut. 30:19–20

We don't always get to choose what will happen in our lives—and neither, we might add, does God. That's the consequence of living in a world in which we're not puppets. That said, we are not left reeling in a meaningless universe where neither God nor we have any power or agency. While we do not have full control over the consequences of our actions, and God may not be telling which sperm to fertilize the egg (to use Kushner's example), that doesn't mean our choices do not matter or that God isn't involved in our lives and in the world. The unreasonable amounts of granola and spinach the writers of *What to Expect* offered me as defense against tragedy are not effective as magical talismans, but they may give us some inklings about how to make healthy choices, about how to begin to choose "life" each and every day.

Both Niebuhr and Kushner want readers to trust that God is not watching us testily, waiting for us to screw up the miracle incantation or overstep the bounds of the righteous life so that *He* can justify making our lives miserable. Rather, God is with us. God is with us—supplying strength to help us through each day, courage to face the unknown, and love to move us through dark nights and uncertain ultrasounds. If something dreadful happens in these weeks that makes the tiny not-quite-a-person growing inside us incompatible with life outside the womb, God will lament with us, sharing in the loss of someone we've somehow come to love in such a very short time. God is not against us, but for us. God does not want us, or our babies, to die, but to live.

Stage 10: Realism

As the second trimester all too slowly became the third, I obsessively counted the passing weeks, waiting for that mystical "point of viability" at which the fetus can be born safely, and reasonably be expected to live on its own without significant medical complications. Forty weeks' gestation is "fully cooked" (as Josh says), but babies born after at least twenty-six weeks are usually able to survive. Once we'd reached that developmental milestone, I felt I could begin, with a measured and reasonable hope, to anticipate the arrival of a baby. While it was still best for him or her to keep cooking, if the baby debuted early, the chance of tragedy was greatly diminished.

This loosening of anxiety's grip allowed us to be more realistic, to finally hear voices of comfort and assurance over the din of our fear. An older friend advised, "Stop reading *What to Expect When You're Expecting.* Those folks are fearmongers." When Josh and I would read advertisements for companies that allowed you to stock your baby's own personal cord blood as an insurance against disease, we were able to critique the company for turning a profit by preying on both the fears and the self-interest of new parents, instead of reaching for our checkbook and wondering where we'd find the money for something so exorbitantly expensive.

Stage 11: Anticipation

As we rounded the corner past thirty weeks, I was so full of baby that my organs seemed pushed every which way, crowded into the few remaining spots in my body. Two effects of this were nearly constant heartburn and a decreased appetite. I couldn't imagine that my due date was still more than two months away; was it possible for me to get any bigger without exploding? ("Just wait," my mother answered helpfully.) And while there's no medical evidence to support this, I felt convinced that all that baby left inadequate room for proper brain function.

"Pregnancy brain," it's called. I was less forgetful than preoccupied. The impending arrival of a child, the imminent expansion of my family was now, finally, *the* thing in my life and on my mind.

No longer did I bother with the overstuffed computer bag; as long as I had my *Baby Bargains* book with me at all times, I was good to go. Scouting cribs, attending showers, washing and folding tiny onesies—these were my priorities. I was still working, tending to my duties, but my heart was elsewhere.

More importantly, I was finally enjoying the pregnancy. I could commend my body for all the good work it was doing. I may have had six chins and upper arms as thick as a redwood, but this baby was thriving. We were in the homestretch. We had everything to look forward to.

Stage 12: Discomfort

In the last two weeks, the only thing there is to look forward to is not being pregnant anymore. The arrival of the baby is exciting, too, of course—but mostly the woman is dreaming of evicting her little occupant. No matter the season, she is hot, sweaty, and out of breath. Medical wisdom maintains that weeks thirty-eight through forty give the baby's lungs and other bodily systems time to develop and otherwise prepare for life on the outside. This wisdom doesn't matter to the pregnant woman. She would give anything not to be pregnant. Forgetting all she learned about free will and the divine respect for the laws of nature in the second trimester, she prays to God to break her water. Forsaking recommended obstetrical practice, she considers slurping castor oil or going jogging or pathetically begging her husband to make awkward love to her.

Stage 13: (Momentary) Relief

My labor was atypical.

That morning, the maternity ward was unexpectedly crowded and the anesthesiologist uncommonly busy; thus I was given an epidural dosed to last all day and into the night. I hardly felt a thing and spent the day watching *Law & Order* reruns on hospital cable.

But some things were as they have been throughout the ages. Finally, the moment came. I pushed. We cried. Joy, awe, and wonder overtook us. Someone wiped off our newborn daughter (a girl!) and placed her on my chest.

The first thing I said as I looked at my daughter was "Holy. Shit," uttered through tears and laughter. The hospital staff burst out laughing. The swearing, bleeding clergywoman was apparently a pleasant surprise in the delivery room.

I looked my beloved husband in the eye and questioning each other silently— just to make sure we still agreed on the result of our forty-week negotiation over moniker—we named her together. At some point, the placenta ("huge and pretty disgusting," in Josh's estimation) made an appearance. The delivery staff took the baby to show her off to my family, the room cleared out, and then a nurse brought our daughter back to us and I nursed for the first time.

Gratitude for my body, for my husband, for the richness of life and this work of creation flooded through me. We cried some more, and then a nurse brought me the most delicious hospital-issue turkey sandwich anyone has ever made. Or so I assume—I wolfed it down too quickly to really notice.

They removed the epidural and sent me off to try to go to the bathroom. I fainted, luckily into the arms of a nurse and not in the toilet.

Back on the delivery bed, the leisurely postbirth pace now vanished, an examination revealed a tear in my cervix that was bleeding. I'd need to get sewn up.

They knocked me out, wheeled me into an operating room (not enough light in the delivery room), and left a very bewildered Josh sitting holding a brand new infant, scared witless.

I was fine; the procedure didn't take long. Josh, though, couldn't believe how quickly we'd moved from rapture to terror. Josh is not someone who prays, but in those tense moments, with every fiber of his being, he flat out *needed* to know that I would be okay.

This is how life goes with children, with love. There are so many things that call us to respond: good and bad and everything in between. We move quickly from joy to pain. And when it comes down to it, after those forty long weeks, we don't have time to worry, don't have time to blame ourselves or cast aspersions on God and others when things don't go well. There's life to be led, a child to raise. Thanks be to God, who promises to be with us through it all.

CHAPTER 3

Called by Name

On names, and identity, and making a place in the world

I KNOW, I KNOW.

My daughter's name is Harper. My name is Lee. Like Harper Lee, the writer. Yes, we like *To Kill a Mockingbird,* and yes, I've read it several times and own two copies, and yes, when we were looking for names, we scanned our bookshelves for ideas. But I swear to you—and you'll just have to believe me on this—that our daughter was six weeks old before I realized that if you paired my name with hers, you get the author of that high school lit class staple.

I remember the moment I figured this out. I was in the bedroom folding clothes—either hers or mine, I can't remember, there was so much laundry in those early days—and I was thinking about signing our names to something, a birthday card perhaps. It was a novelty to have three names to sign. I imagined writing "Harper, Lee, and Rob," and realized what we had done. I think I dropped whatever I was folding and smacked myself in the forehead. Our dear child was doomed to a lifetime of unwanted comments about her name.

I couldn't believe I'd missed it; I'm particularly sensitive to the complications of names. You put Rob's name together with mine and you get a certain Civil War general. Our last name is Moses, which, in addition to inspiring all kinds of minister jokes (really, go ahead, I haven't heard that one before), also ruled out any biblical first names for our children. (This was especially true for boys: Isaac Moses? Noah Moses? We just couldn't do it to our kid.[1]) And with my first name, I've spent my whole life contending with comments like, "I thought you were going to be a man!" I get mail addressed to Mr. Lee Moses. I was once assigned to a boys' PE class. On the phone, customer service representatives are routinely incapable of puzzling out the existence of a woman named Lee. (My progressive-leaning, equality-minded parents chose gender-neutral names for both their daughters because they'd read somewhere—it was the 1970s—that women with nonfeminine names were more successful. There were family connections, too; Lee is my mother's middle name as well as her grandfather's name.)

I did not mean to make things complicated for our daughter. I didn't want her to have to explain her name. We just wanted something different, something we liked, and something that went with Lynn—my sister's name, which we planned to use as a middle name. One night early on in my pregnancy, we were tossing around possibilities and generally vetoing each other's choices. He frowned at my Elena. (Why? It's so pretty!) I did not like his Gordon. (It should have been the perfect choice; we have Gordons on both sides of the family. But I just couldn't picture snuggling up with a baby Gordon.) When it seemed we had exhausted every name in the *Big Book of Baby Names,* I got up and glanced at our book collection, which includes everything from our college texts to Dean Koontz (his) and Jhumpa Lahiri (mine). "What about Harper?" I said. He didn't veto the name right away, so it stayed on the list and eventually ended up at the top.

Her hospital wristband may have said "Baby Girl Moses," but she was Harper Lynn from the moment the midwife declared her a girl and laid her on my chest. "Hello, Harper," we said, as she squinted up at me and screamed.

My dad sang "Sweet Harper Lynn" to the same made-up tune he'd used with our names when my sister and I were babies. My mom called her Babes; Rob called her HarperGirl; my sister even tried out Harpsichord (which didn't stick, but I always kind of liked it). I called her Peach Pie early on, though I don't remember why. Funny Girl is a regular nickname these days, as she dances around the kitchen. So is Babycakes—and I laughed when she said to me one day recently, completely earnestly, "Mama, you're my Babycakes."

It was such a delight when she could say her own name and even more exciting when she could spell it—or at least mimic back to us "H-A-R-P-E-R." Now she's on the verge of writing it herself. She's got the hard lines of the H down, but the angles of the A and the loops of the R and P are a little tricky. She can read her name, though, and knows if a card in the mail is addressed to her.

Someone made a sign for her bedroom door, "HARPER'S ROOM," and her grandparents bought her a kid-size rocking chair with her name painted on it. It was like we were marking territory for her—a person lives here; a person who is somebody; a person with a name.

It's a daunting task, naming a child. The expectant-parent advice books list *choose a name* on the same pre-baby to-do lists as *set up a crib, buy a car seat,* and *pack a bag for the hospital,* but it's really a different category of preparation. After all, her name is the first gift she's given, and she'll keep it longer than anything else we pass on. She'll write it on every school notebook, every "HELLO MY NAME IS . . . " name tag, every form she fills out for the rest of her life.

How do you pick a name? How do you decide who this person will be before you've even met her? Bromleigh and Josh had two girl names picked out, just in case the baby they gave birth to wasn't, in fact, Fiona. (She was.) We had one girl and one boy name each time; we didn't know the gender with either. The first time around, we loved the name Harper Lynn from early on but had a boy name that we weren't crazy about. When I was pregnant the second time, we settled on Jonathan Bruce quickly yet had a girl name that was okay but not great. That was either good luck or some kind of sixth sense about what we were having.

When Harper was born, the moment I remember most clearly was the look she gave me when the midwife first handed her to me: she arched her head back and looked me straight in the eye. With Jonathan, the moment was different: the midwife had just delivered him and held him up in the air before laying him on my chest. It had been a long labor, and in the last few minutes, the baby's heart rate had slowed, so they'd called in the pediatric doctors, just in case. The room was filled with people, but all I could see was that baby, lifted up in the midwife's hands. (Remember that scene from *The Lion King,* when Rafiki presents the newborn Simba to all the animals of the Pride Lands? It was like that, but with fewer jungle animals and no Tim Rice–Elton John soundtrack.) There was a split second—though it felt like an eternity—when everything was silent. But then he gasped, and wailed, and the doctors left with their scary equipment, and the midwife handed him to me so we could get acquainted. "The Baby" turned out to be Jonathan, a boy. *A boy,* I thought. *Who are you?*

How are we supposed to know, in that moment when we give a name to a baby we've just met, who this little somebody is?

Developmental psychologists generally agree that babies don't know, for quite a while, that they are separate people from their parents. It takes a good year and a half or even two years before babies become self-aware beings who realize they are different and separate from their caregivers. It seems to me that naming a child begins the differentiation process because, on a very basic level, names help us distinguish between each other. My daughter is Harper. Not Mom, not Dad, not Jonathan. *Harper.* Who she is—her identity—is defined in part by who she is not. But her identity is also defined by the relationships that surround her: She is daughter to Rob and me, sister to Jonathan, friend to her classmates at school.

My sister would have loved to name her daughter after our grandmother, Lois, but the child's last name is Lane, and that just seemed cruel.[2] Instead, she went with Elizabeth Lee, after me and her sister-in-law, but they call her Eliza. Eliza: her own name, because she is, of course, her own person, someone separate from her parents, an identity still forming. But Elizabeth Lee Lane: deeply connected to her family, to aunts who adore her. She comes from somewhere. She is not alone in the world.

I know a family who adopted their second child through an international adoption. On the plane ride halfway across the world to meet their daughter, they debated what to do about her name. Should they keep the Chinese name she already had or give her a new name to go along with her new home country? They decided on both: She is Ella Bo-Lei, and they call her Lei Lei. Her blended name reminds her that she has two homelands. Her roots are in China, but she also has a home with her parents in the United States.

Sometimes, last names become the signifier of who belongs together, but not always. Bromleigh didn't change her name when she and Josh got married, and they gave their daughters Josh's last name, so when Bromleigh has to call the preschool or the pediatrician, she identifies herself as "Bromleigh McCleneghan, Fiona Hammond's mother." (It's a mouthful; but I'd give anything for one of those syllables in my own short name.) The fact that she doesn't share a last name with her daughters doesn't make them any less a part of her family.

I use both my maiden name and Rob's last name. We debated about that before we got married, and I couldn't decide what to do. (It takes me awhile to make big decisions—have I mentioned that?) Should I keep the Hull that connects me to my parents and sister? Or take on Moses, so I'd match my husband and kids? So, I use both, in a variety of combinations; usually, when I'm dealing with something related to the kids or family stuff, I just use Moses. In professional settings I add the Hull. I never can remember, when I go to the polls to vote, whether I'm registered under H or M. It's imperfect, but so are relationships.

Names differentiate—and relate. Naming a child says: You are separate from us, you are not a part of me any longer, and also: We love you, and there is a place for you here.

You are separate from us.

Naming our children is the first step in sending them off, pushing them away from us. No longer "The Baby," they are people, apart from us, never to be a part of us in the same way again. This is inevitable, of course. From the moment they're born, they're moving away. We give them names not to keep them close, but to send them off. A name says, "You are not a part of me any longer."

The poet Kahlil Gibran writes:

Your children are not your children.
They are the sons and daughters of Life's longing for itself.
They come through you but not from you,
And though they are with you yet they belong not to you.[3]

Jonathan and Harper will always be my babies, but they are moving away from me. From that first moment after each child's birth, from the moment we gave them names, we were sending them out into the world. They do not belong to us.

On the surface of it, this is terribly sad. I look at sweet Jonathan's sleeping face and want to gather him up in my arms forever. I watch Harper's growing legs and wish I could will them to slow down, just for a minute. I can hardly bear the thought that my children won't always be so small, so dependent on me, so willing to snuggle their bodies into mine.

But it is also just the way of things. It is Harper's job right now to push back against nearly everything I'm giving her; that's the only way she'll forge her own identity apart from me. When she's particularly mad at me lately, she'll scream at me before slamming the door to her bedroom, "You are *not* the best mommy!" (*I know, my darling,* I want to tell her in those moments, *I know.*) And once, recently, she was so angry about something I'd done or said that she threatened to send me to China. I don't think she knows anything about China except that it is very, very far away. When I pointed out that if I left, there wouldn't be anyone to make dinner, she said I just had to go for the afternoon. She is figuring out who she is, apart from me.

She tries on different identities, too. That's part of what playing dress-up is about. But even when she's not wearing her Superman cape or her chef's hat or her sparkly ballerina dress, she's often pretending to be Mom to her beloved Elephant or her baby doll. (In these scenarios, I am often the grandmother, an identity with which I am not entirely comfortable at this point.) Right now, she tells me, she wants to be a mom, an artist, and a teacher when she grows up. It occurs to me that she'll try on all kinds of identities over the next twenty-some years, some of which I'll know very little about. What if she wants to be a cheerleader? Or a physicist? She is not a part of me anymore.

We love you, and there is a place for you here.

But as much as her name differentiates her from everybody else, it is also—I hope—a way of claiming a place in the world for her. From the name on her birth certificate to the handmade sign on her bedroom door, Harper's name means she belongs here. When she started a new preschool class last summer, we arrived in the new classroom on the first day and found that her teachers had already set up a cubby for her: a hook for her jacket, a basket for her things, and a sign with her name on it at the very top: HARPER. She knew she belonged.

I have not always been crazy about my own name. It's short and hard to hear. (One of the many reasons I'm glad I met my husband early on: I didn't have to shout my name to strangers in noisy bars.) Everybody thinks I'm a boy. Especially when I was a kid and über-sensitive to the comments and imagined scrutiny of my peers, I longed to be one of the many Jennifers or Amandas in my class. But once, when I was about ten or eleven, my family was walking through a mall and passed a store selling Lee jeans. There must have been a sale going on, because the store was plastered with signs that declared, "It's Lee Week!" My dad—never one to embarrass easily or let anything stand in the way of something for his daughters—went in and asked the manager what they planned to do with the signs after the sale. The manager—maybe he had daughters, too—gave my dad an extra one on the spot. For several years my parents hung it in the family room on my birthday, and I stood underneath it and posed for a picture. I was dorky, sure. But loved? Absolutely. A name tells us that we are loved, that we belong.

In the forty-third chapter of Isaiah, the Lord speaks to the people:

> But now thus says the Lord,
>> he who created you, O Jacob,
>> he who formed you, O Israel:
>> Do not fear, for I have redeemed you;
>> I have called you by name, you are mine.
> When you pass through the waters, I will be with you;
>> and through the rivers, they shall not overwhelm you;
> when you walk through fire you shall not be burned,
>> and the flame shall not consume you.
> For I am the Lord your God,
>> the Holy One of Israel, your Savior.
> I give Egypt as your ransom,
>> Ethiopia and Seba in exchange for you.
> Because you are precious in my sight, and honored, and I love you.

I have called you by name, you are mine.
Isaiah is writing to the people of Israel, scattered far from their homes by invading armies. He writes to remind them of the promises of God: that they are God's people; named "Israel" by God;[4] brought out of Egypt by God; saved, protected, and strengthened by the God who created, called, and named them.

I've always been struck by how personal, how intimate, this text is. This is a conversation between a people and their God, but these are also the whispered words of parent to child: "I have called you by name . . . Because you are precious in my sight, and honored, and I love you." Isn't that what we mean to say to our children whenever we call out their names? When we fill out all those endless forms, when we label their jackets and hang signs on their doors, isn't that what we are trying to tell them? You are precious, and honored, and I love you. This is true even in those moments when we say their names in utter exasperation at the latest mess they have caused. Their names are a promise that they are ours, forever—even when we're angry, even when we're far apart, even when we walk through fire or overwhelming waters.

Except, of course, that they are *not* ours. Not completely.

Those waters that Isaiah mentioned were ferocious, threatening—a metaphor for the tragedy and devastation the people of Israel had seen. But they always make me think of baptism. The waters of baptism have their own kind of ferociousness, I suppose; they are as fierce and life-changing as they are cleansing and life-giving.

The practice of baptism is a place where my tradition differs from Bromleigh's. Her girls have already been baptized, in the United Methodist tradition, as babies. We Disciples practice "believer's baptism," which means we baptize older children and adults, encouraging them to decide for themselves about committing to being part of the body of Christ. (Bromleigh's girls, and other baptized babies, will have a similar opportunity through confirmation when they're a little older.) Our practice comes from our founders' commitment to a New Testament practice of faith, which they understood to include the baptism of adults by full immersion into the water. Jesus, after all, was baptized as an adult.

Alexander Campbell, one of the founders of the movement that became the Christian Church (Disciples of Christ), wrestled with the meaning of baptism, especially as he and his followers were moving away from the tradition of baptizing infants. He came to understand that baptism was a public demonstration and acceptance of God's forgiveness—"a sign of God's grace toward us and a way of our saying 'yes' to that grace," says contemporary theologian Clark Williamson—and also an entry into the church universal, the family of God.[5]

Nowadays, I should note, though we practice believer's baptism by immersion for those who've never been baptized, we don't insist on it for folks who've been baptized in other traditions. In fact, we discourage rebaptism; we believe God's grace is bestowed in all kinds of ways. Our tradition's organizing document—our affirmation of faith—reminds us, "through baptism into Christ, we enter into newness of life and are made one with the whole people of God."[6] It's a way of claiming our place in the life God offers us.

Harper is still several years away from making that decision herself. When she does—if she chooses to—she'll walk through those waters and rise with dripping hair to claim the name God has already bestowed upon her: Beloved. She'll claim the place that is already there for her in the family of God. She will know the grace upon grace that is already hers.

She is mine—but she is God's. We named these children, and they are ours to take care of for a little while, but they do not belong to us. So—maybe—in the same way that we mark territory for Harper by putting her name on things, making room for her in our lives and our home, baptism does the same thing—marks her as God's beloved, reminds her there is a place for her in the great family of Christ, and affirms that she has been called by name, that she is precious, and honored, and loved

Bedtime

On Ferber, and freedom, and faith

BEDTIME WAS ALWAYS A BIT OF A ZOO IN MY CHILDHOOD HOME. My younger sisters, Whitney and Taylor, and I begged our parents to sit in our rooms or lie on our beds, telling us stories and singing us songs until we fell asleep. My dad told stories of "The Super Sisters"—Super Brom, Wonder Whit, and Terrific Tay—who routinely journeyed to the homeland of the Smurfs in their magic cloud for days of adventuring and fun. The songs comprised an eclectic mix, with several frequent repeats on the playlist: George Gershwin's lullaby "Summertime" from *Porgy and Bess*; the Civil War folk song "When Johnny Comes Marching Home"; and "There's a Kind of Hush," the last top-ten hit for Herman's Hermits back in 1967, the year my dad was in the eighth grade and listening to WLS-AM with his older sisters.

My parents both worked outside the home—my dad as a pastor, and my mom, in those years, as a Christian education director and co-owner of a business called The Work Room, which did everything from costuming dance shows to designing and constructing decorative displays for shopping malls. (Giant bears, snowmen, and banners often overtook her sewing table at home; the greatest peril of my childhood was the danger of stepping on the pins that were often hidden in the thick brown carpeting in our family room.) They worked incredible hours, spread out over days and nights and weekends. They were home a lot, too—I ate lunch at our kitchen table with my dad nearly every day from kindergarten through the sixth grade—but they were frequently exhausted. They'd spread out on the floor next to our beds and drop off long before my sisters and I succumbed to the darkness and heavy eyelids. We had energy left to resist.

Much of that energy was nervous energy, exuded in attempts to avoid sleep entirely. I was afraid of the dark and the Salt Vampire (from "The Man Trap" episode of the original *Star Trek* series); Whitney was afraid of fires and the ghost of a pet hamster who'd had an unfortunate run-in with our dog in her bedroom; Tay has just always liked to be surrounded by blankets and bodies. And so my poor parents would lie there, waiting forever until they were certain we couldn't possibly be awake, and then try to sneak off, silently crawling out of the room, praying the floorboards wouldn't creak. Inevitably one of us would stir and complain about their exit. Many, many nights, Taylor (the youngest, our baby) ended up in their bed, and Whitney climbed in with me. And nearly every night my parents cursed their perceived failures to avoid or remedy this bedtime craziness.

Despite the fact that we girls enjoyed all the stories, songs, and nighttime togetherness, my parents have spoken for years of the nightly ritual as a source of regret. When I was first pregnant, they cautioned me: Put that baby in the crib. Get bedtime figured out.

I had every intention of heeding their warnings. Josh was totally against having the baby in our bed, convinced we would smother her or she would be swallowed up by our big down comforter. I was going to continue to have primary child-care duties for the first months after my maternity leave ended, and I would be relying on her taking long daytime naps so I could get work done. We read several sleep-training books, with their clearly laid out plans for getting babies to sleep well and independently. Each had its own underlying "philosophy."

◊   Babies have to be empowered to put themselves to sleep. (You're emotionally crippling them if you deny them this training, one author seemed to suggest.)

◊   The family's life should not adjust to the baby; the baby should adjust to the family. (You're silly and weak if you let a teeny baby boss you around and set your schedule, I read between the lines.)

◊   Allowing your baby to cry it out may seem cruel, but it's a short-lived pain for the sake of a hassle-free schedule later. (Suck it up.)

◊   Children, even babies, have to respect their parents' authority. Spoil that baby, and you'll pay for it later. (This is Christian? I wondered.)

My reactions might have been ever so slightly defensive or hyperbolic, but reading up on bedtime introduced me to just how ideological much of the parenting literature can be. During my pregnancy, though, I wasn't entirely turned off by all these strong positions. Their claims became my aspirations: I would have a baby who slept all the way through the night within three months. Armed with my "toolbox"—a white noise machine, a sling, and photocopies of the schedules and charts in the back of these books—I would escape the lack of order that apparently plagued my parents.

I would be brave and stand my ground; I would find and adhere to a bedtime routine in a way my parents couldn't. I would let my baby cry. *I* knew it wasn't the end of the world. But we wouldn't let this yet-to-be child cry indefinitely. Who was I? A monster? My grandmother ("Let them cry; it's the only way")? We would use a *modified* cry-it-out strategy.

Of course, when our daughter Fiona was born, as anyone but I could have expected, all bets were off. But not because things were more desperate than we had anticipated.

One of Josh's colleagues swore by a sleep-training method that promised to have your baby sleeping twelve hours a night within twelve weeks. The plan seemed reasonable, even as it promised something miraculous. The approach requires that parents gradually increase the amount their babies are eating during the day (so they get less hungry and wake up less frequently at night). That's hard to keep track of while nursing, though, so mothers were advised to pump all our breast milk. This advice met with two major stumbling blocks in our household. First, I was unreasonably terrified of my breast pump for a long time. Okay, maybe not *terrified*—but definitely intimidated. The pump came with an instructional video that I could not bring myself to watch; I could not get my head around how ridiculous I felt milking myself with a double electric breast pump. And in those early months, when I was still on maternity leave, I had no incentive to be brave.

But the even bigger problem was not a problem at all. I loved nursing. I loved being so close to Fiona. I loved watching her drop off while suckling. The pull of her tiny mouth on my unaccustomed nipples was painful at first, but for me, the pain subsided with time and the liberal use of food-grade lanolin. Within a few weeks, nursing was downright convenient. We never had to load up the diaper bag with bottles or spend money on formula. And for months, naptimes and bedtimes were not only nearly painless, but sweet. I would nurse her into what Josh called a "milk coma" and then set her gently in the crib. She woke up to nurse—and would not be denied—but as long as the breast was quickly offered, Fiona was a happy, happy baby and a good sleeper. I was remarkably well-rested during my weeks away from work.

My relief at this development cannot be overstated. Now that I was parent to an actual baby, other cracks in the confident acceptance of these sleep models started to appear, however. While knowing that "having a baby changes everything," I began to harbor considerable doubt that we could become the sort of people who would maintain the strict schedule required by the "twelve hours" method. In retrospect, I see it would have taken a miracle.

Even more than a miracle, though, it would have taken a change of heart. My life manifests a certain ambivalence about order and schedules. One of my favorite things about my work, one of the things that drove me into the ministry, honestly, is the fact that no day includes all the same tasks. I am too manic (too "creative"?) to work nine to five; I love having days where I meet with people and run programs all day, and other days where I sit in coffee shops reading and writing. Blame it on my parents (why not?), but I don't mind working days, nights, and weekends, as long as I can play hooky sometimes and never have to keep track of my sick days, and the decision to go into the office late on the morning after a late-night meeting falls squarely on my shoulders. Maybe it's not so much a problem with schedules as with other people having authority over my schedule.

Whether it's a sign of some personality flaw or a virtue of my calling, in the tension between structure and freedom, my affinity is for freedom. And, looking at life in our little family, it seemed this was the best direction for us. Given that my work schedule was never the same—some nights I was home to get the baby to sleep by 7:30 and others I was out late due to one of those aforementioned meetings—it made sense that our baby should learn to be flexible, too.

Madeleine L'Engle, beloved children's author and Christian essayist extraordinaire, writes about how she found herself making a similar choice for her family. When her first child was born, her husband was an actor and often would not get home from the theater until two in the morning. She tells of other young mothers she knew whose husbands were also working in the theater. These women would be up at 6:00 a.m. to feed their babies, but then would be too exhausted to talk to their husbands when they returned home. The men, rather than unwind in solitude in a dark and lonely apartment, would go out drinking.

L'Engle didn't want that to happen to her, to them. When she was still in the hospital following Josephine's birth, she had to fight to nurse, since "nobody nurses babies nowadays" (her daughter was born in the 1940s). Having won that battle, she was soon faced with another. The hospital staff wanted to eliminate the baby's middle-of-the-night feeding. That would be a good thing for many families, those in which parents were working nine to five. But that wasn't their life. So the new mother suggested that because she was usually up at two, she would rather skip the 6:00 a.m. feeding. She recalls, "I was told in no uncertain terms that it was the 2:00 a.m. feeding which would be cut. I replied in equally certain terms that if my baby was brought to me at 6:00 a.m. I would turn my breasts to the wall. I won."[1]

Reading this story, and L'Engle's reflection ("I made a choice, a free yet structured choice"), bolstered me. This is what we were doing. We would not be ruled by my grandmother's expectations or my parents' regrets or the admonitions of sleep-training experts who knew nothing of our lives. We would do what was right for our family.

Over time, then, nursing became a panacea. Hungry baby? Nurse. Tired baby? Nurse. Cranky baby? Nurse. Teething baby? Nurse. Startled baby? You get the picture. I could take her anywhere and keep her out late. She went to the theater and restaurants, to friends' houses and meetings. Life was full and my sense of modesty was modified dramatically, but we'd found freedom where we'd expected to be homebound and restricted by a baby's schedule.

Josh and I had always imagined we would share equally in parenting duties, but the replacement of the experts' toolbox with nursing meant I was the one who always put Fee to sleep; I was the one who always took her when she cried. I lost sleep, but for a long time I did not mind. My beloved felt differently, I think. Because nursing was our cure-all, his toolbox felt significantly emptier. For those seemingly endless first months, Fiona cried as much when handed to him as to anyone. "She hates me," he'd lament.

We learned soon enough that there were other problems with our strategy. I was the only one who could get Fiona to sleep. It turned out she liked cuddling as much as I did (maybe more!) and would wake up protesting when I tried to put her down in the crib. When I returned to work and my father-in-law became her daily caregiver, he could only get her to sleep by pushing her around in a stroller—during the winter, he'd push her in a ridiculous loop through our kitchen and dining and living rooms for hours on end.

I feared I would never be able to wean her. I grew frustrated that she always wanted *me.* I lamented how hard it was to leave her at night, knowing she would cry inconsolably for whatever poor sap we got to watch her. Josh was left with a baby who inevitably cried while I was gone at those evening meetings, refusing bottles and any other form of solace. He's a teacher, and his schedule and commute require that he leave the house by six most mornings. Up since 5:00 a.m., he'd fall into bed as soon as I got home on meeting nights, leaving me to get Fiona down and leaving us with no time to check in with one another, no time to reconnect.

What had begun as a rejection of outside structures and schedules felt increasingly difficult to maintain. We tried to change our ways. We put Fiona in bed drowsy but still awake, with a pacifier and a "Sleep Sheep." We would sing to her, leave the room. We tried to use Dr. Richard Ferber's system in which parents leave the baby alone for increasing amounts of time, until eventually, the infant goes to sleep without the parents in the room. It works for a lot of people, and we envied our friends who'd endured the weeks it had taken to "Ferberize" their babies. But, whether it was the system itself or our failure to execute it properly, it just made Fiona mad. She'd cry hysterically, angrily, until we could no longer endure her increasingly hoarse shrieking.

Through conversations with friends who had children Fiona's age, Josh and I learned that no strategy works with all kids all the time, and we were comforted by the knowledge that all parents are seemingly in this mess together. But while identification of this harried communion helped alleviate some of our regrets, we still longed to figure bedtime out. Also comforting was our increasing affinity for attachment parenting—the idea that babies just want to be held, to know they're safe and loved. We didn't feel any particular need to develop Fiona's independence while she was still months away from the end of infancy. I read anthropologist Meredith F. Small's book *Our Babies, Ourselves* and was reminded that culture shapes both our methods and expectations in parenting; not everyone throughout history and around the world insists on cribs and independence and crying it out.[2] This was particularly helpful to me as a Christian. My theology regularly prompts me to question the assumptions of U.S. culture—taking what is useful and holy to me and eschewing the rest—but in my role as a new mom, I was pretty reliant on the wisdom of "Mommy culture." And yet, as Fiona got older and months passed, we also wanted to be able to have time together as a couple. We wanted to be able to go out on a date.

Years earlier, on our very first date, Josh and I had sat over dinner and compared professional notes. At the time, he was teaching fifth grade in an elementary school on Chicago's South Side. Just about all the students received breakfast and lunch at school—that is, almost all of them were living in poverty. The school had some great teachers and some terrible teachers, too few resources, and too many students. Josh excels in his field generally, but the key to his success at that school was his understanding of the critical importance of classroom management.

"Kids need some structure. They need to know what they can depend on. They need to know that there are rules and expectations—for everyone, including the teacher—and that the rules are fair. If they can trust that, basics like listening and paying attention become routine, and they can use their energy to actually learn," he mused over mediocre Italian food.

I sat there pretty well enraptured. Teachers are hot, man. Men who love kids? Be still my beating heart.

We talked politics: In addition to a mostly calm learning environment, kids need a full stomach if they're going to learn. If their parents leave for work before they wake up, or if they can't afford a good breakfast and instead stop to get a bag of chips at the corner gas station each morning, their bodies can't stay alert, their minds can't focus on the critical work of learning. I couldn't believe my luck: He was cute, *and* he understood the importance of funding Head Start.

Eventually, we talked theology. (I masquerade as a functional social being, but I am such a nerd. Talking about theology on a first date. Sheesh. But he didn't seem to mind. And that is why I married him.) I was reading Paul Tillich a lot in those days and heard in Josh's description of his classroom management style a bit of Gospel according to Tillich. I tried to make my case, largely to convince my as-yet-unchurched date, that my career path wasn't totally insane.

Tillich thinks our faith is limited by understandings of God as some strange man in the sky with unending powers and inscrutable motivations. Tillich would prefer we think of God not as far above us but as the ground on which we stand, the power that moves beneath and through everything that is, the power of love and creation, of life and all that is: the "ground of being."

As a native German, Tillich was steeped in Lutheran theology (Martin Luther was German, too). And, to my thinking, Tillich's slightly inaccessible "ground of being" language emerges from Luther's description of faith as trust. Faith is not primarily about accepting certain propositions or blindly believing ridiculous things. Faith is about trusting in God. Trusting God to be present. Trusting that God is powerful and good. Trusting that God will show us grace.

That trust is the ground on which everything else is built. It's the foundation of everything else. In Matthew 7:24-27 Jesus tells the story about the houses built on sand and rock: One washes away when the rains come; the other can withstand just about anything.

Faith in God is the rock, the trust that frees people to do anything,
to build lives that are strong and whole. It is (and this is why I was
going off about Tillich over drinks on a hot summer Tuesday) the
genius of good classroom management. Knowing that there are
certain givens, certain things we can trust, engenders the courage
and confidence (in theology, we might say "the assurance of grace")
kids need to learn and explore the world. This assurance is what
we all need—and definitely what I needed to get up and get out
of the house and overcome the crippling doubt that sometimes fell
upon me in the first months of Fiona's life. *We brought a baby into
this world? What, are we crazy?*

Of course, just having a firm foundation doesn't solve all our
problems. Josh and I had thrown away all our sleep-training strategies in a burst of confidence, sure that as long as Fiona could trust
that we would always be there in the night, that she never had
reason to fear, we'd be doing right by her and helping her develop
the sort of trusting spirit she'd need to grow into a person of faith.
And that was true. But we hadn't counted on the toll our lack
of structure would take on our marriage. We hadn't anticipated
wanting to throttle her as she got older and her refusal to sleep
became willful. It's awfully hard to be that loving, trustworthy presence when you are entering hour three of the Bedtime Battle for
the umpteenth night in a row.

On those crazy-making nights, Josh and I found some conso-
lation in the knowledge, once more, that we are not alone. As
our kids have gotten older, friends with a wide array of bedtime
approaches have assured us that every parent faces tantrums at one
point or another. Kids seem to cycle through easy periods and
harder ones; times that are more rife with conflict and months of
joy and rapture. When I told my friend Laura Jean that I was extol-
ling the virtues of her and Tim's steely wills in establishing a routine
with their daughter in this chapter, she laughed. "As we speak, my
child is pitching a fit in the other room. Some routine!"

Once parents discover that there's no entirely painless way to do bedtime and naptime, we have to figure out what it is we want our kids' overriding experience to be about. My parents, for all their regrets, gave my sisters and me the reassurance that we would never be left alone. We knew they would always be there for us. We felt loved and heard. We knew our fears were important to our parents. They took them seriously and would sit with us until hamster ghosts and Salt Vampires were vanquished or, at least, fell asleep in the closet.

Developmental psychologists and social scientists suggest that the task of parents, particularly as kids get older, is to help their children feel grounded enough to successfully navigate change and risk. No problem, right?—since we adults have that all figured out, we should have an easy time conveying it to our children! Living in this tension—between structures and freedom (Tillich calls it dynamics and form)—is a part of human life. We never figure it out, and if we were to try to settle on one side or the other in any sort of ultimate way, we'd run into trouble. We don't want to be ruled by strict forms that don't give us room to breathe and grow and adapt, but we also don't want to flounder in our freedom, going every which way.

While it is easy to succumb to self-doubt when you're wondering if the baby is asleep "enough" to put her down, or if you're trying to evaluate whether her cries are escalating or subsiding, or, generally, if you're exhausted, I maintain that there's something really critical about bedtime—about parents and kids facing the long, dark night—that warrants this reflection. Sociologist Peter Berger writes in his book *A Rumor of Angels* about the human need to order the universe and uses the example of a mother tending to her child after he awakens, crying, in the night. Berger writes that she will tell him in soothing tones that "everything is all right."[3]

In a factual sort of way, everything in this world is not all right. There are dangers in the world, grave injustices, threats to us as individuals and to all living things. Kids know this. They see it from very early on, and they see all too clearly when the adults in their lives are afraid. Berger asks, in light of this, "Is the mother lying to the child?" When the mother is reassuring her son that he can trust in her, that he can trust in the world, in God, "in being," is she just telling him a fib to get him to go back to sleep? Berger says no:

> Every parent (or, at any rate, every parent who loves his child) takes upon himself the representation of a universe that is ultimately in order and ultimately trustworthy. This representation can be justified only within a religious (strictly speaking a supernatural) frame of reference. In this frame of reference the natural world within which we are born, love, and die is not the only world, but only the foreground of another world in which love is not annihilated in death, and in which, therefore the trust in the power of love to banish chaos is justified. . . . *The parental role is not based on a loving lie.*[4]

Loving parents—of the sort I'd like to be—aren't lying. They're witnessing to faith that there is a loving God. We may not be sure in every moment that we can trust that there's an order and goodness to the universe; we may not always dare to believe that God, or we, can vanquish the boogey men, both real and imagined, that threaten. We may be uncertain about how we can best help our kids learn to adapt and flourish in the world; in fact, we may still worry about how *we* are navigating the tension between the structures that shape our home lives and the freedom we need to breathe and adapt to changes in our work, our relationships, and our kids. But we try to trust that all will be well—that Jesus Christ is victorious over death and that everything else will fall into place from there. I try to trust that God is good, at bedtime and all the time.

In other words, Fee needs a bedtime, but we're not gonna be jerks about it. We will continue to tell endless stories and sing another song, and we will occasionally leave her to yell at a baby-sitter, so Josh and I can get some time alone. And when I lie next to her (for her terrible bedtimes have graduated from a crib, to a toddler bed, and now to a twin "Big Girl" bed), rubbing her back after returning from a late meeting to find her father frustrated and her still awake, I will resolve not to ruminate on my despair that we're in for years of this mess but will rather turn to the words of Julian of Norwich, and offer a lullaby in prayer: *All shall be well, and all shall be well, and all manner of things shall be well.*[5]

Good Work

On rest, and work, and getting things done

ROB FINDS ME IN THE KITCHEN, PASSIVE-AGGRESSIVELY SLAMMING dishes into the dishwasher. I am thinking dark thoughts about the injustice of it all: how I am the one who always gets stuck with the dirty dishes, the one who takes care of everything around the house, the one who makes sure the bills get paid on time. I say none of this out loud, however, because it is utterly unfair. Rob has spent the evening mowing the grass, giving Harper a bath, running to the grocery store. It is 10:30, and neither of us has stopped moving since we got home from work. We are weary.

He can read my mood, because we've been married six years and have played out this scene many times, so he approaches cautiously. "Can you be done?" he asks.

He doesn't mean my pouting. He's asking—kindly, really— what else I need to do before I can be finished for the night, before I can sit on the couch for a few minutes and watch the news or put my pajamas on and crawl into bed. But there are still clean clothes to fold, food to prepare for tomorrow's dinner, and I'm not prepared for my morning meeting.

I long, most days, to be done.

I watch other parents dash from one activity to the next, from office to school to baseball diamond, gasping for breath, and I am occasionally shocked to discover that I am one of them. Harper isn't even old enough to be involved in activities, and still, we always seem to be rushing. When I leave the office at the end of the day, there is always another phone call to make, another e-mail to send, another article to read. At home, the dishes pile up faster than we can wash them. We're amazed at how many dishes three people can use in the course of a day and how many times the floor needs to be swept. There is always a load of laundry to be done, another bill to pay, a bathroom to clean.

There's also an expectation that somewhere in all this, we'll find time for rest from our labors. "Pamper yourself!" all the parenting magazines command, urging me to get a pedicure, take a walk, go out with friends, or hire a babysitter and go to a movie. But there are still unwashed dishes, unfolded laundry, and unswept floors, so even those rare moments of quiet are tainted by the pressure of all those unfinished tasks. I would never rest if I waited for the work to be done.

The command to rest is one of the most ancient in the Judeo-Christian tradition. It's right there in the Ten Commandments, given to the Israelites in the wilderness as they were learning what it meant to be God's people: "Remember the sabbath day, and keep it holy. Six days you shall labor and do all your work. But the seventh day is a sabbath to the LORD your God; you shall not do any work" (Exod. 20:8-10a). A whole day of rest, without any work. For centuries, faithful people have practiced sabbath-keeping as a way to put aside the worries of the world and commune with the Divine.

The sabbath commandment itself is rooted in God's own day of rest after six busy days of creating the world: "And on the seventh day God finished the work that he had done, and he rested on the seventh day from all the work that he had done" (Gen. 2:2). That word *finished* glares at me from the page, and I search desperately through other translations, but it's there in nearly every English version. The hard part about Sabbath-keeping, it seems to me, is the stopping—especially when the work isn't done. Must I really fold all the laundry before I can sit down? Must I cross off every item on my to-do list before I go home? Must I really *finish* all the work before I rest?

"God," I think irreverently, "did not have a toddler at home."

Abraham Joshua Heschel, an American rabbi who wrote eloquently about the sabbath and its importance in the Jewish tradition, calls the sabbath a "palace in time."[1] The seventh day, he suggests, reminds us that the world has already been created and will get along without us for a while. Heschel notes that rest—or *menuha* in the original Hebrew—means "much more than withdrawal from labor and exertion, more than freedom from toil, strain, or activity from any kind. *Menuha* is not a negative concept but something real and intrinsically positive." He quotes the ancient rabbis: "What was created on the seventh day? Tranquility, serenity, peace, and repose."[2]

I don't know many families with young children who use the words *tranquility, serenity, peace,* and *repose* to describe their lives.

I know that quiet time spent with God is important, and I adore that image of Heschel's "palace in time." I know my life can get overrun by all the tasks of the day. Carving out and protecting sabbath time helps me pay attention to my relationship with God. I've always loved the idea of an early-morning prayer time, when I sit with my Bible and my coffee in my quiet kitchen and look out the back window and ponder God's goodness. About twice a year—usually just after New Year's and again in early September, when school starts and the church program year begins—I decide I'm really going to do it. I pick out a devotional book, get the coffee ready the night before, and set my alarm early. I usually stick with it for a day or two, and then something happens: Harper gets sick and we're up all night, or I have an early meeting, or I sleep through my alarm and am lucky to get out the door on time. I always feel vaguely guilty when my morning prayer "habit" fades, because, I suppose, it's yet another thing on the should-do list. But I *don't* feel disconnected from God when I stop. As good as that quiet time sounds, it's been my experience that God is found not only in the still moments but also in loud, busy, never-ending days.

Rob and I both have full-time jobs outside our home. We knew we wanted to have children, but I never had any ambition to "stay home with the kids," and neither did he. I never felt I had to choose between work and family. I assumed I could do both—and that I wanted to. Like most things about parenting, however, our prebaby idea of what that meant was completely different from our postbaby reality.

When Harper was born, I had a good maternity leave: nearly three months with full pay and benefits, and for the most part, work left me alone. Rob and I had talked about what to do with "the baby" (as we called her before she was born) once I went back to work, but we hadn't made final plans. Child care just loomed out there as something else to figure out in addition to the diapers and the sleeping schedule. Rob assured me repeatedly, in my many moments of angst as my leave neared its end, that he did not expect me to bear the burden of child care alone. The reality, though, was that I had the breast milk and the more flexible job, so much of the juggling during those first few months fell to me.

Our first arrangement was an experiment, and it didn't work that well. The church I was serving had a well-equipped nursery, and I wanted to keep Harper nearby so that I could keep breast-feeding. We arranged for a college student in our congregation to meet me at the church when she wasn't in class and watch Harper downstairs in the nursery, bringing her up to me when it was time to nurse. When the babysitter wasn't available, I planned to have Harper with me in my office.

Keeping her with me sounded like a good idea. Rob helped me set up the pack-and-play in the corner, and I made a cute little pink-and-white sign to hang on my door when we were nursing. People stopped by to tell me how adorable she was. My colleagues were generously accommodating and graciously managed to tell me they didn't really mind her screaming while they were trying to talk on the phone.

But there were a number of problems with this arrangement. Our babysitter's class schedule, like that of most college students, was sporadic at best. She was free in the morning one day, the afternoon the next, and some days she had class right in the middle of the day. It also turned out that packing up all the baby supplies every morning was more trouble than it was worth. So eventually she began coming to our home to watch Harper, and I would take my breast pump to work. But I'd usually have only about two hours of solid work time before I'd have to rush home so she could get to class. Then, I'd just stay home and try to work from there, or pack everything up and take Harper back to church, where I would pray that she'd fall asleep so I could get something done.

Harper didn't exactly cooperate with our plan, either. I had imagined her sleeping while I worked or playing quietly on the floor. But she has never been one to do anything quietly (a trait she must have gotten from her more extroverted father) and has generally been happiest when someone is paying attention to her. The pack-and-play sat unused in the corner, and I spent most of my time walking up and down the church hallway, trying to calm her down enough to go back to the office. I could occasionally make a phone call while she was eating, but I called only people who would understand if she started wailing in the middle of our conversation. One afternoon, our custodian accidentally walked in while Harper was nursing. I wasn't bothered; I was completely covered up, and by then so many people had seen my breasts it didn't matter to me anymore. But he was so embarrassed that he couldn't make eye contact with me for a week.

I couldn't concentrate, and I wasn't very productive. Tasks I used to handle easily started falling through the cracks. I felt bad that I wasn't doing my job very well, and I felt bad that I was lugging Harper around town instead of letting her fall into a regular schedule at home. "This isn't working," I muttered to myself several times—before finally admitting that it really wasn't.

I'd been breast-feeding this whole time, but once Harper was in full-time child care, my milk supply started to falter. "She needs more milk," the child-care provider told me nearly every day. I took Harper to the pediatrician's office, where the lactation consultant watched her nurse, assured me I was doing everything right, and suggested I try some herbal remedies and get lots of rest. "And if that doesn't help," she said, "you may want to think about working parttime."

Her words haunted me as I dropped my daughter off at the babysitter's and headed back to my office. I didn't think I'd have to choose, but there it was: my baby or my work?

It wasn't that stark a choice, of course, but it felt like that at the time. And it wasn't that difficult either: Despite my great love for my daughter, I never really considered cutting back on my work. My working parttime would have demanded lots of negotiations with the church and would have had huge financial implications for us at home. But beyond those concerns, I love my job. I think it's important. It's part of who I am. I was going to keep working. If, as seemed to be the case, I wasn't making enough milk for my baby, I was going to have to do something else.

I put it off as long as I could. I did everything the books and doctors suggested to increase my milk supply: I ate oatmeal for breakfast, drank the awful fenugreek tea, took the More Milk Plus pill that was supposed to "boost milk production." And I pumped. Oh, did I pump. Five times a day, most days: I'd get up early, before Harper stirred, and sit in the dark living room in my pajamas, still half asleep as the pump pulled at my sore breasts. Then, three times while I was at work (I made a new sign for the door, not nearly as cute) and once more before bed. Sometimes, I would forget the late-night pumping until I was already under the covers. "Dammit!" I'd yell in the general direction of the universe as I climbed out of bed and headed for the kitchen, exhausted and angry. This was not particularly good energy, perhaps, to seep into the primary sustenance of my child.

It helped, for a while—all the pumping and the endless cups of tea (which, contrary to a friend's advice, was *not* any better with honey). But slowly, the stash of milk in the freezer started dwindling. One day at the grocery store, Rob bought a can of formula and put it in the cupboard, unopened. "I don't want it to be a big deal when we finally decide to use it," he said. The can frowned at me every time I opened the cupboard door.

I don't remember when or why I finally gave in. I do remember sitting on the couch, fighting feelings of inadequacy, while Rob mixed up the bottle in the kitchen. The problem wasn't that I was opposed to formula. I'd read all the debates for and against and decided I didn't really have a stake in the matter. And I'm not a purist. By then, Harper was eating Cheerios dropped on restaurant floors, so I could hardly argue that it wasn't healthy. The problem was that I had to face the reality that my decision to keep working was, in fact, having an impact on my child's life. I had to make a choice after all.

Life got easier after that, I have to admit. I got more done at work because I wasn't constantly stopping to pump. I didn't have to get up so early or stay up quite so late. I didn't have to wash pumps and bottles every night or remember to take milk to the babysitter's every morning. I kept nursing a few times a day until a month or two past Harper's first birthday. I intentionally didn't notice the last time we nursed. It just got more and more sporadic until one day I realized we hadn't nursed for several weeks. She was drinking whole milk then, from a sippy cup instead of a bottle, so it made sense.

It turns out that this was only one instance of the constant choices I must make between the vaguely defined realms of "work" and "home." Will I stay at the office and get ahead for next week or pick up my daughter and go to the playground? Will I get the kitchen cleaned up right after dinner or go play with blocks on the living room floor? Will I have a lazy Saturday morning with my family or get up early to finish a project? Will I do the bare minimum at work so I can get home sooner or the bare minimum at home so I can do well at work? Is there any middle ground?

I am lucky to work with people who understand—and even value—my commitment to both work and family. At a potluck dinner at church one night, after a particularly long week, a church member came up and gave me an unexpected hug. "That's for being a working mom," she said. I was embarrassed, a bit, that my frazzledness was showing—but mostly I was grateful that she understood.

I believe that maintaining good boundaries between work and home will keep me sane. I bring home as little work as possible, and I've discovered (on days when the day care is closed) that taking a toddler to work is even harder than managing an infant there. But I am also becoming convinced that the two spheres are not completely separate. I am as fully *me* in my role of mother as in my role as pastor. I am not one without the other, which is why I do both.

This awareness is not much help, however, when rest is hard to come by and the work never seems to be finished.

On a day when I was feeling particularly overwhelmed with the tasks of life, someone read to me a passage from *The Miracle of Mindfulness,* in which Buddhist monk Thich Nhat Hanh suggests that if we do the tasks of everyday life—like washing dishes—just to get them done and move on to the next task, we will inevitably rush from one task to the next, missing most of the goodness of life. But if we are "mindful" about the work we are doing—if we are "washing the dishes to wash the dishes"—then we are more aware of ourselves and our surroundings: "The fact that I am standing there and washing these bowls," he says, "is a wondrous reality."[3]

I only sort of half agree with this—and not just because it is hard to mindfully wash the dishes when there is a toddler pulling

on your pants, begging, "Watch Elmo? Watch Elmo?" I'm not sure
there's always something holy about everyday chores; sometimes
you just wash the dishes because you want to have a clean bowl for
cereal in the morning. But it is true that there is goodness in the
work we do. I'm grateful (when I let myself stop and think about it)
that I have dishes to wash and clothes to fold. I'm grateful to have
a family to eat dinner with, even if it means the floor needs to be
mopped every night. I'm grateful for a job I love, most of the time,
and a house to clean.

I won't lie; it's a lot, managing a full-time job and a full-time
family. There's a lot said about "work-life balance," but that implies
that there's a particular equation, and if I could just figure out what
it is—working a little less, being home a little more, or the other
way around—the scales would even out, and I'd be at peace. But life
doesn't seem to work that way, at least not for me. My life does not
easily divide into discrete categories like job and family or work
and rest. There are not many quiet moments. There are days when
home feels a lot like work, and there are mornings when I'm glad
to get to my office because at least there aren't smashed up bananas
all over the floor. It's hard to imagine it all balancing out; it's even
harder to imagine taking a whole day off each week to practice
sabbath.[4]

Rest is important, and so is quiet time in the presence of God.
It's important to stop sometimes and be reminded that we are not
indispensable, that the world will go on without us. But the work
is important, too. It occurs to me that maybe the most important
word in the Genesis creation story isn't *finished*. It's *good*. At the
end of each day, God looks on all the work and declares it *good*.
Maybe it's not just the creation but the very work of creating it that
is good. And maybe the work that God has called me to do—the
holy work of tending to a congregation and caring for my children,
even the mundane work of washing the dirty cereal bowls—maybe
there's goodness and wholeness in that work, too.

After all, even after God closed up shop on the sixth day, the work wasn't really over. The work of creation continues as God's grace forms and re-forms our lives. I need look no further than my daughter, making "worms" out of orange Play-Doh and singing to herself, to believe that God is still at work. Harper is so busy all the time—exploring her world, learning new words, creating, imagining, discovering. That is her work right now—all that learning—and she delights in it. It is very good work. And while Rob and I don't always delight in mopping the floor or folding the laundry, I'd venture to say that that's good work too, and that God is at work even there, forming us into the parents our kids need us to be. So, sure, the work doesn't ever get completely finished; the to-do list never fully crossed out. But maybe it's not the finished-ness of our work that gives us reason to rest; perhaps it is the good-ness—the God-ness—of our work.

Harper woke up earlier than usual one morning with a kind of mournful cry as she transitioned from sleep. It was a haunting noise, and I worried that something was wrong. But by the time I got to her room, she was fully awake and standing in her crib, grinning at me. "Mommy's bed?" She asked, already thinking ahead. So we gathered her things (at that point, she slept with her elephant, two green blankets, and one pink blanket, which she insisted on having with her at all times), and I carried her back to our room.

Rob rolled over and squinted at us sleepily, then helped her get settled. She squirmed a bit, arranging the blankets, getting her head in just the right spot on the pillow. She was tickled to be lying between us: "Hello, Mommy!" she said to me, then flipped her head to Rob. "Hello, Daddy!"

As she started to tell her elephant a story in a language only they understand, I caught Rob's eye above her head and we smiled.

"This is good," I thought, and we rested a moment before the day began.

Cuddling, and Other Not-As-Precious Things about Incarnation

On intimacy, and being human, and assorted bodily fluids

CALLIOPE, MY BABY, NOW A TODDLER, HAS WATCHED MORE TELEVI-
sion than is good for her this morning. She was up early, and it
was my plan to park her in front of *Elmo's World: Springtime Fun*
on my laptop while I snuck off for a much-needed shower. I am a
congested disaster right now and can barely keep my eyes open for
all the crud pushing against my face from within. I had hoped the
hot water would help me shake the "walking undead" feeling with
which I'd awakened.

But Miss Calliope was too sweet, too cuddly. At twenty-one
months she still likes a bottle for comfort (don't judge me), and
thus, as I got the video ready, she climbed into my lap and lay back
in my arms to enjoy her milk, her mother, and her hero. Change
of plans: I'm going to sit here and learn about birds and bugs and
bicycles for an hour as I stroke her hair, hold her close, and kiss her
hands, as she tries to shove them in my mouth.

That last activity is a habit she developed early on and one
she shares with her older sister. Some time when they were very
small, as I nursed each of them, their little arms would flail about.

As they began to develop some semblance of motor skills, both of them reached for my face. They'd put their hands on my lips and in my mouth. I don't know why; my mother says I did the same thing when I was an infant. What's amazing to me is that the practice carried on, even after we were done nursing. Fiona, until we finally forced her to give up her pacifier at three, would suck on it as she fell asleep. If I were lying next to her or holding her, her hand would snake on up to my lips and sneak in. If we were in the car, coming home from G-mama's house late one night, she would take her pacifier out of her mouth to whine, "I want to put my hand in your mouth!" I don't know why; do other kids self-sooth like this? Does it count as self-soothing if she needs my mouth (or that of her father) to make it work?

I wasn't sad to see Fiona leave behind her days of longing so routinely for my presence and my body, including the wet contours of my mouth. Kid hands are often gross. In those days, I couldn't sing her lullabies or tell her stories at bedtime, because my mouth was full, receiving a nightly dental check-up from an untrained nonhygienist. Though I love to sing and had been assembling my mental playlist of soothing melodies since before she was born, we had to wait to make those a part of our nightly routine.

Josh was far less tolerant of the hands-in-mouth thing: He'd hold their hands or simply say no when the girls reached faceward. And Fiona eventually stopped trying with him. I can't say exactly why I've allowed it to persist. Maybe because these children have felt like such a part of my body for so long. Maybe because, while nursing, I grew accustomed to the strange notion that my body wasn't really my own and its boundaries were somehow more permeable than I'd thought possible. Or maybe it's simply because I'm really, really bad at saying no to them, though I feel a bit guilty now, as I watch Fiona become an evermore confirmed nail-biter and feel convinced this is related to some pseudo-Freudian oral fixation that I inculcated in her. Whatever the reasons for this tradition, I am very sure it contributes to the phenomenally effective mechanism we have developed in this household for sharing germs.

But when my baby (who is really no longer a baby—she talks and knows her colors and demands that I put her down so she can walk into her day-care classroom) climbs into my lap, when she reaches for me, I am content. Even on a day like today, when I really need a shower, when the morning routine really should get started sooner rather than later—even today—I can sit with her and be happy.

There are people, I am told, who don't really like to be touched, who prefer to maintain their own personal acre and police the borders with vigilance. I am not one of those people. Oh, sure, there are people who are not invited to touch me—people like the guy who sells church photo directories, who thinks we are buddies and tries to hug me whenever we meet. But, really, I am happiest when surrounded by bodies.

I am sure this has roots in my childhood. My happiest early memories involve playing with my sisters and parents. Whitney, Taylor, and I were all over each other when we were little. Thanks to a variety of aforementioned (chapter 4) circumstances, we'd cram into one bed together, but not just at bedtime. We'd tickle; we'd chase; we'd do makeshift acrobatic routines on the arms of the couch. I wouldn't call our activities "roughhousing" so much as "piling." I'd lie on the floor, Whit would take the middle, and Taylor would climb on top and lay down, and we'd see how long we could balance. We'd also pile on the sofa, our legs and arms and heads all jumbled up, the configuration not mattering much as long as we could all see the TV.

When I got to college, I missed my family, but at first, I couldn't articulate exactly how I experienced their absence from my daily life. We talked frequently enough, and we wrote (letters! How recent was *that* time!), and I was so busily overjoyed with new friends and new ideas and a new city that I struggled to recognize that there might be *any* loss associated with moving one thousand

miles away from my piling partners. Somewhere around finals of
that first semester, though, I realized I would have done just about
anything to score a hug—a nice, warm, loving, platonic hug. I had
made friends, but we hadn't broached that sort of intimacy in those
first months.

The various forms of physical intimacy aren't something most
of us reflect on with any amount of diligence or regularity. Our
culture seems far more concerned with the ins and outs of sexual
relationships than the closeness of parents, friends, or siblings. But
often becoming a parent causes us to pay attention to this, for here
are bodies to which we have near total access and for which we
have near total responsibility, bodies that are nonetheless not our
own. Even in a marriage, unless we've walked through significant
health problems together, we tend to draw barriers around certain
features of our embodiment in the name of "keeping the romance
alive."

While it feels strange commiting this sentence to paper, as
though I'm sharing something far too intimate, if obvious, I know
that a good part of what makes Josh and my marriage work is the
physical nature of our relationship. He *knows* me, knows the ins
and outs, the curves and the lumps of my body, just as I know his.
When my sisters and I were little, we played this game where we'd
put a closed eye up against a part of another's body—an elbow, a
tiny knee, a shoulder—and, on noting the perfect nesting place
that eye socket created for those tiny parts, we'd gleefully declare,
"It fits!" Please do not ask me how this game was born or how it
became such a regular feature of our childhood time spent amusing
ourselves in the family room. But after nine years together, Josh
and I *fit*. When we stand next together, I can lean into him *just so*.
When I am stressed out, he can wrap his arms around me, and I can
bury my head in his shoulder in exactly the right way to maximize
comfort and the assurance of grace.

When Fiona was born, I marveled at how a body that had been
a part of mine could be both so familiar and so foreign, how we

could be so intimate and yet so inherently *separate*. I am, to borrow a phrase, only *sorta-crunchy*,[1] by which I mean that I nursed, and I loved nursing, but now that I'm not nursing, I absolutely cannot get my head around the fact that I shared that with my kids. It's natural and beautiful and inexpensive . . . but they *sucked on my boobs!* All the time! In front of people! Is that even decent? (Of course nursing's decent. It's just intimate. And we're not always accustomed to seeing or engaging in intimate interactions in anything but the most private of settings.)

I remember how strange and new it felt to hold this other person so close, to work to get her to attach to me, and to bear the pain as she got used to eating and I got used to feeding. The amazing physical intimacy I felt with these girls extended beyond the actual act of nursing, of course. As I held each of those babies at my breast, I found myself channeling my inner ape: I'd look down at my infant daughter, suckling away, often sleeping, and marvel at her beauty, at her existence. I'd touch and count her fingers (so far, so human), but then I'd notice a little bit of ear wax and slide my finger along the ridge of her ear to remove it, or I'd be captivated by a semidetached scale of cradle cap that begged to be liberated. I have, perhaps, several tendencies that *may* indicate OCD, and so I *must* pick at things. It's totally gross, I know, and I imagined that to the casual observer (lurking in our nursery?), I might just as well have been picking nits out of her fur. I can swear before heaven, though, that I never felt tempted to ingest anything I gleaned from their heads, unlike some of our primate relatives.

I wasn't the only one exhibiting simian characteristics in our house, though. Have you noticed how toddler bodies, with their round and bulging bellies, and their pert, extruding backsides, are shaped like gorillas? Have you noticed how toddlers make a face that's all determination and defiance when they're chucking something at you (something that is, one hopes, not feces like the apes of myth and legend are always throwing)? Or how they sneak off to squat and concentrate in a corner while they fill a diaper? Having a kid around is like having twenty-four-hour access to those animal-in-its-natural-habitat *Nature* documentaries on public television.

These myriad reminders of our creaturely status point toward the Christian profession that God is our creator and we are the creatures—creatures with some dominion over and responsibility for other creatures, but creatures nonetheless. We're made (as the story goes) from the dust of the earth, and as such, we are made of the same stuff as stars. And mealworms. But the creation narratives in Genesis also tell us that we're made in the image of God, that we're created good.

The writer of Psalm 8 ponders this strange paradox of our base physicality and our relationship to God:

> When I look at your heavens, the work of your fingers,
>   the moon and the stars that you have established;
> what are human beings that you are mindful of them,
>   mortals that you care for them?
> Yet you have made them a little lower than God,
>   and crowned them with glory and honor.
> You have given them dominion over the works of your hands;
>   you have put all things under their feet,
> all sheep and oxen,
>   and also the beasts of the field,
> the birds of the air, and the fish of the sea,
>   whatever passes along the paths of the seas.
>
> Psalm 8:3–8

It's easy to see the goodness of God's creation when we're holding our newly born, beloved children, assuming they're pretty healthy. Several years ago there was an episode of *Sex and the City* when Miranda was acquiescing to her partner's request to have their son, Brady, baptized, but she objected to most of the liturgy and especially to a phrase that conveyed the doctrine of original sin. I am not so naïve as to imagine that the writers of *SATC* had any interest in portraying Christianity *well*, but I've always regretted that in the program, the (albeit fictional) priest just let her take her red pen to an ancient and living tradition rather than try to explain this complex doctrine to her. To say that our children are born sinners is not to say they are not born good. It's simply to say that they're born human: made in the image of God and yet prone to living as though they are not.

What does it mean to be human, though? This whole book is, in a way, evidence of Lee and me puzzling this out for ourselves and our families, a way of exploring the theological meaning of all these experiences we're having as parents. For us, such theologizing is not so unusual. We're pastors. We deal with these sorts of questions in our daily work, and we'd done so before we became parents. But having a baby—not just being pregnant and giving birth but also caring for an infant—has impressed upon us that we're not just meaning-making beings, and we're not just those who relate to God in prayer, song, and worship. We're animals—animals to which God gave the spirit of life, but animals nonetheless.

Lee and I were together recently (a rare thing, as she lives in the South and I'm in the Midwest, and our jet-setting days seem long past), and we were trying to remember when it was that we *really* became friends. We went to grad school together. We tried to encourage Rob and Josh to become man-friends, since neither of them was into theology and both were into *The Lord of the Rings*. (I recall that they went to see the Dracula thriller *Van Helsing* together, perhaps among the few people who saw it in a theater.) But for Lee and me, I think we moved from being casual friends to becoming really close when Harper and Fiona were born. We shared the easily blossoming intimacy of new mothers. It can take a long time to become close friends in adulthood, especially for those of us (cough, cough) who are ridiculously insecure about informal social interactions. ("That couple might be too cool for us," Josh and I have been known to worry.) But Lee and I could talk about leaky breasts and infant constipation and the horror of the nasal aspirator. About the recovery from labor and those awesome mesh panties and the gigantic, mattress-sized pads with ice packs in them that we wore. Though we were miles apart, our bodily experiences, and our experiences of our daughters' brand-new bodies, gave us some significant points of connection and drew us together.

The fact that we human beings have bodies, and we experience life through those bodies, shapes the way we understand ourselves and the ways in which we build communities. Though the range of possible beliefs that people hold across this wide world is nothing short of mind-boggling, there are a few things we can agree on—and many of them have to do with our bodies. People need access to clean water; we need food, preferably nutritious food. We require shelter, and in most environments, we require some protective skin covering (if not strictly requiring Louis Vuitton). We also need other people. (Those who live in utter solitude don't tend to fare that well.) People who will care for us and protect us from harm are even better. In addition, while tyrants and eugenicists may disagree, it's pretty well established that human beings need other things to thrive as well: love and freedom, truth and beauty, and the possibility and resources to fulfill our potential.

The Christian tradition has "sacramentalized" the first several of these needs, bringing these physical requirements of survival into the life of the church and imbuing them with religious meaning. We are washed and made new, "born again" not just through the waters of the womb but through the waters of the Spirit. Just as water itself gives and sustains life, the waters of baptism remind us of the sustaining power of God's love. "Those who drink of the water that I will give them will never be thirsty," Jesus says in John 4:14. Christians also gather at a table to eat together, to share a meal of bread and wine, that becomes to us the body and blood of Christ. United Methodists haven't really developed any of the complicated doctrinal notions describing what *happens* to the bread and juice. (For Methodists, it's always grape juice. Mr. Welch was a Methodist! Fun fact.) But this is what we pray:

Pour out your Holy Spirit on us gathered here and on these gifts
of bread and wine. Make them be for us the body and blood
of Christ that we may be for the world the Body of Christ,
redeemed by his blood.[2]

The food we eat that nourishes and sustains us, that becomes
a part of our very bodies, reminds us of the God who took a body,
whose life nourishes and sustains us. Just as we take on the characteristics of the things we eat (there is truth in the old adage "You are
what you eat"; nursing mothers are especially aware of this as their
babies respond to every gas-producing food we ingest and every
glass of diaper-rash-causing lemonade we consume) by ingesting
Christ's body, we become more like him.

In Holy Communion, in our eating and drinking, our bodies
become the means by which we relate to God in Christ and are
transformed. This practice is central for Christians and has been for
centuries. Sacramental theology in some Christian traditions suggests
that the sacraments—like baptism and Holy Communion—allow
us to experience God in special, unmediated ways. It's notable, I
think, that those special, unmediated ways are offered to us through
the very physical, bodily acts of eating, drinking, and bathing. And
yet, the reality of our embodiment has long been a source of embar-
rassment for some in Christian tradition. Followers of Gnosticism,
an early Christian heresy (of course, the Gnostics didn't think they
were heretics) believed humanity would be saved *by* special knowledge (*gnosis* is the Greek word for "knowledge") and that we'd be
saved *from* all the trials and tribulations this material world foists
upon our bodily selves. Gnostics—and others—have viewed our
bodies not only as the sign of our mortality but also as agents of
our sinful natures.

Bodies have gotten this bad reputation as the means by which
people engage in all sorts of sin—from gluttony to violence to a
whole host of sexual sins. And it's not just the Gnostics who gave us
this notion. The apostle Paul is forever feeding such thinking with

his teachings about a soul/flesh dichotomy. "For we know that the law is spiritual; but I am of the flesh, sold into slavery under sin" (Rom. 7:14), he writes, which is to say that from a very early age, we are willing to hurt ourselves and others and God. We're willing to break God's law, which Jesus sums up like this: Love God with all your heart, mind, soul and strength, and love your neighbor as yourself (Luke 10:27). Nursing babies bite their mothers; toddlers hit their siblings and playmates; elementary school kids shoplift; teenagers shoot their classmates and harass them online; college kids assault each other and abuse their own bodies. As adults—both individually and collectively—we manage to sin a whole lot. So much that, as theologian Reinhold Niebuhr pointed out during the Cold War, we've actually figured out how to completely destroy ourselves and our world.[3]

We sin—and, frequently, we sin with our bodies. Our passions have long been associated with our bodies, and both of these are frequently associated with sin—love and lust, pride and violence, fear and self-preservation at the expense of others. Our passions are powerful, and that makes us nervous. As a friend once told me, our preference is to claim that our passions are simply controlled or easily damned or somehow diminished in importance so that we don't have to account for the sway they may actually hold over us. But the passions in themselves, despite their power, are morally neutral. It's the line between perfectly healthy responses to those passions and unfaithful responses that is easily and often carelessly blurred and crossed. It's one thing to want to dodge the speeding bullet; it's quite another to throw the guy standing next to you into its path.

We sin, and sin leads to death—metaphorically and otherwise. Sure, when Callie bit me as an infant (on purpose, with this totally naughty look in her eye!), the path to death was quite a bit longer and far more easily interrupted by grace than the wrongs we intentionally commit as we grow older. But just two days ago, a kid took a gun into his high school in Ohio and shot five other teenagers, several of whom died. Josh reported on the most recent death as we lay in bed last night and said the most devastating thing ever: "That could be one of our girls one day. We could send them to school, and someone could bring a gun, and that would be it."

I almost threw up when he said that.

He's right, although it hurts me to admit it. We're all mortal, we all die, and in this broken and "teeming" (to use theologian Serene Jones's apt description)[4] world, many—far too many—people die much too soon, victims of unnecessary violence. Far too many people die of preventable diseases. Far too many people die of starvation or from a lack of access to clean water. Three teenagers killed in Ohio, 133 in Syria. Even the best parents can't protect all these children; Josh and I can't even protect the two for whom we're most responsible from everything the world might throw at them. Even if we never let these precious girls out of our sight, they'd still get sick sometimes . . . and they'd hate us to boot.

But just because it is true that we cannot protect our children from "the world" does not mean that we throw up our hands in despair, abnegating our responsibilities. We can work for stronger gun laws. We can teach them to respect themselves, their bodies, and those of others. We can teach them about what it means to be incarnate beings.

Human life happens in bodies, and while I'm not usually one to say that everything that happens is "of God," we might infer some things about what God hopes for humanity by observing these bodies—which change, which allow for connection, which create and give and sustain life. There is something at work in the universe that brings forth life, and that mystery is what we call God. Christianity makes several central claims about God that stand over and against the claims of other faiths: namely, that God is three-in-one and that God became incarnate, took on a body in the life, death, and resurrection of a man named Jesus who lived two thousand years ago in what is now Israel and Palestine.

The doctrinal phrase that's been used throughout the church's history to express the meaning of incarnation describes Jesus as "fully human and fully divine"—as if that settles the matter, as if that pairing makes any sense at all. If nothing else, this doctrine claims that the theological centrality of Jesus lies not simply in his self-sacrificial death on the cross. This doctrine suggests that the fact that Jesus was God-in-flesh means something to us. And I think part of what it means is that our bodies are not to be despised, even though they make us vulnerable to the world's dangers and to the temptations of "earthly delights" (wink, wink, nudge, nudge). Though they might periodically (or even frequently) be led astray, our bodies are part of who we are—and even part of how we know God. Paul, complicating his earlier dichotomy, cautions us to appreciate the value of our bodies and to treat them accordingly:

> Do you not know that your bodies are members of Christ? . . . Or do you not know that your body is a temple of the Holy Spirit within you, which you have from God, and that you are not your own? For you were bought with a price; therefore glorify God in your body.
>
> 1 Cor. 6:15a, 19–20

Paul's words here both convict and inspire me, and I want to reflect this teaching in the way I exercise my own embodiment: if our bodies are temples of the Holy Spirit, if they are members of Christ, then we are obligated to care for them and to listen to them. There's a long history, however, of Christians and other religious folks who make it their life's work to deny their bodies, to pursue asceticism, and to train themselves to ignore the urges and insights of their bodies. True, those ascetic strains are not without biblical origins. In the Sermon on the Mount, for example, when Jesus is talking about adultery and its precursor in lust, he says, "If your right eye causes you to sin, tear it out and throw it away; it is better for you to lose one of your members than for your whole body to be thrown into hell" (Matt. 5:29). These ascetic readers might interpret Jesus to be saying that we should ignore our bodies or train them into submission rather than allow them to drag us into sin. Still, despite the presence of verses like this, I think the larger thrust of the theological tradition insists on the integrity and wholeness of the human person. To emphasize the sinfulness of the body or a part of the body, to separate the metaphorical right hand from the soul or spirit or other parts of the body, is to miss that theological insight.

Seeing our bodies as integral parts of ourselves often takes more than just reading the Bible in a new way or rejecting ancient heresies (even in their modern manifestations), especially, perhaps, for women. Kim Barker, one of the three authors of *Birthed in Prayer: Pregnancy as a Spiritual Journey*, testifies to this difficulty. She writes about being labeled as obese as a child: "From that moment on it seemed that my body and I were no longer one. My body was a problem I had to fix." She continues: "By sheer force of will I had to ignore what my body was telling me, as I could no longer trust it. Hunger was not real hunger but greed. Desire was deceptive and could not be acted upon. My mind had to plan and control my eating because clearly my body had failed me on that count."[5]

While her childhood self might not have used such language, Barker saw her body as sinful, as deceptive. But by mistreating her body over the years, through anorexia and bulimia, she actually experienced the pain and weight of sin—of being separate, alienated, from the things of life and health and wholeness.

There's a terrible theological paradox at the heart of Christianity. We're separate from God and, therefore, prone to sin, hurting ourselves and others. That separation is seen most fully in the fact of our embodiment. Our mortality, our disconnection from others, and the limitations on our knowledge and our ability to commune with God are all part of what it means to be human. The theological problem is a logic issue. We're responsible for that sin and separation—Adam and Eve's fall and all that. But how can we be responsible for something we didn't cause? Why isn't it God's fault for making us this way?

I can't really give an adequate explanation for this paradox. But I've come to this conclusion: We can't define our bodies as the location of sin. Sin is not in our bodies. While human beings are both inherently embodied and inherently sinful (and live with the implications of both of those inborn existential conditions), those two categories are not (contrary to some strands of Christian tradition) necessarily linked in a relationship of cause and effect. Rather, our bodies are a part of who we are. They shape how we experience the world; they give us a means of being in relationship, of showing love.

For Kim Barker, part of getting healthy was finally embracing her body as a friend and not an enemy. Near the end of her second pregnancy, she came to the realization that "My body was as much me as my thoughts and feelings." She reports writing in her journal:

> I don't have to fight my body. . . . It is me. It speaks to me of what it needs. . . . It is not involved in some subversive plot against me. I am caught up in a culture that turns me against my body and encourages me to respond to it with fear, loathing, hatred; to punish it, to control it, and to suppress all its appetites—for food, for touch, for rest, for sex, for nurture. *Why?* Who benefits?[6]

Way back in chapter 2, I talked about the suggestion of feminist theologians that women tend to sin through self-abnegation, by acting as though we don't matter, by abusing ourselves. I don't want to suggest that little Kim Barker, carrying a note regarding her weight home from the school nurse, was responsible for the sense of shame she felt about her body or the cultural bias regarding body size. But she bore the brunt of it and, ultimately, she was the one who had to seek freedom from that shame and grief and pain. It was critical for Barker to fight the power of this sin in her life, this

need to control herself, and to learn to trust her body again, to find
health and holiness and to appreciate herself as a child of God who
manifests the goodness of God's creation. She had to seek reconciliation with her body and with God.

Barker's understanding of her body may have been especially
fraught, but even if our experiences differ, her writing prompts us
that this reconciliation with our bodies is something we must ultimately work out as individuals before God. We are all individuals,
with unique minds and experiences and souls and bodies, and one
consequence of that individuality is that we have to learn to listen
to our bodies, because, finally, no one else can do it for us. This
reality became apparent to me on one incredibly long night with
Callie during her infancy. She was not a gassy kid most of the time,
and she was an unbelievably good-humored baby. But that night
I walked back and forth with her lying lengthwise on her belly
over my forearm for hours, patting her back, trying to relieve the
gas pressure that was making her so miserable. And I remember so
clearly thinking: "This is it, the height of futility: attempting to help
another person pass gas."

That night with Callie was one brief reminder of the ways
we are separated from others by our bodies, but life with kids is
full of similar examples. There's just something about excretion
and digestion that drives this reality home over and over in the
early years of parenting. When the time came for Fiona to be potty
trained, we were incredibly lucky, because the teachers at her day
care had already started the process. We thanked God for peer pressure ("Don't you want to be like Tess? She likes to use the potty!")
and Skittles. We also thanked the good Lord for the good people at
the Sesame Street Workshop, who put together *Elmo's Potty Time*.
We watched that video constantly for months. "Trying, and trying
again . . . ," we sang. "Accidents happen . . . and that's okay!" we
cheered. Josh and I really appreciated the blues number Elmo's
daddy sings as well. Fiona thought it was okay.

But the thing that moved me so (why, yes, I did cry regularly while watching *Elmo's Potty Time*)—other than the "trying and trying again" song that featured all these kids taking on daunting tasks and courageously, adorably refusing to give up—was the question that undergirded the whole thing: "What is your body telling you?" Given how many women I have known and loved who for years experienced their bodies as Kim Barker did—as a source of shame and guilt, of distrust and fear—it is important to me and Josh that we do all we can to help our daughters avoid such experiences. Elmo's refrain thus became ours as well: "Fee, is your body telling you that you have to use the potty? Fee, is your body telling you that you're hungry?"

We did not, I confess, always rely on our two-year-old's expert testimony. Josh and I put her on the potty at bedtime, before car rides, after drinking juice. Periodically we still have to convince her to "at least *try*" before we get in the car to drive the forty miles to my parents' house. But it seems so right, so critical to me that we teach her to ask herself these questions, that we teach her how to listen to her body.

As she ages out of Elmo, Fiona may find other sources stressing the importance of our bodiliness, not least of which is the Bible. Our bodies, Paul notes in that passage from 1 Corinthians, are a primary way we connect with the God whose Spirit dwells within us, but they are also the means by which we connect with one another. Lee and I both gave birth to our kids, and our husbands are their biological fathers, and that is certainly one way in which we are connected bodily to our children. But our mutual friend Alex is just as biologically connected to her three adopted children: She delights in their cuddles, has picked at their ear wax (I'm guessing; I shouldn't assume Alex is as gross as I am), and has come to recognize their distinctive smells and shapes and ways of living into their bodies. We all connect with our partners and our parents and our siblings and our dearest friends through our bodies. One way I knew I'd been welcomed and accepted into the congregation I serve was that the kids started seeing me as an acceptable person to hug, and the little ones felt safe and welcome to the point where they'd come climb in my lap while I read a story. Our bodies can be means of sharing grace, hospitality, and love.

For all the possibilities of connection, though, the paradox I notice in cuddling with my girls these days is that, despite the holy connection we share, they are, in fact, separate from me. And not just in toilet-related matters. No matter how long I want to hold them, they tend to get their fill of bodily closeness before I do, and they squirm away, off to the next great adventure.

They are their own people. They have their own bodies and, increasingly, their own lives to lead and their own preferences about how to pursue them. My baby, for example: She's a thrill seeker. Her two favorite things to do right now are to bypass the baby gate so she can climb the stairs unassisted, and to stand on the child-size green wicker rocking chair we own and surf back and forth. Josh and I used to worry about how cautious Fiona can be. ("She'll never learn if she doesn't try anything new!") But with Callie, we long for a bit more caution, since she seems intent on concussing herself on a regular basis. I pray she outgrows this before the stairs become rock faces and the kid-sized rocker a tightrope. I pray she listens to her body's desire for self-preservation and not just the adrenaline. I pray this as her mother, and only with a desire for her always to be safe.

But human life isn't only about being safe: There is no grace in never messing up, no glory without risk. Theologian Kristine Culp, who writes regularly about theological anthropology—how we interpret what it means to be human in light of our under-standing about God—coined a brilliant phrase for describing our creaturely existence as those made in the image of God. She says this life is one of "vulnerability and glory." We are vulnerable to disease and sin and our own limitations and, finally, the mortality that meets all living creatures. But we are also prone to, invited toward, and participants in glory, in the fulfillment of what is right and good and just. All this—all our vulnerabilities, all our hopes for glory—are played out before God.[7]

The diapers, the potty training, the leaky breasts, the bloody recovery, the late night fevers, and unbearable smells, as well as the cuddling, the connection, and the communion—this is life with kids. This is what it means to be human. This is life before God.

CHAPTER 7

Saying Grace

On stories, and songs, and nurturing faith

IN A BOOK ROB AND I READ TOGETHER THE YEAR BEFORE HARPER WAS born, Marcus Borg tells the story of a little girl who creeps into the bedroom of her newborn brother shortly after their parents bring him home from the hospital. "Tell me about God," she whispers to the baby, "I've almost forgotten."[1]

When Harper was just a few days old, Rob and I lay in bed listening to her newborn gurgles in the next room. We often ended our days that way in those first blurry weeks, falling into bed once she was settled, exhausted but unable to sleep.

"What do you think she's thinking about?" I asked.

"Maybe she's forgetting about God," he said.

I burst into tears. "That is the saddest thing I've ever heard," I sobbed.

He was instantly contrite, having grown accustomed to my then regular emotional breakdowns. "I'm sorry. I thought it would be funny."

"Well, it wasn't!" I reached for a tissue. "What if she really does forget?"

"Then we'll remind her."

It was then that the enormity of our role hit me. Of all the overwhelming tasks parenting seemed to require, nothing quite compared to this one: How would we keep this little soul from forgetting about God?

Our daughter has always been an amazing sleeper, giving us full nights of rest long before I care to admit to other sleepy-eyed new mothers. But in the first few months, those long stretches of sleep were paid for by an hour or two of rocking and walking and singing late into the evening.

Somewhere along the way, I started memorizing hymns. I would stand in her room with the hymnal propped up on the changing table, Harper sideways across my chest with her head in the crook of my left elbow. I'd sing a verse, then step away from the changing table and see how much I could remember, singing it over and over until I didn't need to cheat anymore or until she was asleep enough to set in her crib. I picked seasonal hymns, such as "Let All Things Now Living" at Thanksgiving and "Awake, Awake, and Greet the New Morn" in Advent (which, despite its name, works pretty well as a lullaby). I always cried during the last verse of "Amazing Grace."

As Harper got older, we stopped singing quite so much. Pretty soon, she just needed a book and her stuffed elephant and generally wanted to be left alone to go to sleep. Sometimes, actually, she would sing herself to sleep with a little ditty of her own that Rob and I came to call "Be-Bop." It really did have a tune, which she varied with different syllables. There was a "Bop-Be" verse as well as the regular "Be-Bop," and on occasion, "De-Dad." Sometimes it was a sad, slow tune, as if mourning the passing of another day. Sometimes it was bright and cheerful. I often wondered if there were words in her head as she sang. I wondered if she were remembering our late night hymn sings.

I wonder if those hymns are embedded in her memory, even if she won't remember my singing her to sleep. It's kind of mind-boggling to think about the ways we do—or don't—influence our daughter's subconscious. In the final weeks of my pregnancy, I started working my way through *The West Wing* on DVD. I'd watch an episode every night as I lay on the couch with my feet up, willing the swelling in my ankles to subside. When Harper was born, I was midway through season 3, and I discovered that the time it took to watch an episode was about how much time she needed to nurse. Especially on those long days of maternity leave when it was just the two of us and we had not yet mustered up the courage to go out into the world on our own, I welcomed the familiar faces and witty conversation of the *West Wing* cast. When I could tell Harper was getting hungry, I'd pour myself some water, find my place on the couch, and push PLAY. I kept the volume low, but still I imagine that thirty years from now, a grown-up Harper will be flipping through TV channels late one night, settle on a *West Wing* rerun, and suddenly find she has an urge to have a snack and call her mother.

Now, though, she's long since graduated from nursing to regular food, and our family is trying hard to sit down to dinner together most nights. It seems like the responsible thing to do, even if we only manage five minutes of actual sitting, and even if "dinner" consists of frozen pizza. We also started saying grace before we eat, something Rob and I didn't really do when it was just the two of us. One of our favorites is "Johnny Appleseed," which we started singing when Harper was still in a high chair, banging gleefully on the tray in front of her. We usually start out quietly, drawing out the "Ohh . . . ," while drumming our fingers on the table, and then we're off: "The Lord's been good to me, and so I thank the Lord, for giving me the things I need, the sun and the rain and the apple seed. The Lord's been good to me." And then the fun part: "Johnny Appleseed, Amen!" with our arms flung high in the air. Even before she could sing along, Harper always joined in for the amen.

It took me awhile to realize just how important those few moments of giving thanks had become. One evening, when my day had run long and I was late picking Harper up from day care, she yelled at the top of her lungs all the way home. Sixteen minutes of bloodcurdling screams (it would have been eleven minutes, but the screaming made me take a wrong turn that sent me down a series of one-way streets). As she thrashed against the straps of her car seat, tears squeezing out of the corners of her eyes, I drove silently, too weary to even attempt a chorus of "The Ants Go Marching One by One," our usual ride-home song. I'm not sure what set her off. Maybe I didn't let her climb into the car seat herself, or she was mad that I'd been late, or she'd hoped Daddy would pick her up instead of me—or maybe she, too, was just weary from the day.

The screaming continued when we got home, the frustration of whatever happened in the car quickly exacerbated by hunger pangs. Rob and I looked despairingly at each other and took turns holding her while we got dinner ready. I sighed when I looked down to discover snot stains on the shoulder of the shirt I'd planned to wear back to work for a meeting that night. Finally—*finally!*—dinner was ready, and we sat down, Harper still yelling as if the world were ending. Suddenly, though, the crying stopped, and she started tapping the tray. "Ohhhhh . . . ," she said, looking at us expectantly and waiting for us to start singing. So we sat and sang together, and I marveled that in the midst of her despair, she remembered to give thanks to God.

We occasionally forget to pray, to be honest, especially on those nights when simply getting home seems like an accomplishment. Sometimes, in the middle of dinner, Harper will stop eating and pat her hands on the table, looking up at us with a little hint of a giggle, and sing, "Ohhhhh . . . ," waiting for us to join in. "The Lord's been good to me, and so I thank the Lord. . . ." It's as if, in the middle of a bite of pizza, she remembers just how good God is. I am grateful for the reminder.

Saying grace is a good place to start, I suppose, but nurturing faith in my daughter—reminding her about God, if that's really what we're doing—requires more. I discovered not long ago that in the vast library of children's books we seem to have accumulated in the past several years, only a very few are explicitly related to the Christian tradition. They are an odd few: One is about the donkey who carries Mary to Bethlehem, another has an audio component that says, "It's fun to pray!" when you press a button, and a third is a strange little book about Booker the Bear who reminds us in rhymed verse that God is in control. Frankly, I feel silly reading them and generally reach for *Goodnight Moon* or *Max's Bedtime* instead.

One night, as I passed over those Bible storybooks yet again, it occurred to me that I want her to learn the Bible stories at some point, and I wondered: If Rob and I don't tell her those stories, who will? (I had a similar revelation not long after she was born: I was hurriedly changing a diaper and did a less-than-thorough job of wiping her, as if I were thinking, *Well, someone else will clean her up better later.*) If we are going to "remind her" about God, hadn't we better start with the basics?

Those Bible stories—the breath of God that swept over the deep, Noah and his ark full of animals, Sarah's laughter, the wandering in the wilderness, the starlit Bethlehem sky, the twelve baskets of loaves and fishes, the stone rolled away, the rush of a mighty wind—those stories are the reason I believe in God. I want her to love them as dearly as I do. But where do I start? What do I say? "Harper, this is the story about God." How do you tell this story to someone who's never heard it?

In the sixth chapter of Deuteronomy, the people of Israel are commanded:

> You shall love the LORD your God will all your heart, and with all your soul, and with all your might. Keep these words that I am commanding you today in your heart. Recite them to your children and talk about them when you are at home and when you are away, when you lie down and when you rise.
>
> Deut. 6:5–7

Rob and I once stood in front of our whole church and promised to do this. In our tradition, we dedicate babies instead of baptizing them. For us, the baby dedication is more about the commitment of the parents, who stand at the front of the sanctuary and hope their child won't be the one who cries when the minister holds her. When asked if they promise to nurture the child and lead her to full discipleship of Christ, the parents respond, "We do, with God's help." We made those promises, as our daughter squirmed in a little green jumper and tights she wasn't used to wearing and both sets of grandparents watched.

I was the mom that day, but with most dedications I'm a part of, I'm the minister—the lucky one who gets to hold the baby. I'll confess it's one of my favorite parts of the job, and not just because the babies are cute. It's also because of the way the church looks on, claiming that little one as part of the family, reminding the parents that raising that child in the faith is the task of the whole community. The first baby dedication I led as a minister was for a set of twins, long before Harper was born. It was my first year in ministry, the first year that Rob and I both had full-time jobs. We were thinking about buying a home and putting down roots. We weren't yet thinking about a baby of our own, at least not seriously, but my uterus was sending crazy signals to my brain, and I craved babies. If there was one in the room, my arms ached to hold her, and I would hover around the mother, too self-conscious to actually ask, until invited to take a turn.

So when this mother brought her six-month-old twin girls to be dedicated, I was thrilled there were two, because it meant the other minister and I could each hold one. They wore lacy white dresses and little bonnets that made them look like something out of the nineteenth century. After the prayer and the words of dedication, we set off down the aisle carrying the babies to introduce these little girls to the congregation. "Look, Caroline," I whispered, as I tilted her head up to see the people in the pews. "This is your church family. They love you already." She looked at me with big eyes as the folks in the pews smiled at her.

Several years after her own dedication, Harper has become a good church kid. "Church!" she says, gleefully, as we pull into the parking lot, and I find myself praying she'll remain so cheerful about coming to church after a childhood of being the pastor's daughter. For now, though, she loves it. And why not? She is often the only child in a sea of grandparents who dote on her as if she were their own. At potluck dinners, she begins on a chair next to me but usually ends up across the room, eating strawberries from someone else's plate or running up the ramped hallway with one or more of the preteen girls who have become her fan club. Someone always keeps her from standing on the folding chairs or knocking over the table of desserts.

"You turned out okay," my mother says, when I worry aloud that Harper spends too much time at the church, and I'm reminded that my own life was shaped by church people who passed me around and looked after me. There are far worse fates than to grow up in the church.

> Do you covenant with God and this community to live your lives as a testimony to the living Christ such that Harper may come to know Jesus Christ as teacher, friend, and Savior?

We do, with God's help.

It's quite a thing to promise, when I stop to think about it. Will we live our lives in such a way that our daughter will come to know Jesus Christ? The first time Harper said the word *God*—I don't even remember the context, I just remember the word—it took my breath away, and I realized that as much as I want her to know God, I wanted her to wait a little while, at least long enough for me to figure it all out for myself so I could teach her. At moments like that, I remind myself of that sanctuary full of people who looked on, smiling, at Harper's dedication, the people who made those promises with us. I'm glad we don't have to do this alone.

When I finally decided we needed something more than Booker the Bear and the battery-operated prayer book, I went looking for a new Bible storybook to give to Harper for her birthday. The shelves at our local Christian bookstore offered a dizzying array of choices. Most were filled with pictures of Caucasian cartoon characters, which made these ancient and holy stories seem no more significant than a Saturday morning TV show. I finally settled on a lift-the-flap-book that had decent pictures and a good selection of stories. Some time later, I was thrilled to find a storybook Bible called *Children of God,* written by Archbishop Desmond Tutu and illustrated by artists from around the world. Tutu manages to capture the meaning and grace of each story in kid-friendly language without dumbing it down, and the illustrations depict a world of beauty, where all children of God are known and loved.[2]

The pictures are essential, of course, to pre-readers; I suspect these images will be forever tied to the way Harper hears these stories. (I was tickled the first time we read about the Garden of Eden from her new storybook: "They're cold! They need shirts!" she declared when she saw Adam and Eve covered only by tiny fig leaves.) The stories themselves, though, are the important part, and that's where it gets tricky. The Bible stories we generally think of as children's stories often carry R-rated themes and raise questions for which even the most well-versed Bible scholars don't have easy answers. Noah's ark may be full of cuddly animals, but the rains outside come from a God who intentionally flooded the earth. We celebrate that Daniel was saved from the lions' den, but we don't go into much detail about what would have happened otherwise. Equally frightening is the notion of being swallowed, like Jonah, by a big fish. Why do we think all Bible stories about animals are for children?

The New Testament stories are tricky, too, especially as Jesus approaches the cross. The stories about Jesus in most kids' versions either skip too quickly to the resurrection or linger too long on the crucifixion. (Bromleigh recounts that she recently had to reassure Fiona that no one would try nail *her* to a cross. "Enough with the atonement theology!" she said to me.) Granted, this is a tough balance for any kids' book to achieve; it's tough for adults, as well.

I am torn between wanting to protect my daughter from the darkness of the world and wanting her to know that through the darkness, God's light still shines. That's the paradox of our faith, though,
and it's the truth that comes to us through these stories, passed
down through the ages. As troubling and awkward and difficult to
understand as these stories may be, they have carried the good news
for generations. On the days when I can't quite answer all the questions, I trust that the story will be enough.

Now that Harper is a little older, she goes to a church-run
preschool that holds a chapel service for the kids each week. I
found her singing "Jesus Loves Me" one day after chapel and started
singing along. She grinned at me, delighted that I knew the song.
These days, when we're not singing "Johnny Appleseed" before
dinner, we say a table grace she learned at school and taught to us:
"Protect us, God, the whole day through, and everything we say
and do. Thank you, God, for friends that care. Thank you for the
food we share. Amen."

It surprises me sometimes to hear her singing songs and
retelling stories that I didn't teach her, but it shouldn't. Her
preschool teachers have taught her many things I haven't: numbers,
letters, the months of the year, and how to use a bug-catcher. But I
guess I always thought I would be the one to teach her about faith.
I have to remind myself that the promises Rob and I made included
the community. Raising this child to know and love the Lord is not
only up to us.

She doesn't always get the details quite right, but she's learning.
One afternoon she told me, in great detail, the story of Samuel
and Eli, in which Samuel hears someone calling him and thinks it
is Eli. Three times, he goes to Eli, but Eli sends him back to bed.
Finally, he realizes it isn't Eli at all. "Who was it?" I asked Harper.
"Jesus!" she said, excited to deliver the surprise ending, apparently
unaware that Jesus would not appear on the scene for another one
thousand–plus years. A minor detail for three-year-old theologians.

Another day, I asked her what the story at chapel had been about. "I don't know," she said, busy wrapping her baby doll just so in a blanket.

"Was it about Jesus?" I prompted. (Having led a number of children's sermons in worship, I knew this to be a relatively safe guess.)

"Yeah!" she said, and then went on to explain, "He said, 'We're all kids . . .' No . . . , 'God is a big kid.'"

I looked at her. "He said, 'God is a big kid?'"

She scrunched up her nose. "No, that's not right."

"Maybe he said, 'We're all children of God,'" I suggested.

"Yeah, that's it," she said, and went back to wrapping up her baby. Close enough, I thought.

Will we keep these words in our hearts? Will we recite them to our children? Will we live our lives as a testimony to the living Christ?

I hope so.

I hope we'll always make time to give thanks, even when we're not feeling very thankful. I hope we keep telling those stories and singing those songs. I hope she will keep asking questions. I hope church people will always be as good to her as they are now, and even if we never find the words to describe it to her, I hope she will come to know the grace of God.

My mother-in-law, on a visit when Harper was not quite two, brought a book of bedtime lullabies. Most were secular—"Frere Jacques" and "Twinkle, Twinkle, Little Star." Most I'd never heard of. But midway through the book was this one:

All night, all day, angels watching over me, my Lord.
All night, all day, angels watching over me.

It was familiar, somewhere down in the depths of my being, though I hadn't heard it for years, probably since my own childhood. It took me awhile to find the melody, and even then I'm sure I changed keys several times. (There is surely a lesson about grace in my daughter's acceptance of my tone-deaf lullabies.)

I sang it through a few times and then turned the page to try a different song, but Harper reached out and flipped back. "Again," she commanded, so I sang it again . . . and again . . . and again. After several times through, she was perfectly still, and I thought she might have fallen asleep, so I began humming. She sat up and shook her finger at me. "No," she said. "Sing."

So I did. She sat still in my lap as we rocked and sang about the ever-present love of God in the deepening night.

We're not alone here, Rob and I. These aren't our stories in the first place; they aren't our songs. They belong to the great cloud of witnesses that has carried them through the ages. They belong to the people of God, the community of faith, who will surround our daughter and remind her about God when she needs reminding. But I don't think she has forgotten.

I'm the Mommy, That's Why

On authority, and experts, and looking for truth

FIONA WAS BORN AT A UNIVERSITY TEACHING HOSPITAL. WE CHOSE TO deliver her there because we trusted the level of care the medical staff provides. (As residents of a densely populated area, we have options that many people simply don't.) Also, the hospital had a neonatal intensive care unit (NICU), which would be important on the off chance that anything went wrong during the delivery. Aesthetic considerations did not come into play, which would be obvious to even the most casual observer of this hospital's exterior. The design style could be called Eastern Bloc Functionalism; the color palette, gray concrete. The red signage was pretty, but that was about it.

All but one of the rooms on the maternity ward were doubles. But on the tour we took as part of our birthing class, the nurse in charge assured us that the floor was rarely filled, and every mom would almost certainly have a room to herself as she recovered. Audible sighs of relief escaped the lips of nearly every expectant parent in the group. No mom wants to spend her recovery, and the first precious (read: exhausted, emotionally draining, tear- and blood-filled) hours of parenthood, in a room smaller than a college dorm with an equally unfamiliar roommate.

As it happened, on the day Fiona was born, Labor and Delivery was full to bursting. (Now there's an image!) The ward was so crowded that I ended up getting my epidural hours before my

contractions even grew painful, because the staff told me that if
I waited, the anesthesiologist might be busy with a more complicated birth, and I might miss my shot (literally). I was unprepared
and unwilling to entertain that as a possibility.

After leaving Labor and Delivery, I was assigned a bed in a
double room in the crowded maternity ward, and Josh, the
exhausted new father, was expected to spend the night next to me
in a vaguely reclining vinyl-covered chair. Every square foot of the
room on "my" side of the curtain was taken up by furniture—the
hospital bed and chair were so close to that there was hardly room
for visitors to stand. And the bassinet, when they brought the baby
in, was placed flush against the end of the bed.

In other words, despite our exhaustion, Josh and I couldn't get
out of there fast enough. We were so uncomfortable that our apprehension about taking home an infant to parent faded into the background, as I pushed for permission to take that first shower, as we
asked to meet with the lactation specialist, as we less-than-graciously
inquired after our discharge papers. The phrase "chomping at the
bit" comes to mind.

And then, after an interminable length of time (thirty-six
hours, tops), we were finally allowed to take our little darling and
go home. The apprehension returned slowly—first, as we noticed
that the onesie we'd brought for Fiona to wear for her introduction
to the outside world was, at size S, way too big. The next challenge
came as we struggled to buckle her into her new car seat before we
left the hospital room. Then Josh had to try to figure out how he
could manage to retrieve the car from the hospital parking garage
while simultaneously pushing me down the hall and out the door
in the legally mandated wheelchair. That's when it finally hit: We
didn't really have a clue. Not a clue—about how we were supposed
to parent, about how to pick out clothes that would fit her, about
how to tell if something was wrong or she was just fussing.

We lived just a mile from the hospital, but it took us about twenty
minutes to drive home. I sat in the back next to the baby—just in

case she needed me for anything—while Josh (who even under normal circumstances is a naturally cautious and extremely responsible driver) drove us home at the speed of molasses moving across a kitchen counter.

It's easy, now—now that Fiona is in her fifth year and has never been seriously harmed in all that time, now that we've also managed to conceive, birth, and not criminally neglect a second child—to laugh at how worried we were then. At how many things tripped us up. At how frequently we went looking for advice.

My younger sister (now in her early twenties and one of the coolest people I know) was born when I was eight and a half, and I spent a good part of my late childhood and early adolescence participating in her care. I changed diapers; I played; I babysat. I enjoyed these things, most of the time—and those experiences contribute in large part to why Taylor and I are so close as adults, despite the age difference.

I babysat other kids, too, during both high school and college. I work with kids. Josh works with kids. We are good with kids. It's fair to say that I had far more experience with babies than many other first-time moms of my generation. But we were still worried about so much, Josh especially. We wanted to do this right. So, in the first days home from the hospital, we diligently practiced getting our "burrito" swaddle just right, and Josh made little spreadsheets and tables to document Fiona's wet and dry diapers, how many minutes she was nursing at each feeding, and on which side. (Josh and I saved those charts, by the way. We'll probably whip them out when suitors start showing up.)

This sort of recordkeeping can be helpful, to make sure this new creature is properly adapting to life on the outside, that all systems are up and running. And I really did refer to the nursing chart when I went to feed her. Since we seemed to be nursing constantly, I could never remember on which side she'd left off. Having been warned by baby books and lactation consultants, I knew how absolutely, critically, vitally important it was that I alternate, so that my little Fee would get the appropriate mix of fore and hind milk. Never mind that I'd never heard of fore and hind milk before, I took the word of these varied experts as gospel.

I suspect Josh and I were so keyed up because Fiona's arrival, at a slightly less than average but nonetheless robust seven pounds two ounces, impressed upon us in a way we hadn't quite anticipated just how tiny and helpless she would be. I had felt like a whale for months, had grown fleshy and pillow-like. I had assumed my baby would be equally fleshy and pillow-like. With all the kicking and bladder-punching she'd done in utero, I also assumed she'd be a little more, I don't know, active. Have a bit more muscle. But she was so tiny and couldn't even lift her head! She slept all the time and reminded us of a baby kitten, not quite ready to open her eyes to the wide world.

At one point during my pregnancy, I'd gone through a period of reading books and articles that emphasized just how creaturely we and our babies are. I took great comfort in the knowledge that babies have these funny reflexes related to our simian ancestors, that their eyes, unable to focus on much, can find that large, differently colored nipple that sustains them. Fiona, though she may have been able to see my nipples, certainly couldn't do anything to get her little mouth in range of them. I had to hold her head and prop her mouth open in a tricky little maneuver as I tried to get her to latch.

"Babies!" Josh and I would laugh and shake our heads. "It's like they can't do *anything* for themselves."

Babies' unbelievable and incomparable helplessness isn't the only thing that intimidates new parents, though. There is so much at stake; the weight of responsibility for their well-being is the heaviest burden many new parents have yet had to bear. If that responsibility weren't intimidating enough, *everyone* has an opinion on how to go about caring for an infant, about how to parent a child wisely or faithfully or organically or according to the recommendations of the American Academy of Pediatrics. If they all provided the same advice, that chorus of witnesses might prove helpful, but the variety of instructions, and the voracity with which they are offered, is more bewildering than anything.

This voracity (and the teensiest bit of self-righteousness, maybe) that is exhibited by many parenting experts, both accredited and self-appointed, is lampooned by the wonderful comic and writer Tina Fey in her book *Bossypants*. In one chapter, as she discusses the decision to nurse or bottle feed, she reminds readers that they should take her advice seriously: "Remember, I was pregnant once, *and* I'm on TV: Those two things combined make me an *expert*."[1]

Experts abound, and I, wanting the best for our baby, sought out their expertise. Our house is full of books, and in the "reference" section of one of our many bookcases, right under my massive and unnecessary cookbook collection, is a full shelf of books about babies, pregnancy, and parenting. Books about when to call the doctor and when to expect your baby to pass certain developmental milestones and when to call the doctor if you don't see the developmental milestones. Books about how to clean the umbilical cord stump and how to give your infant a sponge bath.

A lot of this information is wildly helpful; much of it is not. One book says to put rubbing alcohol on that smelly stump, another says leave it alone. One says you must have your baby boy circumcised, to help with hygiene and reduce the risk of penile cancer (no joke); another says the practice is cruel and must not be done; and a final one says to take it or leave it, depending on how "conventional" you're feeling. One says if you give your baby a pacifier or a bottle before six weeks old, she'll develop "nipple confusion." (Just typing that phrase, I scoff inwardly, "Yeah, right." But we totally believed it with Fiona, and then had to work to get her to take a bottle at two months old. She ultimately kept nursing and using the bottle and took to the pacifier as though we'd dipped it in sugar. And wouldn't give it up. She finally traded it in—in a negotiated trade—for a doll she picked out at the toy store around her third birthday.) Another expert insists that bottles and pacifiers are terrible for a child's teeth, and still another says to just give the kid bottles from the get-go.

The frustrating thing for us was how much advice was available and how very little we had in the way of criteria to help us wade through it all. To remedy this, we simply became the new parents who call the pediatrician's office each day with a new variation of the same question: *Are we doing this right? Is it going to be okay?*

But who else could we trust? Our parents didn't remember a lot of the information, having not spent time with babies in nearly twenty years; plus, when Josh and I were infants, people were just (*just!*) starting to figure out that smoking around babies was bad news, and the campaign to lower the incidence of SIDS by placing babies on their backs to sleep was still ten years away. So, you know, we loved our parents and were grateful and all, but we sometimes took their advice with a grain of salt. (My mother was known to have a particularly nonchalant take on reducing risk around babies. She used to sit me up on her sewing table next to her—several feet off the floor—and let me sort buttons into a muffin tin. Buttons, one can imagine, are not typically considered the best toys for children under age three. She has, to be fair, worked very hard to convince us that she would never, ever endanger our children. We believe her, of course, but we still tease her without mercy.)

These questions about what constitutes an expert opinion and whom we can trust for advice and information lie at the heart of much of the shift in Western culture from something called *modernity* to what we call the period we're now in, *postmodernity*. (For the record, Josh thinks these are stupid names; any time I mention *postmodernism,* he says something derisive like, "As if that's even a thing!" The man makes a compelling argument.) Despite the obtuse terminology, the ideas bandied about in philosophical circles reflect and shape the culture in which we live and in which we parent our children. *Modernity*, in philosophical terms, is actually a lot older than we might first suppose; it has to do with how cultures began to differentiate between the power and authority of different institutions—like church and state, for example—and to speak about the rights and responsibilities of individuals over and against those broader institutions. For a long time, what was good for the king or good for the church was considered good for everybody . . . or, you know, *good enough*. Gradually that began to change. One thing that remained, however, was the sense that there was a Truth that could be revealed or discerned or recognized by human people—one capital-T Truth that was true for everybody. You see this perspective (and you likely had to take notes on it, if you attended a liberal arts college) in the writings of thinkers like Immanuel Kant, who wrote about the "categorical impera-tive."[2] He described this imperative as something that is universally, morally good—and it compels us to treat others as we'd like to be treated, and as part of that, never treat someone as anything other than an end in themselves. That is, don't use people or treat them as no more than props in your life's drama. They are characters, too.

That's all fabulously great stuff (sounds sort of like something Jesus was known to say, in the Sermon on the Mount, for example). But there came a time when people started to realize that, even if there were just one capital-T Truth out there, people other than educated, rich white guys should have a chance to interpret it. Women, for example, and people of color, and poor people, and non-Westerners. As those other folks started to add their voices to the conversation about meaning and value and Truth, a funny if unsurprising thing happened. People began to disagree on the content of meaning and value and Truth.

Okay, that's not entirely true. People have always disagreed about things. But what's different is that our ability to arbitrate truth claims—to appeal to given authorities to decide who's right and who's full of nonsense—is now greatly diminished. And that creates big problems for those of us who want to talk about what life *should* be like or how people *should* behave.)

And, honestly, that's where we remain today. We disagree about what makes something true and what gives someone authority. My shelf of parenting books is a pretty clear demonstration of this; the parenting rack at a bookstore would render the differences of opinion even more obvious. (My shelf has less variety because I refuse to spend money on books with which I know I will patently disagree. That might limit my research, but I am comfortable refusing Jenny McCarthy and James Dobson space on my already crowded shelves.) Any parent who's been overwhelmed by the range of options and opinions thrown at us (like so many mashed peas) can confirm that this shift is not always pleasant. It's bewildering if not outright frightening to chip away at the one conception of truth we've held to. Human beings experience change as stressful. When a change in the things we consider authoritative accompanies the change of bringing home a baby, it's a wonder we don't all just crawl into the cradle, adopt the fetal position alongside our progeny, and join them in whimpering.

This changing understanding of Truth, of where it comes from and who has the authority to speak and share it, has been enormously threatening to many Christians over the years. Some believers see it as a blasphemous rejection of God's final and absolute authority. In the early twentieth century, as Americans (by way of their clergy) were beginning to adopt some of the new ways of doing biblical interpretation, and as Darwin's *On the Origin of Species* was making its way into common understanding, a number of Christians gathered to articulate what they saw as the "fundamentals" of Christian belief. These items were non-negotiable, and no fancy-schmancy German literary analysis was going to do away with the Christian affirmation of the historical reality of the virgin birth or the literal existence of a first man named Adam and a first woman named Eve.

The Bible, as the infallible word of God (and words of God), became the emblem of Truth. These Christians who called themselves *fundamentalists* wanted us to read the Bible, study the Bible, and order our lives according to its instruction. Obviously, that seems fairly unobjectionable on a surface level. Christians should read the Bible. It's the question of how we read it, and how we interpret what we read, that tends to raise hackles. This brand of

Christian gets caricatured a lot these days, but I can understand how it might be hard to resist poking fun at those who pay good money to buy billboards along the interstate that say things like, "'I can think of ten things that *are* carved in stone.' —God."

As those Christians dug in their heels, others broadened their sense of the sources of authority. Some, in this past century, pretty much did away with the Bible as authoritative and read it for poetry or general inspiration, but they weighted its wisdom along that of, say, Oprah. These folks are infuriating to the fundamentalists, and, actually, they infuriate me, too—because, as much as we all love Oprah, the Bible is *the* text that Christians have shared and read and argued about and relied upon and been guided and challenged and inspired by for millennia. That said, we've learned a lot in the past several millennia, and I would prefer a physician with a degree in medicine over a faith healer well versed in the Bible to treat any illnesses my kids might acquire.

The denomination in which I serve, the United Methodist Church, has as part of its heritage twenty-five "Articles of Religion" that John Wesley (Remember him? Founder of the Methodist movement, eighteenth-century Anglican priest) adapted from the Articles of Religion in the Anglican Church that governed the church in his day. Article 5 is about the Bible: "The Holy Scripture containeth all things necessary to salvation; so that whatsoever is not read therein, nor may be proved thereby, is not to be required of any man that it should be believed as an article of faith, or be thought requisite or necessary to salvation."[3] My best interpretation of that suggests that the Bible's authority is carried not in the exact words of each verse but in the way the Bible leads us to new life in Christ. Anything that's not in the Bible may well be true (the Holy Spirit isn't limited to speaking through Scripture), but it only adds to what's revealed about new life in Christ.

Christian parents, then, can and should look for the Spirit and wisdom of God beyond Scripture. But there is without a doubt a lot of garbage available as well. Terrible ideas about discipline or authoritarian models of parenting often masquerade as biblical or Christian. The Internet has made the challenge of postmodernism all the more real, because everyone with a modem and a keyboard can portray herself as an expert. (You don't even need to be on TV, Tina Fey!) Our old models of authority—of claiming the absolute and inarguable truth of Scripture or the church or the government—just don't hold water anymore. With so many voices flooding the cultural atmosphere, it can be difficult to suss out which voices can be trusted and who actually knows what they're talking about. I may have a hunch that Jenny McCarthy doesn't have a clue about vaccinating children. (Her authority to speak apparently comes from being (1) mother to an autistic son, (2) a former Playboy bunny, and (3) a celebrity with money to pour into supporting terrible science.) But how do I move from that hunch and address my own need to make wise decisions for my kids?

Not to beat the Methodist drum too incessantly, but the leading contribution of my tradition to wider Christian understanding is something called the "Wesleyan Quadrilateral," which was actually articulated not by Wesley himself but by Albert Outler, a scholar who studied Wesley in the mid-twentieth century.[4] The quadrilateral affirms the Articles of Religion by holding that Scripture is the primary way in which Christians come to hear the story of God and Christ that witnesses to salvation. But (and here I offer you, dear reader, my highly academic and well-studied biblical hermeneutic, or way of reading the Bible) there's a lot of stuff in the Bible:

Some of it is a bit mind-blowing in its metaphorical detail. (Anything considered apocalyptic literature.)

Some of it is repetitive. (Kings and Chronicles record similar periods of history from different perspectives.)

Some of it is contradictory. (For example, Peter and Paul could not agree on a lot of things as they began to plant, grow, and lead churches after Christ's resurrection, but both men spoke with authority for early Christians and for us today.)

So, Outler suggested that Wesley suggested that Christians can know what is true by running any question or reflection through a quadrilateral comprised of Scripture, Tradition, Reason, and Experience. So, suppose I'm considering the question of whether I should breast-feed my baby? Scripture doesn't say much about this, although there are a few places where God is described as nourishing and sustaining God's people as a mother nurses her child. Tradition keeps shifting (our grandmothers may have never even considered nursing; our mothers might have, depending on the decade they were having babies), so that's kind of open. Reason says there are health benefits and it's free—but also that there are countless reasons why a mother or child might not be able to nurse. And experience can break either way.

Now, there are those who might consider that four-part exercise sort of useless. Should I breast-feed or not? Where is my clear answer?

The quadrilateral doesn't usually offer a clear answer—and not just on questions of parenting. What I find useful about it, though, is that it is open and flexible in helping me discern what's true, and it allows me to ascribe some authority to my decisions, rather than being entirely random. The fear of a slippery slope to randomness and baseless assumptions is what troubles so many religious people about postmodernism. We're afraid that if we admit that Scripture might be ambiguous on some issues or that our commitments to certain things are more culturally conditioned than biblical, we're conceding that there's nothing true, nothing about which we can be sure. (Check out some of the patriarchs and their many, many wives to get a sense of what "biblical marriage" often looked like. I can tell you that it's not always one man and one woman.) We're afraid that a world in which "anything goes" will squeeze all decency and holiness out of the world.

But to confess that truth is complex and often mysterious and sometimes downright difficult to discern is not to say there is no such thing as truth. It is to say, however, that there may be *more* true things than we previously supposed or that the true things are a bit more abstract than we'd once understood them to be. Is breast-feeding good? Yes. Everybody says so. Is it for everyone? No, it's not for women with health problems, women who rely on prescription medications that could harm an infant, women who adopt, kids whose biological moms aren't around, women whose work schedules don't allow it, or women for whom it just doesn't work. Is this something to fight about? Most likely not. Does this mean bottle-feeding one's baby diet soda is an appropriate substitute for breast milk? Decidedly not.

Tina Fey seems pretty comfortable with the decisions she made about nursing and then bottle-feeding her first child, but she rails against the women she'd encounter at parties or on the playground who seemed to believe it was their responsibility to make her feel guilty for her choices. Fey is a humorist, of course, but I think she hones in on one of the important realities of humanity. We are more likely to be strident, pushy, or self-righteous when we're not sure of ourselves, when we're afraid.

Unlike Fey, I don't go to fancy Brooklyn parties (well, rarely . . .), but some of my very own middle-class Midwestern peers have nonetheless adopted the George W. Bush stance on war in their parenting: "If you're not with us, you're against us." (To be fair, he was quoting Jesus's words from Matthew 12:30 and Luke 11:23.) If you're not aligned with the same experts, choosing the same pre-school theories (Montessori or Waldorf or Chicago Daily Math?), you clearly hate me and my kids. Based on my armchair understanding of psychology, I assume this defensiveness comes from my peers' lack of confidence in themselves and their parenting choices.

Personally, I prefer the alternate wisdom Jesus offers in Mark 9:40: "Whoever is not against us is for us." There are as many ways to parent well as there are kids, I am sure. Waldorf and Montessori schools can *both* nurture self-directed hippie kids. So, in becoming a parent, I wanted a way to claim my own authority—to decide what was right and good for my family, to wade through "the literature"—in a way that wasn't defensive, but healthy. I wanted to base my parenting decisions on something in addition to my own intuition and personal convictions, without simply reacting to the biggest title on the parenting bestseller list. Josh and I struggled to figure out our authority as new parents and as a couple, too. Yes, I had a lot more experience caring for babies than he did. Still, I didn't want to claim I knew everything about baby care just because I am a woman and the mom (and also because I didn't know everything). With him, no less than with our kids, I wanted to refrain from tossing out "Because I'm the Mommy!" as a conversation closer. I wanted my authority to be grounded in more than just my gender or my role.

Josh and I make a good couple, I think. We take turns being right and try not to make a big deal about it when the other has obviously made a mistake. But we disagree sometimes. An example: I have perhaps the teensiest, tiniest, little lotion addiction. Which is to say, in all seriousness, that I have really dry skin—like many other members of my family. If I don't apply lotion at least a couple of times daily (and drink enough water, and stay out of the sun, and so forth), I get really uncomfortable. Red. Itchy. Josh's ethnic heritage is predominantly Greek and Italian. He has perennially soft, lovely, Mediterranean skin. He did not, maybe, believe that I actually need all the lotion I use. And so when I wanted to use all the nice smelling organic lotions we'd received at various showers on our baby, my inclination was vetoed. "Just wait," he said. And I did. Perhaps I gave in because Fiona resembles Josh more than me in a lot of ways, so I assumed her skin would take after his as well. At any rate, I held off. During the first six months of Fiona's life, we didn't put any lotion on her—not daily, not after baths—because we'd read a recommendation somewhere that said not to: Babies' skin has to learn to regulate itself with outside moisture levels—or something like that.

One day, her skin was bright red, more beet than tomato, and it seemed to be raised. What sort of demon rash had overtaken our precious girl, we wondered? Off we went to the pediatrician, who took one look and offered a diagnosis: "This kid has dry skin. Go put some lotion on her. See if she gets better." As it happened, she didn't just have dry skin, but pretty bad eczema. "Cream" became part of our morning and evening ritual.

I was gracious in my victory, mostly because Josh loves his daughter so very much that I didn't want even to hint that we'd prolonged or exacerbated the issue. But I was kind of ticked off for a while. Why didn't he trust me? I was mad at myself, too. Why hadn't I asserted myself? Was it because I wasn't really sure? Or just because I didn't want to argue?

I consider myself very lucky that I can trust that Josh and I both absolutely want what's best for our kids, even if we don't always agree on what that is. The assurance I get from that knowledge generally helps me claim my authority as a parent—and it's getting easier over time. I know this, because while we took Fiona to the emergency room before her first birthday (Diagnoses: Stomach bug. Treatment: $1,000 hospital bill, a drive home, and bed.), Calliope has never been. With Fiona, I pumped and pumped and then cried when we first gave her formula; I nursed Cal whenever I was with her, but that kid started getting formula in her bottles the day I went back to work after my maternity leave. Woe to the firstborn, who carries the burden of all our angst! Woe to the secondborn, whose childhood lacks parental vigilance!

It's not just the passage of time and having two kids that eases this authority business for us. I do believe we've gotten better at running through the quadrilateral about hard things and trusting one another and ourselves on easier things. That trust is absolutely critical, it seems to me—but so is knowing what this trust is based on. Fiona is four and a half now, and Calliope nearly two, and in the span of their childhoods, I've come to believe that I'm a pretty good mom. My girls love me, and I love them. They're healthy, thriving, curious, and funny, and they are, for the most part, a joy to be around. But the only certainty I would claim as I parent regards very small and uncontroversial issues. (I'm pretty sure children should sleep at least once every night, that they should not drink soda, and that their mothers really ought to try to limit their consumption of that beloved sugary garbage if they're ever going to manage to be a good example.) My confidence as a parent does not come from any sense that I have all the answers. Quite the contrary. My confidence comes from accepting the fact that I do not have now, nor will I ever have, all the answers. All I can do is try, and try faithfully, to make good decisions for my kids.

It is ridiculously scary to believe there is no one right decision—that things are complicated and hard, and they're never really guaranteed to get any easier. I am so lucky. So lucky. So far, the hardest medical decision I've faced as a parent was around whether or not to get Callie ear tubes (Yes.) and the most difficult behavioral challenge concerned how to react when Fiona told me that her preschool girlfriend had made a comment about kissing a boy's penis. (Oh, dear sweet Lord. I cursed Josh for not being in the car with me that night, talked in my best nonalarmist tone about how a boy's penis is one of his private parts and thus not really for anyone else to touch or kiss, and then went to chat with the preschool "principal" the following Monday, just to make sure everything's okay in that other little girl's home life.)

But I know a woman who found out she was six weeks pregnant as she went in for a mastectomy. And I know a committed Catholic couple who dreamed of having a huge family like the ones they were raised in, whose first daughter had a life-threatening genetic ailment. After their daughter's successful stem-cell transplant, the couple wondered, should they have more kids? Another woman I know was forced to face the question of whether she should end her marriage to her beloved husband when he was diagnosed with Huntington's Disease, and his grief drove him to a belligerence that kept him from parenting their young children. In her wonderful memoir *Bad Mother,* Ayelet Waldman tells the story of how she and her husband responded when a routine amnio came back with devastating news.[5] I don't know, cannot say, what I would have done in any of these situations, but part of becoming a parent is knowing that we must make choices, and that we always do so with limited knowledge.

In place of certainty, though, we can look to hope and faith, we can try to trust, and we can make the most of the knowledge we do have. We can also know that even though there is often not one right path to choose in raising our children, there are better choices and worse choices.

I don't, honestly, want to make good parenting decisions just so I have snappy comebacks to self-righteous pseudoexperts and other bossypants parents. I want to parent well because I love my children. I don't want to be right just to be right—just as, I imagine, God doesn't long for us to respond to the divine voice just because "he said so." We want to live as God intends, want to parent well, because God's dream (as Desmond Tutu puts it in the wonderful children's Bible Lee mentioned in chapter 7) is Good and True, and participating in the things in this life that are Good and True makes this crazy life worth living.

Thinking of my quest to discover and claim my parental authority in these grace-filled terms has become a more pressing need for me as my girls have reached the point at which asserting their own will over and against mine is as natural to them as breathing. I gravitate toward babies now more than ever before, risking spit-up and other hazards simply because babies don't fight with me. (Also because they are very cute, and they smell nice.) Babies, I am reminded as I hold my brand new nephew, don't throw blocks when they're mad about bedtime; babies don't throw a fit when their parents make perfectly reasonable requests like, "Wash your hands before we eat, please," or, "You need to wear socks if you're going to play in the snow."

Just as I am relatively convinced that God isn't threatened by the acknowledgment that truth is more complex than we're prone to believe, I also can't allow myself to be threatened by the knowledge that other people parent differently than I do—or by the fact that my children are periodically insolent little beasties. I want to be a good parent—to teach my kids the categorical imperative, to raise them to have faith in God and to serve all people in the name of Christ. And I absolutely cannot do that if I can't trust that I have some authority as a mother and as a human being.

Mary Beth Hicks, a columnist and mother of four, says that asserting parental authority in healthy ways is one of the corner-stones of raising "GEEKS" (Genuine, Empowered, Enthusiastic Kids)—which are, presumably, the sort of kids we'd all like to have.[6] Hicks says that we assert healthy authority neither by becoming an overbearing drill sergeant nor by being a "friend" who enables and allows for our child's poor behavior and lack of boundaries. Hicks urges us to set and maintain high expectations and boundaries for our kids, while still being warm and nurturing. She reminds parents that authority is hard to lose; your kids, though they test you, can't actually take away your authority. You can only give it away. That is to say, a parent is more likely to sacrifice his authority by engaging his kid's tantrum, or allowing the child to escalate a situation, than to lose his authority because the kid rejects it or usurps it in some ultimate way.

Parental authority is meant to be *authoritative*—claimed, and used, but responsibly. One thing that should have been obvious to me in those early months and years of Fiona's life, but that I just could not see then, is that we have power over our children. Not just authority, but power. And it's a common cultural trope that people don't respond well when their power is threatened. They act out, they lash out. So what I long for is to parent authoritatively, to recognize and name my power without ever abusing it. What's at stake for me in figuring all this out is nothing less than figuring out how to never, ever hit my child again.

When I was pregnant with Callie, Fiona went through this extremely frustrating phase during which we seriously considered selling her to the circus. Both naptime and bedtime were a daily struggle. It took hours to get her settled down. She'd talk and talk, and then be silly, and then sort of mean, and then she'd get up and jump on the bed or hit the wall, or hit Josh or me when we tried to make her stop all that. One afternoon I was just at the end of my rope, and I told her as calmly and sternly as possible that she either needed to lie down right that very instant or I was going to . . . I don't remember what. Give her a time out? Take her television privileges? Take a toy? We went through so many ineffective tactics in those weeks, it's hard to remember.

At any rate, I tried to assert my authority—sternly, calmly, maturely, by the book—and she spit on me. She did. Right in my face. And I slapped her. Did it without thinking. A reflexive response.

As soon as I felt my hand on her cheek, I wanted to die. I couldn't believe it. I mean, my primary objections to light spanking are that it's an ineffective practice and it just seems sort of unfair for a big ole grown-up to hit somebody smaller, even if it's for good reason. Josh was never spanked and is totally opposed to it, and thus in addition to feeling incredibly shameful, I also despaired that he'd leave me. Hurting children: That's definitely on Josh's top-five list of unforgivable sins.

Fiona, for her part, was confused and just laughed.

I apologized immediately to Fiona and told her that it is wrong to hit, and grown-ups should never hit children, and people should never hit those they love, and basically restated everything I believe about human relationships—everything I'd just violated. If she'd known how to roll her eyes at that age, I am sure that's what she would have done.

But even though I thank God that this incident seemed to affect me more than her, that's not a risk I'm willing to take again. And so I have to learn—not just assent to, but know in my core—that my authority as a mother will never simply come from stomping my foot and saying, "Because I said so." "I'm the parent, that's why" always failed to compel me to listen when I was a kid; I can't imagine it would work any better (or I'd feel like less of a hypocrite) if I pulled it out myself.

But if not "I'm the mommy, that's why," then what?

The younger kids in the Sunday school at our church start their hour of Christian education with "Chapel Time," which I lead. Each week this year, we've been learning about a new biblical image or metaphor for God, guided by illustrations and meditations from Marie-Hélène Delval's wonderful book *Images of God for Young Children*.[7] God is covenant. God is mystery. God is justice. About the image "God is a parent," Delval writes:

> A parent says to a child, "Come, I will show you the world! Come, I will teach you about life!" when the child has grown up, the parent says, "Go on—it's up to you to make your own way!" The parent watches the child leave, happy and proud to see the child walk alone, free. But the parent still loves the child. Always![8]

Miss Calliope and Miss Fiona will probably reject multiple hundreds of my requests in the next days alone. As I attempt to live into my authority, as I attempt to trust that I'll always be their mother, whether they listen or not, I want to remember the endgame. How I exercise my authority—how I claim it and how I teach them to respect and honor and question it—will surely affect how they go out into the world. I want to be proud and happy; I want them to be free, wise, and brave. So, I'm going to try a new response—the best one I've got in a complicated world where there is little certainty—and I'm going to cling to what I know to be true: *Because I'm your mother, and I love you.*

Washing the Diapers

On gratitude, and justice, and
living in a broken world

THIS CHAPTER BEGINS WITH AN INARTICULATE QUESTION AND ends without much of an answer. The question is something like this:

How do I make sense of my very abundant life when people all over the world do not have enough?

Or maybe it's something like this:

How do we do right by our family and still maintain our commitment to working for justice in the world? And what do we do when those commitments conflict?

Or maybe it's simply this:

How do we live in this world?

But let me back up for a minute.

On a hot afternoon last summer, a day when reports about the famine in east Africa and the stock market's tanking again were topping the headlines, I attended a meeting of church leaders and community organizations. We had gotten together in an attempt to figure out how to best serve the many people in our community who had fallen behind in their rent or utility bills. Funding was scarce; county and city budgets had been cut, as had the budgets and staff of nearly every agency in town. Social workers and shelters were getting slammed with requests for help, as more and more people found themselves without jobs and needing help. Churches

wanted to help but didn't know how to fit into the system, especially given their own limited staff and resources.

We went around and around for more than an hour, suggesting
systems and procedures, policies and protocols, but it didn't really
matter: even with all our pooled resources, the best system in the
world couldn't overcome the reality that there just wasn't enough
money to help everyone who needed it. The meeting ran long,
and I was already late to pick up Harper, so I slipped out before it
ended, feeling more than a little discouraged and despairing.

I tried to switch hats on the way into the preschool parking
lot, squeezing in between all the SUVs and minivans, waving to
the other moms and dads who were running, harried from their
workdays, to pick up their kids. *I don't have to solve all the problems of
poverty right this minute*, I reminded myself. *I just have to pick up my
daughter, get home, and get dinner on the table.*

But after my daughter was safely buckled into the car and we
were headed toward home, we turned onto the main thorough-
fare that runs from downtown to our neighborhood, and there she
was: the homeless woman we see standing on that corner nearly
every day. She stands holding a cardboard sign, her bicycle propped
against the fence next to her, and stares with vacant eyes at the rows
of cars stopped at the light. She is thin, with short graying hair,
which, last winter, she tucked into a thick wool hat. She stands up
straight, feet together and shoulders back, as if she learned moun-
tain pose in a yoga class and is practicing.

I avoided making eye contact. I don't even know what her
cardboard sign said.

I tried to keep Harper chatting away so she wouldn't ask me
(again) why the woman was there, and I wouldn't have to come up
with an explanation. I don't know what her story is, what leads her
to stand on the street corner as driver after driver avoids eye contact
on the way home to a comfortable house and a hearty dinner.

The light turned green, finally, and we left her behind as we
turned toward home. When we slipped into the air conditioned

coolness of the house, as Harper went off to her room to get out her paints and I turned toward our full cupboards to pull out some dinner, I felt—not for the first time—the incredible disconnect between the crushing needs of the world around me and the incredible abundance of my life.

Sometimes, I don't know how to live in this world.

I'm writing this chapter in the days before the tenth anniversary of September 11, 2001. The attacks that day not only killed nearly three thousand people but also woke many Americans from a deep and isolated ignorance that had convinced us the world's troubles had nothing to do with us. The ongoing wars in Afghanistan and Iraq have killed many thousands more, including civilians whose names never make it onto our newscasts. Now, soldiers who were just children at the time of the attacks are joining the ranks of those who die on those battlefields. Just this morning, CNN announced that there's a new terror threat being investigated. The country and the world remain deeply broken.

It's easy, though, to forget all this, especially on beautiful summer evenings with just a hint of fall in the air. The weather broke recently, easing back from the mid-ninety-degree days we'd been having for months. The soaring temperatures and high humidity, combined with the extra thirty pounds of pregnant belly I'd been carrying around all summer, meant that I'd hardly been outside at all. I felt like I'd missed the season completely, having stayed huddled up in my air-conditioned office or car or living room. So when the first of September brought a cooler breeze, we hurried to turn off the air and open the windows. I felt like I could breathe again.

On one of those cooler evenings, Harper and I packed a picnic dinner and met Rob after work at our neighborhood playground. It's a lovely park located on a relatively quiet street, so Harper could run from the picnic table to the slide and back, while Rob and I caught up on the details of our day. (A more prepared mother, I thought at one point, would have brought hand wipes and made Harper wash up between bouts of playing and eating, but I shrugged and gave thanks for my child's healthy immune system.) We drank lemonade and ate tomato sandwiches and devoured what might be the last of the good summer peaches. After we were done, Rob went to push Harper on the swing, and I stayed at the table, packing up the picnic leftovers. I watched them playing, but mostly I listened: Harper's squeals of delight drifted off into the evening as she soared higher in the swing; Rob was unable to keep his own laughter from joining hers. What a good life this is, I thought. To have good food, time to be together, a safe place to play, healthy bodies.

Harper woke up with giggles this morning, discovering that she had flipped herself around during the night and was sleeping with her feet on her pillow. She sang her way through breakfast and danced out the door to school, where she'll be surrounded by friends and highly qualified teachers who are teaching her to read. We made cookies last night to share on a play date this afternoon. We're full of excitement about the baby who is about to invade our lives, whose arrival could happen any time, after a very normal and uncomplicated pregnancy. Here in this little corner of the world, life is very good indeed. We want for nothing, and we are grateful.

But gratitude can't be the last word, can it? It can't be enough for us to compare our lives to the lives of most families in the world and simply be thankful for what we have. There must be something else, some other way of responding to the chasm between rich and poor, between the haves and have-nots, between the lives of abundance we lead and the scarcity and pain around us. Surely we are called to do more than give thanks that we are not one of those families being turned away from the homeless shelter because there aren't any more beds available.

Earlier this summer, a slideshow called *Where Children Sleep* made its way around cyberspace.[1] It featured pictures of children from all over the world alongside photographs of their bedrooms. Some were hard to look at—because of the extreme poverty in which some children live and because of the extreme luxury of others. A four-year-old American girl's bedroom was decked out in pink and decorated with the ribbons and tiaras she'd won in beauty pageants. The floor of a Tokyo bedroom was cluttered with the toys and electronic games of a ten-year-old. An eight-year-old boy in Cambodia lives with his family on top of the town dump.

I wish I could say that Harper's bedroom—with its hand-me-down bed and consignment sale dresser—fell somewhere in the middle of the spectrum of those pictures, somewhere at least midway between the extreme poverty and the overwhelming extravagance. But the truth is that she has way more stuff than most children in the world. We try to limit the acquisition of new toys to special occasions, but she still has more than she plays with. The English major in me will never admit that we have too many books—but it's true that there isn't quite enough room for all of them on her bookshelf, and we have a perfectly good library card.

Once this new baby is born, our children will share a room. "Children share rooms all over the world," I kept saying to myself as we rearranged furniture so we could squeeze the crib into the corner. But the reality is that we have two other bedrooms in another part of the house—one a guest room, the other an office/storage/place-to-pile-the-stuff-we-don't-know-what-to-do-with kind of room. Harper and her baby sibling will share a room not out of necessity, but because of the quirky layout of our home. Their sharing will be nothing like that of the Chinese boy in the slide-show who shares a single bedroom with his sister *and* his parents.

We have an abundance, and we are grateful—but that's not enough. Gratitude is only the first step.

One of the most compelling chapters in Bonnie Miller-McLemore's book on parenting, *In the Midst of Chaos,* is her chapter on justice. In it, Miller-McLemore wrestles with the negotiation needed to honor her commitment to her own children and her commitment to justice beyond the family. "Christian parenting," she writes, "means not only balancing our own needs and those of our children, but also the needs of our own children and those of other children." She describes the decision she and her husband faced when moving to a new town and choosing where to live: "Should we live in an area where people of different economic classes or races or sexual orientation would be our near neighbors? Or should we focus on good schools? . . . What would we convey to our kids by choosing a safer route? If we made the riskier choice, how would we handle the extra demands it would bring when we were already so busy with other things?"[2]

The choices we make in our daily tasks as parents *do* matter to the world beyond ourselves. Decisions about where to live and what schools to send our children to, where we shop and how we spend our money—all these choices affect not only our own families but also our neighbors, globally and locally.

But making these choices gets tricky. Living with other people even in the context of family is already one long negotiation. Who's responsible for doing the dishes? Preparing the meals? Making sure the electric bill gets paid on time? Throwing in a commitment to justice in the world beyond our family just complicates matters further.

Rob and I have wrestled with these dilemmas, and I'd like to be able to tell you about all the good choices we've made. I could tell you about washing the cloth diapers in an attempt to keep all those nonbiodegradable disposable diapers out of the landfills. I could tell you how I buy most of our produce at the local farmers' market, or about how we've made a commitment to giving a percentage of our income to the church and other organizations we feel are making a real difference.

But then I'd have to also tell you that we have two cars, which we drive even to places close enough to walk. We own a house that has more space than three—even soon-to-be four—people need, with a garage and an attic filled with stuff we get out maybe once a year. We are taking up too much space on the planet. We may buy local produce, but we also eat our share of frozen pizzas, and our recycling can is always overflowing with cardboard cereal boxes. We can give away a good portion of our income because Rob and

I both have jobs that pay well, because we were born into families
that could afford to give us good educations, and because we've
been lucky enough to avoid the layoffs of the last several years.

And even the things that feel like sacrifices are not really. We
can use cloth diapers easily because we live in a house with a washer
and dryer. We shop at the farmers' market because we can afford it,
and because we have free time on Saturday mornings, and because
we can drive there and carry the produce home in our car, and
because the food tastes better anyway. My choice to support a local
bakery instead of our neighborhood Starbucks is hardly a hardship.

But still, even those small choices bring up the quandary
Miller-McLemore addresses: What happens when the choice to do
something good for the world competes with the commitment to
do something good for our family?

For us, this dilemma manifests itself in the diapers. Or it might,
when this new baby arrives. When Harper was born, we lived in a
small condo, where the washer and dryer were nestled into a little
alcove between our bedrooms and just across the hall from the
bathroom. Washing the diapers was messy, sure, but it was hardly
inconvenient to dump the dirty diapers into the washer at the end
of the day.

We've moved since then, and now the washing machine and
dryer are across the house and down a set of twisty basement stairs.
I realize how trivial this sounds (some people have to walk miles
for fresh water, and I'm complaining about carrying dirty diapers
across the house?), but that extra inconvenience, added to the presence of a four-year-old who also needs our attention, means that
washing the diapers will be a little more complicated this time
around.

Awhile back, when Rob and I were just starting to imagine
what it might be like to have a second baby, I reminded him that
we still had the diapers from last time. I knew right where they
were, I said, and we just had to get them out and wash them, and
they'd be ready.

Rob nodded, but then said, "I think we should decide now that if it gets to be too much, we'll stop. I don't want it to make us crazy."

"Yeah, okay," I said, because it was late, and there was no sense in getting into an argument about what might hypothetically drive us crazy several months down the road. And I appreciated his intentions: He's looking out for me, for the good of our family. He knows my tendency to stubbornly grab on to an idea and not let go. He wants us to be happy and healthy and sane—and if that means not staying up until after midnight to wash the diapers, then so be it.

But I'm not so sure.

Because right there is the dilemma, I think: What happens when the choice to do right by the world (washing the diapers) means compromising a priority for our family (a rested, less-crazed mom)? And what if the choice isn't even clear? More than one person, on hearing that we're using cloth diapers, has suggested that maybe the environmental impact of cloth diapers, with all the extra water and energy required to wash them, was actually worse than that of disposables. The truth seems to depend on whom you ask; I'll err on the side of keeping the disposables out of the landfill.

But it gets even more complicated: What happens when the very things that bring us joy cause pain for someone else? This spring, we bought a new patio table for our backyard. It has an umbrella and comfortable chairs, big enough for just our family, or for Rob and me and a few friends. We've spent several lovely evenings out there, talking and eating and watching Harper play. It has enhanced our lives, and we've been grateful to have it.

We bought it from a big box store. It didn't cost much. I'm sure it was made in a factory far away and shipped here, using I don't know how much fuel and energy along the way. I'd looked for a used one—though I admit it was a half-hearted attempt, a couple glances at Craigslist and one or two trips to consignment stores. I couldn't find what we wanted, so we went the easy route. I'm well aware that things like that patio table, or the Slip'N Slide we got for Harper's birthday party, things that bring joy into our lives—and actual, real joy, I might add, not the fleeting kind that isn't worth it—things like that are possible for us because of the exploitation of others, workers in conditions I don't even want to think about.

There's a chasm here I can't get across.

The baby squirms and stretches and kicks me in the ribs as I click over to CNN to see the continuing coverage of the September 11 anniversary. It's been nonstop all week. Everywhere I've looked, there have been tributes and memorials, essays and reflections, memories and prayers and commemorations. Some of it has been sad and tragic; some has been hope-filled and courageous. Some has been overly sentimental, some overly patriotic, some overly politicized. Some of it has celebrated heroes; some of it has mourned victims; some of it has disparaged enemies. It occurs to me that to this baby I'm carrying, the attacks of September 11, 2001, will feel like ancient history. Even this ten-year anniversary will simply be something he or she will only read about in history books.

Maybe there's some truth to the old saying that babies are God's promise that the world will go on.

Like her sibling, Harper isn't aware of the September 11 anniversary. She was a mere figment of our imaginations ten years ago, and we've not talked about it with her, so while I imagine she'll pay attention to the twentieth anniversary, she won't remember this one. She won't remember that night back in May, either, when the president interrupted late-night television to inform the nation that Osama bin Laden had been killed. Shortly after that news broke, Bromleigh wrote an article about how to talk to kids about such a difficult topic. (Another of my life's many blessings: wise friends who know how to put their wisdom into words.) In the article she wrestled with how to reconcile the fact that we have taught our children that killing is wrong but then we—our president, our military, on our behalf—kill someone, on purpose. She wrote, "In the world God wants us to have, no one would kill anyone. We would not be in any danger, not ever. There would be no war. [But] in this world, all of our solutions to problems are imperfect, and we do the best we can. With God's help, things get better."[3]

The storybook Bible we've been reading to Harper, the one written by Archbishop Desmond Tutu, talks about "God's dream." It's what Jesus came to show us: the world God wants us to have.

In God's dream for the world, airplanes don't fly into buildings. Towers don't collapse while rescue workers are rushing into them. In God's dream for the world, women don't have to stand on street corners and beg for food. Children don't have to live with their families on top of garbage dumps.

But in this world, sorrow and grief and pain and scarcity live on. We live in the gap here, between this world and God's dream for the world, still working and praying and yearning for the world God wants us to have.

While I don't think Harper is old enough yet to learn about September 11, I wondered about showing her the pictures of those children and where they sleep. I don't want to instill guilt in her about where she comes from and how we live. At this point, these are choices we are making for her anyway. But I do want her to be aware of the world around her, aware that she has it better than most kids in the world. She won't understand this right now, I suppose, but someday I want her to know that not being allowed to play another Curious George game on the computer is not a real problem in the grand scheme of things.

I want her to love and appreciate this life as much as I do. I want her to delight in summer evenings spent swinging with her dad, to play on a Slip'N Slide for her birthday. I want her to know that God made this world, that it is very, very good, and that God delights in our delight of creation and one another. I want her to be grateful for everything she has. But I also want her to understand that we live in this gap between this world and the one God dreams for us, that we are not yet there.

I want her to understand this—and then I want her to do something about it.

We'll help her, of course. She walked with us in the CROP Walk last year. As we talked with her about why we were raising money—to support Church World Service in its hunger ministries around the world—I was reminded of walking in the CROP Walk when I was a kid. I didn't know many hungry people then, or at least I didn't know I did, and participating made me aware that I had food when some other people didn't, and maybe, even did a little good along the way.

Harper has become my regular grocery-shopping companion, now that she's old enough to refrain from pulling all the cereal boxes off the shelf when we walk by. I kind of like having her along. It gives me someone to talk to and keeps me from standing too long in the toilet paper aisle, trying to figure out which package is the best deal. Occasionally, I pick up some extra cans of soup or beans to add to our church's contribution to the local food bank. It occurs to me that I ought to do that every time, and I ought to let her carry the food into the church and put it in the donation bin herself. And when she's a little older, or maybe even now, we ought to talk with her about why people are hungry in the first place.

My denomination's humanitarian aid ministry, the Week of Compassion, puts out a "Sharing Calendar" every year, with facts and reminders and challenges such as, "More than a billion people worldwide lack access to safe drinking water. Give one unit [a quarter or a dollar, or some other amount] for each faucet in your home."[4] Harper would have fun with a project like that. Or we could get involved with an organization like the Heifer Project, which gives hungry families not just food, but the gift of an animal and the resources to support themselves. It would be a good way to talk about where our food comes from, and the difference we can make by making good choices about what we eat. That cuddly sheep on the cover of their alternative gift catalog? She'd love that, too.

And we can talk with her about why we don't need another toy, why library books are just as good as the ones at the bookstore. We can take her with us to the polls on the next election day, even though she's too young to vote, and tell her about what we're doing. We can tell her to turn off the water while she's brushing her teeth and explain why we're washing all those smelly diapers.

There's much more we can do, and I am not willing to wrap up this chapter neatly and tie it with a bow that makes us feel better. I am not going to let myself or my family off the hook. I am not going to say that I'll just keep being thankful for all we have, that I'll just keep buying local produce, that we'll just keep washing the diapers and making the best choices we can, and hope that it's enough. It isn't enough. It might be all we can do, but it's not enough. As long as there are children sleeping in garbage dumps and sons and daughters dying in battle, as long as this chasm exists between the world in which we live and the world God dreams for us, it's not enough.

So, yes, we'll practice gratitude. We'll make choices that are good for other people's children and not just our own. We'll teach our kids how they can help, how they can live faithfully and responsibly in this broken world of ours. But we'll also lift our voices in the words of the psalmist, in those ancient words of lament that for centuries have captured the despair of those who can see that we are not living in the world God wants us to have:

How long, O Lord, how long?

The Rage

On marriage, and anger, and the nature of love

ON A DARK NIGHT I SAT PROPPED UP IN BED NURSING FIONA, WHO was awake for the umpteenth time. The pillows refused to maintain their shape and arrangement, and kept slipping down. I alternated positions every few minutes, eventually resting my head against the wall, wedged between the vertical slats of our mission style head-board. It wasn't comfortable, but at least I didn't have to support the weight of my heavy head in the midst of my exhaustion.

My eyes surveyed the tiny person at my breast, searching for signs that she was falling back asleep. My heart was mostly full of love for her, though I wondered if I might be capable of loving her a bit more if she'd stop waking me up. The gentle fog of sleep cleared as the minutes passed, as the discomfort of my position made half-consciously nursing impossible. I was awake. Wide awake.

My eyes soon left the baby and began to search our room. Adjusted to the darkness, they fell on the piles of unfolded clean clothes, overflowing from multiple laundry baskets. I scanned our floors, taking in the myriad clumps of dog hair, some huddled against the walls and hiding under the dresser, others boldly venturing across the floor.

Finally, I turned my gaze to look at my husband: his gorgeous dark hair and impossibly long lashes, his arms wrapped adorably around the pillow, his torso rising and falling slowly in the rhythm of one who is deeply asleep.

I wanted to kill him.

How can he sleep like that? How can he rest at night knowing that our home is a disaster, knowing that this baby is up again? How can he sleep through her cries every single time? *Why does he just roll over? Why is our house such a mess? As if it weren't bad enough that I never get to sleep, I also have to live in squalor? What does a girl have to do to get some help around here?*

Here are the facts of our lives: Ten months out of the year, Josh gets up much earlier than I do, because he has a lengthy commute and needs to be at work by 7:30 at the very latest. He works a full day, much of which is spent on his feet, and then sits in traffic for at least an hour before arriving at our home. When Fiona was born, I worked next door to our house and was never expected in the office before nine, at the earliest.

I knew exactly why I was awake and he was sleeping: He was exhausted, too, and I had the work schedule and the biological apparatus to feed a baby with the greatest ease at night. It made sense. The laundry and the dog hair were evidence of our shared failure to keep up with the house, but they reminded me of my own frustrated inability to ask him for more help with the requirements of our domesticity. The whole scene contributed to my fury.

In the weeks and months after Fiona was born, at doctors' appointments for both her and me, I filled out the survey screening for postpartum depression, and I always passed it. There was that one day—the day after we brought her home from the hospital—when I cried into my pillow because I was sure Josh and I would never have a moment to ourselves, alone as a couple, ever again. But after that, I felt like I was maintaining a pretty even keel.

That is, I wasn't crying a lot, I managed to sleep a fair amount, and I showered daily. When I went back to work, I didn't sit alone in my office and dissolve into tears over the fleeting youth of my first child and my working-mother guilt. I mourned those things, to be sure, but they weren't killing me. My mother tells me that when I was first born, my dad would routinely return from work in the late afternoon to find her rocking me manically, both of us sobbing from frustration, weariness, and the devastating stress of being alone together all day. My experience was different.

I wasn't crying, and I could still laugh most of the time, and I loved being a mother. Fiona was a relatively easy baby, and I was so grateful to have her in our lives.

There was just this troubling little matter of wanting to murder my husband three to five nights a week.

I called it The Rage, but I couldn't bring myself to talk to Josh about these feelings, about how alone and angry I felt, about how unfair it was that the burdens of our common life seemed to be falling entirely on my shoulders. The hotness of my temper and the regularity of my frustration scared me. I worried that if I opened my mouth to Josh, I wouldn't be able to shut off the valve again, that the complaints would come rushing out, ruining everything we'd built together. Instead, I made reference to it while talking to my mom and to a friend in frequent Facebook chats.

My mother empathized. *Men!* My friend, a pastor, said I needed to figure out how to talk to Josh. She said it wasn't doing me any good to bitch to her about it.

Laura Jean, my pastor friend, was right, of course. Stewing night after night was bound to lead to an explosion at some point, and even if it didn't, my constantly simmering rage was not exactly conducive to creating the loving and laughter-filled home of my dreams.

Children who grow up in homes with alcoholic parents or a family member with profound mental illness describe their sense that their given task as a child was to walk on eggshells and never upset the extremely delicate balance of family life. Don't antago-nize your mother. Make sure not to get in Dad's way. Just do what he asks. Don't argue. Family systems theory and Al-Anon alike describe how the troubled person becomes the center of family life, because all communal efforts are spent trying to keep him or her from going off the deep end.

My parents are healthy and wonderful people, but I definitely left my childhood home having witnessed more than a few of their arguments. Both my mom and dad worked constantly—long hours at stressful yet good jobs that they often loved and felt called to do. If an unexpected and large expense arose, however, there was often not quite enough money. Our house was, in the words of the great Nick Hornby, "a shabby mess, ruined by children."[1] Honestly, given all the stress my parents were under, I am deeply impressed by how relatively infrequent their arguments were.

They both got angry sometimes, but not unreasonably so. My sisters and I beat up on one another in routine acts of sibling rivalry and didn't listen (in routine acts of being frustrating beasties). My dad would snap at my mom, and then she'd grumble about it. He'd rant a bit, and she'd get fed up from listening to him and finally say, "You do not speak to me that way!" *You do not speak to me that way!* In anger, in those tones, in a way that takes out your frustrations about work or kid or money on me.

Inevitably their biggest arguments were about the house. We'd be preparing to host church people, to put our lives on display for people we wanted to think well of us. But my mom would get stuck at work, and my sisters and I would refuse to help, and the dog would throw up on the newly cleaned carpet. The line would be too long at the grocery store, where Dad had stopped for a few last-minute supplies, leaving insufficient time on his return to finish cleaning, set out the food, and shower post-bathroom-scrubbing.

Or, I fought with my dad—about the phone, about curfew, about my tone of voice. I *may* have had a *tiny bit* of an attitude. I needed to be right, always; we both needed to get in the last word.

Fights began and ended quickly, but the takeaway was always that we were sorry for having yelled, sorry we had wasted the time, sorry we had disrespected each other. In a family, *we do not speak to one another that way.*

Whatever my own feelings about anger are, good sized chunks of the Christian theological tradition are willing to claim it as an important, even righteous, emotion in the right contexts (though most of the "right contexts" are related to God's anger at our terrible sinfulness). Gary Chapman, a well-known pastor and best-selling author, has a really helpful book on the subject that contends there are two sorts of anger, *definitive* and *distorted*.[2] The first is the sort that Christians see manifest in God's longing for and demand for justice and in Jesus's rage when he threw the money changers out of the temple. This is the anger at injustice. Righteous indignation. The kind of divine revulsion at sin and wrongdoing that ensures that those who work evil in the world will know punishment.

On those dark nights interrupted by crying infants and murderous thoughts, I would sit in bed and tally Josh's ever more numerous sins against me. He did not share the work of managing our household. He never went to the grocery store unless I asked him to. He was *clearly* being malicious in his unwillingness to decide what we should eat for dinner, much less to prepare it. His temper was too short: he yelled at the dog (who is, admittedly, a terrible dog); he grew frustrated with Fiona's fussing; he grumped about traffic and ignored the baby and me under the guise of "unwinding" when he got home. Ignored us! After all that time he'd had with NPR! I would have killed for that kind of alone time!

But how would he respond if I were to hold the mirror to his face, if I were to lay his sins bare before him? Surely he would be overcome by shame and, hopefully, remorse. Even more surely, if I proved unable to contain my righteous rage, he'd get defensive and angry . . . wouldn't he? The fight was bound to escalate.

Instead of talking with him, I sat and stewed and bit my nails.

And as I stewed, as the heat of my rage cooled, I began to wonder if maybe I was wrong. If my rage was not so much righteous as what Chapman calls "distorted anger." Maybe, just maybe, the man who had vowed before God and all our loved ones to share a life with me, who had ostensibly brought this baby into the world out of love for me, maybe he was not trying to spite me in every single one of his waking (and sleeping) moments.

Chapman suggests that, unlike definitive anger, which signals that relationships embroiled in conflict are in need of reconciliation, distorted anger is sparked by "circumstantial evidence, faulty presuppositions, generalizations, our expectations or personal preferences, even plain tiredness."[3] I was mad at Josh for a whole host of reasons, and while my anger was very real (don't ever doubt that!), it might not have rightly been directed (entirely) at him.

I have long considered myself, if not exactly cool-headed, at least fair. My sense of justice and fairness, cultivated over years in the church, dragged me into ministry; it is presumably fairly well tuned. But after Fiona was born, my ability to engage in semi-objective analysis was gone. I felt exhausted, neglected, unappreciated, overlooked, and taken advantage of. I required a lot more ego-soothing than any one person could provide, especially an equally exhausted working new father. And my anger, as I was beginning to suspect, probably had multiple sources. I wasn't mad at *just* him. My job was extremely frustrating, for one. I was working in a very small congregation, that was, in church parlance, dying. There were things I loved about it: preaching each week, my weekly clergy Bible study, the intimacy of life in community. But I felt like a clerical Sisyphus, the guy from Greek mythology condemned to push a boulder up a hill for eternity, always to have it escape his grasp and go rolling down again. Everything I did seemed to go nowhere, and the church was edging ever closer to financial insolvency.

I was angry at some of my friends, who seemed to have an easier time adjusting to being parents than I did (Lee's baby just went to sleep, in her crib, all night! I saw it happen!) or who quit working (even though, rationally, I knew I didn't want to leave my job). I was angry at my family, who gave us our space, not wishing to be intrusive, not wishing to pressure us with dinner invitations or offers to babysit.

Fiona was rarely the object of my wrath, though I know many parents frequently find themselves on the verge of shaking the living daylights out of their babies. That's no joke. Shaken Baby

Syndrome (SBS), that is, traumatic brain injury sustained by infants whose parents snap from the unceasing crying that characterizes the first months of some babies' lives, is the leading cause of death among victims of physical child abuse in the United States.[4] *Time* magazine reported recently that the incidence of SBS is on the rise in this uncertain and ongoing economic moment, when parents are so stressed and strapped to begin with, before a baby starts screaming at them.[5]

The Centers for Disease Control is quick and right to note that it is never appropriate to shake, throw, hit, or hurt a baby. But, man, it is startlingly easy for even the calmest of parents to reach the edge of madness when these children, innocent though they may be, just *will.not.shut.up.* On the occasions when Josh had solo parent duty, Fiona often voiced her objections to his care rather strenuously, and on several nights, he, following the advice of child abuse prevention advocates, would put her in the crib and leave the room for a few minutes to calm down and breathe, lest he dash her against the wall. It's possible that the only reason I'm here and writing today is because my mother's best friend, Ann, has a daughter, Mandy, who is just a few months older than I am. I am my mother's first child, but Mandy was child number three, so Ann was significantly calmer in those early months of my life; she'd been there before and had lived to tell the tale. My mom had Ann's number posted on the wall by the phone, just above the number for the child abuse hotline.

I consider it no great feat or honor that my rage wasn't directed at Fiona at that point in her early infancy. Borrowing from *The Happiest Baby on the Block,* I attributed her crying to her adjustment to life on the outside; the "fourth trimester" is hard on babies![6] When she cried, it was not to be fearsome but because she was tired, or hungry, or cold, or gassy. She may have been screaming, but she wasn't doing it on purpose. *"She's just a baby!"* I would huff at my poor, defeated husband when he'd call her "a bad baby." My friends, family, and mate, though, were clearly moral—or immoral, as the case may have been—agents who didn't care about me enough and whose behavior manifested all the injustices in my life and the world.

This is what makes me so wary of anger: The way it divides us from one another. In a time when parents of young children need as much love, empathy, and patience in their lives as possible, anger draws lines in the sand, points fingers, and picks fights. Never mind that my friends who had given up working because the cost of child care was so high as to render it useless were lonely and longing for a chance to feel like grown-ups. Never mind that my parents invited us over all the time. Never mind that the members of my church were trying their best, or that my husband was as tired and cranky as I was. Anger seems to grow in the absence of empathy, fed by defensive thoughts and general self-righteousness. There's nothing good, and nothing particularly Christlike, about that.

The Christian and biblical tradition are less than clear on what we ought to do with these inevitable feelings of rage. There's Paul saying, "Be angry but do not sin" and "do not let the sun go down on your anger" (Eph. 4:26). And there's Jesus, saying you don't have to murder your brother to wander into sin. You can just be angry at him; thinking murderous thoughts is trouble enough (Matt. 5:21-22). But our Divine Brother has his own displays of anger: in the temple (Mark 11:15), telling Peter, "Get behind me, Satan! (Matt. 16:23). And then, there's the inclusion of anger on the list of the "seven deadly sins" that's evolved in Western Christianity.

It's no wonder that I couldn't figure out how to talk to Josh, how to cope, or calm down.

In the Old Testament, readers can find a number of references to the anger of God, and Christians have a tendency to talk about that divine wrath in the face of human sinfulness that can only be assuaged through the sacrificial and atoning death of an innocent. I love those prophets, who rant and rave about how angry the Lord is when witnessing the oppression of the poor and the exclusion of foreigners and widows. I do my best to honor them by ranting and raving, in enumerated and profanity-laden litanies directed at my husband or therapist, when I see something unjust or unfair coming to pass in the world. Those who would cut school funding and health care have been getting a lot of airtime in my sessions and in my marital bed. This week, a member of our extended family is being harassed at work, and my normally peace-loving clan has been sitting about casually discussing their desire to deck the perpetrator.

But I can't ultimately get behind a vision of God that pits anger at the center of the cosmic story. I have no interest in that. My theological boyfriend Paul Tillich (1886–1965) addresses the concept of the "wrath of God" in an awfully prescient way, speaking to our nation's pervasive popular Christology (understanding of Jesus), an understanding that makes Jesus's death the only act of his life that seems to matter.[7] The long and the short of Tillich's interpretation is that God is, ultimately, about love. That's the character and nature of God. So God stands against anything that stands against love—and that includes sin and terribleness, and my anger at my husband. So, as long as we are (or I am) persisting in terrible rages, I'm going to experience God's wrath and judgment. And it's going to make me feel just awful, full of despair, because who wants to experience disapproval from anyone, much less God? But, God is also reconciled to us through Christ, who showed us all that even though sin and death are awfully powerful, resurrection, love, and new life are even more so. For Tillich, this is the heart of salvation. Being saved, then, isn't about being plucked from the burning flames of hell through a one-time profession of faith in Jesus. Rather, salvation lies in experiencing the power of resurrection and participating in that power. As we experience that salvation, we will understand God not as raging against us anymore but rather as helping us to overcome sin and terribleness and rage, anything that stands in the way of Love.

This reading of the Christian story makes so much more sense to me than the "angry God demands blood payment" vision that people often assume is the only reading of our tradition. (It's also

pretty much how Tillich won my heart.) In addition to naming
what is self-defeating and death-dealing about sin and anger, it also
expands the understanding of God's justice. Justice for the Lord
God doesn't mean bad folks get what they deserve; it is a broader
vision of how the divine love is made a part of reality in our individual and communal lives.

There was an article in *The New York Times Magazine* a few
years back about how working couples kept their lives in order and
divided housework and child care responsibilities.[8] A majority of
men and women surveyed believe they're sharing the load, but men
thought the divide was a bit more even than their partners. A tally
of hours spent weekly cooking, cleaning, and tending to children
also revealed that the women, on average, were contributing more
labor. There are plenty of reasons for that; some better than others.
My dad did all the cooking in our household during my childhood,
because his job as a pastor let him get away in the late afternoon,
and he loves to cook. (Also, my mother had long, only half-jokingly,
claimed her inability to locate anything other than cat food, coffee,
and toilet paper at the grocery store.) I have the same job my dad
did, with its flexible hours, and my husband has the long commute.
It makes sense that I should do most of the cooking. Plus, I mostly
enjoy it. Josh always does the vacuuming and the floors (which I
hate), and takes care of cleaning up after the dog. But that still leaves
shopping and laundry and bathrooms and dishes, not to mention
amusing the children.

The couples in that *New York Times* article found that the only
way to reach exact parity was to plan and document everything.
And so they did. But that's not what I want for my family. To begin
with, Josh and I are not nearly that organized. But my objections
are bigger than that. The marriages documented were partnerships,
with give and take and compromise, but they also sounded to me
like "tit-for-tat" operations, with the trading and negotiating of
responsibilities and tasks. For some, that sort of order is freeing. To
me, it sounded soul crushing—the sort of arrangement that would

suck all the joy, spontaneity, and grace out of the marriage. I want a bigger sense of justice and fairness in my home. I want the knowledge that we're all in this together, that the ultimate reality is our love for one another.

Even when couples hope for spontaneity, we all can develop habits and patterns of behavior; that's part of living together day in, day out. When a baby gets (figuratively) thrown into the mix, the responsibilities multiply exponentially. It's easy, in that time of transition, to feel like the new patterns are being set forever, to feel that any new patterns are really an inescapable rut. And inescapable ruts tend to breed discontent and arguing.

Lee reports that during the first few years she and Rob were together, they fought every time one of them had a birthday. They each brought varying and unexpressed expectations for what a birthday gift or celebration from a loving and appreciative partner might be. Given the unexpressed nature of these expectations, one of them always ended up disappointed or hurt, and a fight started. Finally, they decided they needed to stop it. They needed a new pattern, a new way of communicating.

When I counsel couples about to get married (something I do a lot, since I serve as pastor at a church with a gorgeous sanctuary, with the all-important center aisle, located on a hill with a scenic view), I always remind them of the sacred nature of the commitment—the covenant—they're preparing to make. But despite how holy the moment when vows are made might feel, and is, that moment does not actually make them *one person*; vowing to live *one life* together does not magically enable them to read one another's minds. They still have to put their feelings into words, still have to find ways to connect, even when things are difficult to name.

As Fiona got older—as I got angry, and then got worried about my anger, and then despaired of my anger—I finally realized this was no way to live. I talked to my counselor, I talked to my doctor, and I got on sertraline (an antidepressant) when I realized my anger was outside of the range considered "normal." I'm a bit ashamed to admit that it took me far longer than it should have to make these moves. But once I was a little farther away from postpartum hormonal rage, I stopped fearing that any conversation about my frustrations with my beloved husband would destroy our marriage. I also realized my rage would never subside if I didn't get the help I needed—not just emotional help from my counselor, but help around the house from my husband.

There's a song by The Submarines in which the singer wonders, "Will you ever let me love you like you did before the fight?"[9] But as weeks and months passed, as that antidepressant started to take effect, I realized that I know how to have hard conversations; I know how to fight fair. I was raised to know what lines were never to be crossed, what things would change the very way in which we loved each other. I knew *how we were to speak to each other in a family.* I rehearsed what I wanted to say. And we talked.

I used a lot of "I" language. Throwing out "you do this and you do that" comes off as accusatory and puts people on the defensive. "I feel like you don't appreciate the effort I make on the meals we share when you don't put away the leftovers or load the dishwasher. I feel like you don't care about me when you don't kiss me when you come home from work. I feel like you're not as invested in our common life as I am, when you watch that much football and ignore that much dog hair. I love you so much and I don't want us to fight, but I feel we both need to make more of an effort on some fronts."

Josh said remarkably little, after a few lame attempts to counter my arguments. But he didn't get defensive; he started tickling me. "What do you mean I'm not invested? My fingers are invested in having their vengeance!" For me, it was a wonderful moment of grace, a sign that he was listening and that my frustration would not come between us. And in the days, weeks, and months following the conversation, Josh did seem to up his efforts.

I still get angry, and Josh and I still fight sometimes. There is, always, clean laundry and dog hair overtaking my home. Each football season, I fear we will divorce—or kill each other. (Madeleine L'Engle quotes her friend, who claimed that she never considered divorce. "Murder, yes. But divorce, no.")[10]

But I, and we, try to remember that we are in this together. We remember that love brought us together, and that our love brought us this wonderful task of parenting. And when I start to get really, really angry, I tell myself the story of another night, just after Fiona was born, while Josh was still on summer vacation. It was so early in her life that we were both still getting up at night, delirious from exhaustion, but committed to being a team.

She had awakened around one or two in the morning. I had nursed her and we had changed her and walked her until she fell asleep in the cradle in our room. Not ten minutes after we'd laid her down, she was awake again, screaming. We both got up, curious as we approached the cradle, wondering why she should be awake again. At that stage of the night, if we could get her down without waking her, she'd normally be out for at least an hour. I picked her up, and she was drenched. Her pajamas were soaked. The sheet was soaked. The swaddling blanket was soaked. It was so much liquid, we couldn't quite believe it. We had just changed her diaper! How had she produced so much, enough to overflow her diaper and saturate every piece of fabric in the vicinity?

We carried her tiny body over to the changing pad, in its temporary spot on top of my dresser, and unzipped her. As we pulled off her PJs, we realized in the same instant that when we'd last changed her, in our exhaustion, Team Josh-n-Bromleigh had forgotten to put a diaper on her at all.

We laughed in solidarity, but that was the moment when our division of labor was born. This is what I have to remember: We take turns because we're better when we each get a break, when we each get a turn to sleep. The solidarity of sharing every task and doing everything together was so short lived because it very quickly became the solidarity of inept (if comical) parenting.

Josh and I don't want to be terrible at this—at parenting or being married. Too many Christians talk noisily these days about what it means to be married, about Adam and Eve, and men and women. But the thing that makes a marriage Christian in my mind is that it's no mere contract; it's a covenant. A covenant, a promise to be together for better and worse, for richer and poorer, in sickness (and hormonal rage) and in health. Josh and I have promised to be faithful to each other as long as we both shall live. Sometimes that feels like a burden, truly: that we must work things out, that we cannot slip into patterns of sulking and stewing. We must deal with this stuff even when it's really hard, even when it requires the work of negotiating and risking argument. But much, much more often this covenanted love is an incredible relief. Just as I will never leave Josh for his failure to vacuum when I want him to, he will never leave me for being angry or worrying or failing to adequately respect the glory that is fantasy football. We are in this together. This is the gospel: Through God's grace, love is stronger than all things, even the rage that threatens. Though the night is long, the light shines in darkness, and the darkness does not overcome it.

Birthdays and Baby Books

On blessings, and festivals, and ordinary time

HARPER WAS BORN WITH A FULL HEAD OF HAIR. IT WAS SO THICK that the technician could see it on my last ultrasound a few weeks before my due date. "This baby has lots of hair!" she announced, and for some reason, I was completely creeped out. It was one thing for a whole human being to be growing inside me, but hair, too?

Sure enough, out she came with thick brown hair that curled over itself and peeked out from under the little hat the nurses kept trying to tuck on her head. I waited for it to fall out in those first few months, as friends told me it might, but not a single strand ever did. It just grew and grew. At two weeks, the hair in the very back was more than an inch long. By six months, we were pulling it into a ponytail on the top of her head (which garnered much conversation and debate among the ladies at church about what such a hairstyle should be called; our favorites were "top-knot" or "spooker"). At nine months, she was sporting a pigtail off to each side.

At eleven months, we had to do something. Her hair was falling in her eyes and getting endlessly sticky with bananas and peas. So one morning—it was the Fourth of July, I remember, because we were getting ready to go to our neighborhood parade—I snipped off her bangs while she was fast asleep. There was no fanfare. We didn't take a picture. I had just nursed her, and she'd fallen into her milk-induced coma. I laid her on the changing table and said to

Rob, "Want me to just cut some bangs for her?" He said okay, and that was it.

Six months later, we took her to a Great Clips, on a Saturday morning when we didn't have much else to do, and she sat stoically on Rob's lap as the hairdresser trimmed off her baby curls. We took a picture then, but I'll always think of that impromptu July Fourth morning as her first haircut.

I did save a little bit of the hair I cut that day, when she was sleeping on her changing table and unaware of the importance of the occasion. I tied it up with a twist-tie and stuck it in an envelope, which I taped into her baby book. Maybe I will take it out when she graduates from high school and show her. Will she be glad I saved it or embarrassed at something so personal?

"That baby book," my mother said after looking through it once, "is the most thorough baby book I've ever seen." It came with all the expected features: a page for vital statistics—time of birth, weight, length—and a family tree listing family members back to the great-grandparents. There's a page for handprints and footprints, blanks to describe what the nursery looked like and what she wore home from the hospital, and a spot for a newspaper clipping from the day she was born. There's an entire page for teeth, complete with a chart of the baby's mouth and blank lines to fill in the date each tooth came in.

I bought the book for myself, a few weeks before she was born. It had been one of the many pre-baby obsessions that sent me running from store to store to find just the right one. We didn't know if she would be a boy or girl, so I avoided both the pink ones and the blue ones. The more books I looked at, the more opinions I had: Some were too small, some too big, some had too many spots for photos, some not enough. *This is my baby's life I'm going to record here,* I remember thinking. *It had better be just right.* I finally settled on a light green one with a boat on the front cover, and erred on the side of overly thorough, well aware that I might never fill in all those blank pages.

There are places in the book to record the *first* everything: first
bath, first vacation, first holiday, first word, first food, the first time
she clapped her hands, her first outing, her first steps. I remember
being stumped about how to determine what her first outing was.
Was it the walk around the neighborhood when she was a week
old? Or our first trip to Target when my mother was in town? Like
the baby herself, the baby book did not come with instructions. But
I obediently kept mementos and photographs, pasting them care-
fully on the appropriate pages, documenting all the details (though
I never did fill in all those teeth).

Memory keeping is big business, and it's no wonder that
mothers are among the most likely to frequent the scrapbook aisles
of their neighborhood craft stores. "I'm worried that I'm missing it,"
a friend wrote on her blog when her first son was just a few weeks
old, noting that she found herself wanting to make a scrapbook, to
document things in a way she'd never done before. "Having a baby
has made me sentimental, and cutesy, and makes me want to record
everything from now on," she wrote. "It's going by so quickly."[1] I
remember feeling the same way. That's why my baby book is so
thorough; it was an attempt to hang on to a time that was slipping
away, an attempt to capture those memories I was afraid I'd forget.

At some point along the way, however—though we still take
hundreds of photos—we stopped documenting everything and
paying so much attention to the firsts. For one thing, there have
been fewer firsts in these subsequent years than there were in those
early months. Once she started eating solid food, we didn't document every time she tried a new food. Once she started walking,
she has just kept walking; we didn't photograph every step. Still,
there have been other firsts. We just haven't paid as much attention
to them, or at least, haven't marked them with the fanfare of those
early milestones. We don't have pictures of her first day at her new
preschool, her first play date, or her first swimming lesson.

Gradually, the big moments turn into ordinary moments. Time
moves on. It can be a little overwhelming, as my friend noted, how

quickly it all passes by, and if we don't have some kind of handle, some way to mark time along the way, it's easy for all the moments to slip on past.

As I watch my daughter grow, as moment blends into moment and year into year, I find it helpful to consider how the church marks time. The liturgical year—the calendar that guides the worship life of the church—starts in late November or early December with the season of Advent, the four Sundays leading up to Christmas. Then the Christmas season lasts for a couple of weeks until the feast of the Epiphany, on January 6. There's a brief interlude before Lent, which is the forty days before Easter, then Easter itself, and finally Pentecost in May or early June. Every year, the seasons help us tell and retell the story of our faith. In Advent, we wait for the Messiah we know is coming, and in Christmas we celebrate his birth. At Epiphany, we remember the magi who came to visit Bethlehem and celebrate the revelation of Christ. During Lent we follow Jesus's journey to the cross. Easter celebrates the resurrection, and Pentecost, the coming of the Holy Spirit, sent to sustain the church after the ascension of Christ.

In the big liturgical seasons, we pull out all the stops. We dress up the sanctuary and plan special services. We expect large crowds. We invite guest musicians and sing favorite songs and tell stories we know well. These seasons give us a handle, a way to mark time, a way to locate ourselves in the year.

There's an important place in the church for the festivals, these high holy days—the Christmases and Easters with all their fanfare. That's true in family life, too. Think of birthdays. Harper just celebrated her fourth, and while we've not yet given in and invited her whole preschool class (I'm in awe of families who do this: just this month, she's been invited to four parties for her classmates, at locations ranging from a dance studio to a horse stable), we make a pretty good fuss about birthdays around here.

Her big day was a Saturday, which meant we spent just about the whole day in celebration. She woke us up, before 7:00, by tiptoeing into our room. "Mama!" she whispered, just loud enough to get my attention. When I looked up at her, standing by the bed in her nightgown and holding her elephant, she grinned at me. "It's my birthday!" she whispered.

We parceled out the presents throughout the day. Being the oldest granddaughter on one side of the family and the only grand-daughter on the other side has its advantages. Boxes from grandparents, aunts, and uncles had been arriving on our doorstep all week, as if it were Christmas. She used up a new paint set before noon, and a battery-operated walking, barking dog made the rounds through the house all day.

We had a lunchtime party with just a handful of guests: two other preschoolers whose parents happen to be our friends, too. I was grateful they could come; since all our family is out of town, we rely on good friends to fill up those special occasions. The kids played in the yard on a Slip'N Slide Rob set up. (It was not nearly as cool as the one he remembered from his childhood. There was also a tense moment when we could not fit the hose onto the Slip'N Slide nozzle. We looked at each other and grimaced: This was our big plan! What would we do if it didn't work? Rob figured out a work-around, thankfully, and that particular crisis was averted.) After lunch, there was chocolate cake with a ladybug on top. We sang "Happy Birthday," she blew out the four candles, and we served the cake and ice cream.

I had my camera handy all day and filled up another giga-mega-something of space on my computer. I managed to capture her expression as she blew out the candles. I caught a shot of her and the two friends sliding into the end of the Slip'N Slide and even managed to e-mail the photos to our faraway family.

At the end of the day, I wrote my annual birthday letter. I didn't set out to make this a tradition, but it has become one, and I've come to look forward to it. It started because of that overly thorough baby book, actually, which had designated a whole page for "A Letter from Mommy." The blank page was in the "Before My

Arrival" section, so I think the intention was that I should write the letter when she was still in utero. I assume it was supposed to be about my dreams for her life or what it felt like to be her mother. That always felt weird to me, and I couldn't ever bring myself to do it.

But that changed on the evening of her first birthday, after we'd celebrated with friends and cupcakes at our neighborhood pool. Harper had obligingly shoved an entire cupcake into her mouth, face, and hair (which, despite the recent bang-trimming, was still incredibly prone to food accumulation). Later that night, after she'd been sound asleep for a couple of hours, she woke up crying, and we went in to discover that she had vomited cupcake all over her bed. There wasn't exactly a spot in the baby book to record that sort of episode, but it seemed notable enough to preserve, so I used that blank page to tell her about a day she'll never remember.

The next year's birthday celebration, thankfully, did not include any vomiting, but I wrote a letter anyway—as I've done every year since—telling her how we celebrated her birthday, offering a small snippet of what she's like right now and what she's interested in, and reminding her that I love her. I try not to be too sappy. (Not long ago I heard a story on a radio podcast about a young woman whose mother had died when the daughter was quite young. Before the mother died, she'd written a series of letters and arranged for them to be delivered to her daughter every year on her birthday, describing what she hoped her daughter's life would be like at age eighteen, at twenty-two, at thirty. The daughter finally found the letters to be too much, too heavy, and had to stop reading them.) I hope Harper will someday treasure the birthday letters and that they don't become an overbearing sentimental burden. For now, I think they are more for me than for her—a way for me to mark time, to celebrate the high holy days, the festivals, of our life as family.

But every day can't be a high holy day. We'd exhaust ourselves, for one thing, and we'd eat too much cake and run out of room on our hard drives for all the pictures. Most of life's moments don't get recorded in scrapbooks. Most of life is lived in the time between birthdays, the regular in and out of ordinary days.

In the church, the season between the big festivals is called "Ordinary Time." It's a strange name that seems to suggest that nothing special happens, as if we could just as easily call it "dead time," as someone recently did in a conversation with me (accidentally, I think). But this time between the big festivals is anything but dead or empty. The word *ordinary* comes from the same Latin root as "ordinal" or "ordered." And that makes sense to me: this is "ordered" time—not empty time, not dead time, not time when nothing happens. Because the truth is, it's not just on those big, important days that life is holy and precious and wonderful. It's on the ordinary days, too. In the church, the ordered days of ordinary time are when we live our lives together. It's when we take on the week-in, week-out tasks of lighting the candles for worship, opening the hymnals and singing together, donating canned goods for the food bank, reading the Scriptures, visiting friends in the hospital, welcoming new babies, and telling stories at funeral receptions. There's holiness, there, in those days of ordinary time.

There's holiness, too, I think, in the regular days of family life, in the rhythm—chaotic and changing though it may be—of waking up, finding matching socks, pouring milk on cereal, buckling the car seat, heading off to school or work, coming home, saying grace before dinner, reading bedtime stories, and turning off the light at the end of the day.[2]

Writer and preacher Barbara Brown Taylor explores the holiness of ordinary life in her book *An Altar in the World*. "Wherever you are," she says, "you live in the world, which is just waiting for you to notice the holiness of it."[3] God does not live solely within the four walls of our churches, she suggests, nor does God show up only for the big festivals. Instead, every bit of creation, every breath we take, everything we do, is infused with the holiness of God, which we could see if we would only take note.

Something like that, I think, is what I mean about ordinary time. Taylor encourages reverence, or the "practice of paying attention." She recommends beginning this practice by spending twenty minutes marveling at something—a body of water, the earth in front of you, the back of your hand.

> With any luck, you will soon begin to see the souls in pebbles, ants, small mounds of moss, and the acorn on its way to becoming an oak tree. . . .You may even feel the beating of your own heart, that miracle of ingenuity that does its work with no thought or instruction from you. You did not make your heart, any more than you made a tree. You are a guest here. You have been given a free pass to this modest domain and everything in it.[4]

This sounds nice, but I have to admit that I roll my eyes a bit at what feels like such an extravagant use of time. I should spend twenty minutes staring at an acorn? I could be getting dinner on the table or folding that never-ending pile of laundry.

However.

I remember marveling at Harper's little newborn body—those tiny little toes, her fingers, her sweet, pouty mouth when she slept, the abundance of her hair. But somehow, the opportunities for *marveling*, or at least our attention to it, slip away as the Festival of the Newborn Baby gives way to the ordinary time of regular life, when that sleepy newborn begins to spend most of her day awake and chatting. Maybe a practice of paying attention, even on the mundane days when nothing particularly noteworthy—nothing scrapbook-worthy—is happening, would help us see holiness in the ordinary moments of our lives.

One night recently, as I was helping Harper get ready for bed, I told her what I'd planned for the next day. I had the afternoon off from work and intended to spend it with her. I reminded her she'd be going to school in the morning for "water play"—a summer treat at her preschool that involves hoses and sprinklers and a visit from the ice cream truck. "But then," I said, "I'll pick you up right after lunch, and we'll do something fun."

"What?" she said. "The library? Or is the museum open?"

"Well," I said, and debated giving away my whole hand before going for it. "I thought we could go swimming."

"Yay!" she squealed.

"And then, in the evening, we're going over to Jack's house for pizza."

"Wow!" she grinned at me. "So many good things!"

(I should note that this entire conversation took place in the bathroom, as she sat, half-naked, on the toilet. Holy in the ordinary, indeed.)

It is delightful to me that she finds such joy in a fairly regular day, that a trip to the swimming pool and pizza with friends is as much excitement as she needs to be happy. Or maybe it's just that she is quite good at the practice of paying attention. *So many good things.*

There's a notion in Celtic spirituality that I've come to appreciate. It's the idea that all of life is infused with the holiness of God, and that every once in a while, we encounter a "thin place" where that holiness shines through. It's like a well-loved blanket that has nearly worn through in spots, so that if you hold it up to the sun, the light pierces through. A thin place in time is one of those moments where ordinary life becomes holy—or rather, it's when we notice that it was holy all along.

Thomas Merton, a twentieth-century monk, wrote:

Life is this simple. We are living in a world that is absolutely transparent, and God is shining through it all the time. This is not just a fable or a nice story. It is true. If we abandon ourselves to God and forget ourselves, we see it sometimes, and we see it maybe frequently. God shows Himself everywhere, in every-thing—in people and in things and in nature and in events. It becomes very obvious that God is everywhere and in everything and we cannot be without Him. It's impossible. The only thing is that we don't see it.[5]

Our family does a decent job, I think, of celebrating the festivals. We throw parties and eat cake and give thanks. But the ordinary days are holy, too, and sometimes we don't see it. Sometimes the holy moments, the blessings of ordinary time, get lost in the rush.

My friend (and fellow pastor-writer-mom) MaryAnn McKibben Dana notes that paying attention gets harder as our children get older. "When they're young," she writes, "you're with them for hours at a time, face to face, looking them square in the eye, *beholding* them as you nurse them, bathe them, brush their teeth." But as they grow more independent—as the days of ordinary time set in—the challenge "is to be attentive at the margins: while sharing an errand together, in the last few minutes before bed, walking home from the bus stop, at the breakfast table. Every moment is an opportunity to savor, to experience joy, to express love. But it feels much harder, as the busyness of life presses in, and as these little people develop their own busynesses to contribute."[6]

In an effort to stay attentive, MaryAnn started a practice she calls her "Memory Project." Every night—or, most nights—she writes down one sentence about each of her three kids, something they did, something they said, something she wants to remember.[7] It is a way of noticing the holiness in ordinary days. MaryAnn acknowledges that she doesn't write in her one-sentence journals as often as she set out to when she started; some weeks, she's lucky if she writes one line.[8] But she notes—thank goodness—that it's the practice that's important, not the completion or the perfection of it.

The practice of paying attention doesn't mean we all have to keep meticulous scrapbooks. Though I'm glad for the keepsake of Harper's baby book, I don't think we need to document every holy moment on floral-print, acid-free paper. I think there are other ways to pay attention. Bromleigh tells me that, although she feels like she's lousy at keeping mementos, Josh puts together a photo book for their kids' grandparents once a year. I know other families who take turns around the dinner table every night, sharing the "highs" and "lows" of their days. Table prayers work, too, reminding us to give thanks.

Bromleigh and Josh have another practice they use to mark time—or, literally, to mark height—Fiona's, that is. Once a year, they stand Fiona up with her back against the wall and measure how tall she is. Fiona has always been small for her age, so it started as a way to ward off worry, to make sure her development was on track. But it turned into a practice of paying attention. Now, as she stands taller and taller, they marvel at how much she's grown since the year before. That's what we hope for, from year to year, isn't it? When we arrive at those big festivals—the family birthday parties or the high holy days of the church—we hope that we've grown, we hope that the ordinary moments have changed us.

There's a song our family sings on birthdays, in addition to the classic "Happy Birthday to You." I like this one a little better, actually. It's to the tune of "Give Me Oil in My Lamp":

Bless this year and this life, keep it growing, growing, growing,
    growing.
Bless this year and this life, we pray.
Bless this year and this life, keep it growing, growing, growing,
Keep it growing 'til your next birthday![9]

It's fun to sing, the tune is catchy, and I find myself humming it for days afterward. But more than that, it's a prayer: that this year and this life—the birthdays and the haircuts and all the ordinary moments in between—will be blessed.

When Christian Feminists Give Birth to Princesses

On boys, and girls, and Galatians 3

I HATE SURPRISES, GENERALLY SPEAKING. I LIKE TO KNOW WHAT'S coming. Suspense of any variety usually does me in. I cannot stop a movie or even a sit-com in the middle; this is why I am only allowed to pick up novels if I have time to read them all the way through. I am impatient. But despite all this, when I got pregnant for the first time, there was very little debate about whether we wanted to be told the gender of our baby when Josh and I went for the twenty-week ultrasound. We didn't want to know.

I suspect my uncharacteristic ability to tolerate this sort of forty-week suspense had to do in large part with the fact that I believed with some certainty that I knew what "brand" of baby we were having. I come from a family of all girls, and a majority of my cousins are women. But Josh's family is all dudes, and since the biological father contributes the deciding genetic material, I figured I'd be birthing a brood of Hammond men over the years. (This is incredibly faulty reasoning, with no basis in science beyond seventh grade biology, by the way.) Although I was certain I could love a boy just as much as a girl and we found a boy name we really liked (as well as a girl name, since Josh was surprisingly unconvinced by my logic), I had pretty much resigned myself to the fact that I would never have a daughter.

Then I had a daughter.

And then another one. (Incidentally, I was also convinced my second child was a boy. But I had been led to this conclusion by what Josh refers to as a "Jedi mind trick" on behalf of the ultra-sound technician. She referred to the baby as "he." I took this to mean something; she probably just gets sick of calling fetuses "it" all day.)

I'd give two reasons for our decision to wait until birth to discover whether we were going to have sons or daughters. First, I was afraid of my reaction to the news. I wanted only to be over-joyed, but I was afraid. Not trusting my subconscious and the depth of my pathos when it comes to gender relations, I was afraid I'd be disappointed to discover that we'd be having one gender or the other; and after disappointed, I'd feel guilty. Better not to know, I reasoned. Wait until there's an actual baby to love; wait until the gender is news given alongside the finger-and-toe count.

Also, we wanted to avoid a single-color wardrobe for our kid, which is what you often get at baby showers when the child's gender is known. Oceans of blue or cascades of pink, probably festooned with crowns and references to princesses. I'm no great lover of green and yellow, but Josh and I agreed that if we were granted the liberty to choose only one motif for our child's first year, we preferred ducks to either princesses or dump trucks.

By the time I was pregnant for a second time, we also realized a third (and hugely compelling) reason to wait: The last weeks of pregnancy are interminable, and walks around the neighborhood or easy crossword puzzles finally stop serving as effective distrac-tions. Only endlessly debating names and wondering about the baby's gender would do. I don't know what we would have talked about without that conversation; nothing kills time like anticipa-tory speculation.

That first reason, though—my distrust of my subconscious—evidences the profound concern I had about how to understand what being a woman (or, first, a girl) means to me, and how to explain and model living as a healthy, happy female in a world that, well, sometimes seems to hate women. Shortly after the birth of our younger daughter, Callie, I picked up journalist Peggy Orenstein's funny and wise book *Cinderella Ate My Daughter: Dispatches from the Front Lines of the New Girlie-Girl Culture*. I was already predisposed to give it a sympathetic read, but Orenstein's page-two confession on learning she was having a girl spoke to my heart:

> I fretted over how I would raise a daughter, what kind of role model I would be, whether I would take my own smugly written advice on the complexities surrounding girls' beauty, body image, education, achievement. Would I embrace frilly dresses or ban Barbies? Push soccer cleats or tutus? . . . During those months, I must have started a million sentences with "*My* daughter will never . . ."
>
> And then I became a mother.[1]

Pervading the United States is a conception of a certain type of woman—educated, liberal, man-hating, and generally godless, a woman who ironically hates her gender and all natural signifiers of it (pink and motherhood chief among them). This woman longs to make her daughters' lives miserable by denying them all the pure joys of girlhood: baby dolls and play kitchens and dress-up and fairy tales and Barbies. Skeptics might say that Peggy Orenstein is just this sort of woman. Orenstein and I are the sort of women who make a big deal about gender, but the skeptics might suggest this is all for naught: *boys will be boys, girls will be princesses*. But Orenstein has spent the better part of twenty years reporting on the state of women and girls in this country, and she's seen the evidence that women and girls face some significant hurdles that men and boys do not. She recognizes that being a woman in America (or really, anywhere) can be a fraught and dangerous thing. It is admittedly less so for educated, white, upper-middle-class American women such as Lee and me, but the fact remains that women don't make as much on the dollar as men, get sexually abused and assaulted far more often than gets reported, and frequently get the short end of the stick economically and legislatively. How do we model for our girls a healthy way to navigate the gender mess when we haven't entirely figured it out for ourselves? Add Christian conversations about gender to the mix, and the mess gets even bigger.

Of course, the not-very-good-news is that boys face hurdles and complications of their own. Jenn, one of my very good friends, frets about how to help her very dear, very wonderful son Carl continue to develop as he grows the side of himself that is sensitive and nurturing. He's in first grade now, but with each passing year, she wonders if he'll leave more of his inherent gentleness behind. Lee kept her daughter particularly close to her in infancy and toddlerhood, luxuriated in her hugs and the availability of her physical affection. She does the same with Jonathan, but as she watches him learn to roll, she wonders if he'll keep rolling away from her, from here on out. How will raising a son be different?

On a larger scale, a community and national scale, issues around gender and sexuality provide even more cause for wonder and worry. Testosterone is a great thing (says the straight girl), but hormones of all sorts can wreak havoc in adolescent lives, contributing to all sorts of challenges in relationships, learning styles, and behavior before settling down as adulthood begins. Worse: millions of men, particularly men of color, are incarcerated. More men of color are in jail than go to college! As I write, the nation is watching in horror the unfolding story of sixteen-year-old Trayvon Martin who, while walking home from a trip to the local convenience store for some candy, was shot to death by a self-appointed neighborhood watchman. Martin was shot, some say, for being a black kid in a country that hates and fears black kids. We're in the midst of what often seems to be a time of never-ending warfare, and in a terrible job market, men (and women, but more men) are heading off to war. My parents breathed sighs of relief when each of their daughters turned eighteen and were allowed to register to vote without also having to register for the selective service.

It's a crazy, mixed-up world we've brought our kids into—and that's before we even start talking about climate change and that huge floating island of garbage off of South America. Like Orenstein, I don't want to be a buzz-kill, destroying all my daughters' fun and making them think "girly things" are somehow wrong. But I want to be attentive to the complexities of what it means to be a boy or girl, created male or female. (Or somewhere in between! There are thousands of intersex people living in the United States today—people whose biological gender is not so clear-cut. One in one hundred people are born with bodies that are not standard male or female. Human sexuality and gender is complicated! Too many Christians dispute these facts in the name of commitment to the Bible and the tradition, but it's my sense that those who deny that gender exists on a spectrum are either fooling themselves or ignoring the medical evidence.)[2]

As part of my attempt to attend to that complexity, I consider myself a Christian feminist—a pairing that probably warrants some explanation. Let's do *feminist* first: I have two sisters. For a long while, my father's only male companions in the house were feline, and, as he pointed out, we had them neutered. This was, of course, a joke. When people suggested to him (as they did, routinely, and, outrageously, in front of his girls!) that he might have been disappointed not to have had a son, he vehemently denied it. I have never, ever doubted my father's total devotion to and contentment with us. I enjoy seeing his delight in his now-acquired sons-in-law, but my father insists that his delight in our men is just because we girls have awesome taste and not because some son-shaped hole in his heart has now been filled. My father's belief that we could be or do anything, and that we were wonderful just as we were, was a critical part of my growing into a confident(ish), healthy-type, adult woman. But I have also known from a very early age that my father's perspective was considered unusual, surprising.

I'm a feminist not just cause I think women are hunky-dory, but because there is a widespread understanding that women are not *good enough*, are not *worth as much*, are not *as good as* men, a view that I feel needs countering. I'm a feminist for all the girls with dads who obviously wanted sons.

I also, as I noted recently elsewhere,[3] spent most of my childhood reading and went through a period of pouring through a series of junior biographies, mostly of civil rights leaders and famous women. Despite the fact that my mother was clearly an equal partner in her marriage and in her household, I learned that there were many women, women *way* back in time (I thought), who were limited in their freedom to pursue their vocations and to make decisions about their lives, because of their gender, because of obstacles thrown up by individual men and by societies that insisted that to be a woman was to be less. Despite the fact that I grew up in a distressingly white suburb, I also learned about racism through books, reading of Martin Luther King, Jr. and Nelson Mandela and Desmond Tutu. I was probably one of only a few kids in my fifth grade class who wondered *why* there were no black people in our town, which bordered Chicago. My exposure to the dangers of racism and sexism from the safe vantage point of school and church libraries gave me, at a pretty early age, the eyes to see and the confidence to name injustice along racial and gender lines.

Although I lived a charmed life in which I knew only the assurance of my parents' love, all those books showed me that my parents' commitment to equal rights and their belief in the essential equality of all people was not universally shared. Importantly, however, I very much equated my parents' views with those of the church and of Christianity, an equation that set me on the path to becoming not only a feminist but a Christian feminist. I was a middle-schooler when I first attended a church with a female pastor, but her existence (and the rumored existence of others!) did not rock my world. The liberal Protestantism in which I was raised and that led me to ministry has no explicit problem with women in ministry. My denomination has been ordaining women for more than fifty years. My feminism, and my Christianity, was simply rooted in an experience of a community that was, at least to my young and curious eyes, pretty egalitarian. The apostle Paul once wrote to one of his churches, "There is no longer Jew or Greek, there is no longer slave or free, there is no longer male and female; for all of you are one in Christ Jesus" (Gal. 3:28). That doesn't mean there aren't divisions in human society, but, I was taught in word and deed, those divisions are not of God. In Christ, we're all one. That's the way things are supposed to be.

In my second semester of college, I learned that not all Christians share the vision Paul articulated in that wonderful verse from Galatians. Betty A. DeBerg's *Ungodly Women: Gender and the First Wave of American Fundamentalism* was on the syllabus of Religion in America 102.[4] Reading it, I learned about other biblical interpretations that have actively worked against female equality, insisting that godly women are subservient, domestic, and silent. I discovered that some people believe outspoken women, while making history, are also sinning against God's intentions for their frailer sex.

That same spring, I read *The Handmaid's Tale,* Margaret Atwood's chilling and fascinating novel about a future dystopia in which the United States (and particularly Cambridge and Boston, where I was attending school) has been turned into a misogynistic theocracy.[5] I must confess that when I first read scenes depicting ritual acts of women's submission, I wondered where the "scriptural" citations had come from; I wondered if Atwood had made them up. Because I was pretty well convinced there was no place in the Bible for something like "I do not permit a woman to teach or assume authority over a man; she must be quiet" and "Women will be saved through childbearing—if they continue in faith, love and holiness with propriety." But I learned soon enough that those crazy, unbelievable verses, the ones that suggested the only good women could do was to bear children and keep quiet while doing so, the ones that were used so creepily in this work of fiction, have also long been attributed to Paul. They're right there, just a chapter into 1 Timothy (2:11–15).

The unwelcome discovery of these troubling verses led to my first paper on feminist theology, which in turn brought me to the not very revolutionary idea that biblical texts ought to be interpreted (and not just memorized or used to beat people about the head). Over the years I've encountered myriad reputable interpretations that attempt to make sense of these words in 1 Timothy. Linguistically and thematically, enough differences exist between this letter and those that can be attributed to Paul conclusively that there are questions about its true authorship. Others suggest the author of the letter is speaking to very specific instances in which women in the congregation were gossiping and disrupting worship. As I hope we've been making clear in these various chapters, Lee and I believe the Bible is a wonderful text, a source of wisdom and beauty that bears witness to the work of God in Christ. But there are parts of it that don't speak to that gospel norm—of the victory of life over death in Christ, of the equality of all people before God that Jesus preached. I think we Christians have to make sense of those, whether by placing them in historical context or reinterpreting them in light of our modern experience and the overriding themes of Scripture.

Being a Christian feminist is, for me, as natural as being a daughter or sister, but the combination makes far less sense to many people. There are still ostensibly Christian publishers putting out "biblical" titles (like *Lies Young Women Believe* by Nancy Leigh DeMoss and Dannah Gresh)[6] that suggest women are more susceptible to deception because our ancestor Eve gave in to the conniving of that dastardly serpent. There are pastors (like Mark Driscoll and John Piper) who routinely preach about the spiritual headship of men and how wives are supposed to submit to their husbands, who will rule over their little ladies as Christ does the church. (I know many equality-minded folks want to redeem this analogy by pointing out that men are supposed to love sacrificially, as Christ loves. That's nice, but it still doesn't work for me. The church exists because of Christ; he is its *raison d'etre*. And I'm not willing to say that about my wonderful husband, no matter what he sacrifices for me in the name of love.)

I recently met a woman who's served as an ordained staff member of her independent evangelical church for twenty-one years, but on the rare occasions when she's allowed to preach, a number of people always get up and leave worship as she approaches the pulpit, because she's a woman, and women are supposed to keep silent in church. There are folks who give 1 Timothy higher priority than Galatians.

In addition, then, to fearing all the demoralizing, disempowering, self-subjugating messages offered to girls in our wider society, I confess to being particularly watchful of the sorts of messages Fiona hears at church. And I am particularly angered by those who would, in the name of Christ, limit girls and women in their attempts to grow into the people God calls them to be.

While I worry about all the negative messages Fee and Callie might hear, I know there's a lot I can do to insulate the girls against their power. I also know that our level of education and our middle-class status and the fact that I work outside the home in a profession I enjoy and that their father and I try to be equal partners in our home—all of these will help protect our girls against these messages. One of the key critiques leveled by women of color against the second wave feminists of the 1960s and 1970s was that the result of their efforts seemed mainly to meet the needs and challenges of middle-to-upper-class, educated white women. And that's a valid critique. I realize I can afford to make a stink about pink, because I have reason to hope—unfair, incredibly unevenly distributed reason—that they will not face the challenges faced by so many women lacking in social networks or financial and educational resources. Mothers who aren't sure their daughters will have enough food to eat or a safe place to live don't have the luxury of being concerned about whether their girls identify too closely with the Disney princesses. But here I am.

Peggy Orenstein actually does a good job discussing the way the princess tide touches on issues of class and race while maintaining her ambivalence about all things pink and princess-related. After all, she grew up as a Disney kid. She watched all the movies. She had a set of Mouseketeer ears. I also grew up with an All-American canon of Disney movies, as well as a wealth of musicals from both Broadway and Hollywood. I continue to know by heart the soundtracks to most of the movies I saw as a kid, which suggests that I watched many of them multiple times. And it's true that many of those movies have a love story and, if not a princess, then a pretty stereotypical heroine at the heart of them.

But Disney is different from when I was a kid and certainly from when Orenstein was growing up. In the days before direct-to-DVD productions of princess stories and Disney Channel sitcoms for preteens, my sisters and I relied on our public library's collection of live-action Disney movies—many from the '60s—to fill rainy afternoons and family movie nights. Generally starring Fred MacMurray or Hayley Mills, these stories—from *The Happiest Millionaire* and *The Shaggy Dog* to *Blackbeard's Ghost* and *The Parent Trap*—were fun and funny. They weren't made for boys or girls, like *Cars* or *The Princess Diaries*; they were just for kids. Now, gender differences are assumed, entrenched, and marketed from the time a girl can hold a baby Ariel doll. Orenstein tells the chilling story of how the Disney Princess brand was born in 2000. Andy Mooney, an executive in the Disney consumer products division, attended a Disney on Ice show. She reports on his dismay:"[He] found himself surrounded by little girls in princess costumes. Princess costumes that were—horrors!—*homemade*. How had such a massive branding opportunity been overlooked?"[7] Within a year, the Disney Princess line had climbed to $300 million in profits.

I object to anything that is so crassly materialistic, especially when it's shilled to my girls. But it isn't just the marketing aspect that troubles Orenstein. She doesn't like the Disney versions of the stories, which often offer one-dimensional female characters whose primary actions are falling in love and, frequently, nearly dying. But I'll cop to liking those stories, however retrograde they may be. My favorites, from an early, early age, were the stories with a romantic plotline. I watched *The King and I* and mostly ignored the stuff about the multiple wives and the analogies about imperialism and slavery, and focused on "Hello, Young Lovers." I lived for duets, and I'm always rooting for the boy to just go ahead and kiss her already. (So many good songs have been written about this moment of hesitation and the frustration it raises, from "Kiss the Girl" in Disney's *The Little Mermaid* to "Show Me" in *My Fair Lady*.) It's strange, maybe, that someone who believes so vehemently in gender equality, someone who wants so desperately for women—and especially my daughters—to know they do not need romance to make them human, would love these storylines so much. But my fondness for romance, strange as it may be, is also why I remain largely unconcerned by Fiona's current love of skirts and why Josh and I deliberated for all of five minutes before giving her the one Christmas present she really wanted this year, when she was four: a Barbie makeup kit. She likes to be "fancy" and has a Fancy Nancy doll and many of the accompanying books. We have had many, many discussions with her in which we reiterate our belief that makeup for four-year-old girls is just for dress-up, not for school or church, though I confess we stumble when she asks why. "Children are so beautiful that they don't need make-up" implies that mommy isn't that beautiful and wants to cover up her natural flaws. "Makeup is just for playing" causes our girls to question why I get to wear it to work.

My concern about her predilections is limited because, at least for now, I have near total control of her media consumption, and

I can make sure she gets inundated with all sorts of models and messages. (I would add that these predilections are not entirely innate: She has grown 300 percent more committed to pink and to things she thinks appropriate for girls since starting preschool; it's peer pressure, I tell you!) I allow her to watch princesses because she also watches *Finding Nemo* and *Bedknobs and Broomsticks*. She can watch *Cinderella* because she also loves *Once upon a Mattress*. She can develop a little tiny preschool crush on Zac Efron, the protagonist in the *High School Musical* trilogy, but then I'll introduce her to the most recent remake of *Hairspray*, in which Efron stars, but which also features a really heavyset romantic lead, interracial romance, a man in drag, and a plotline focused on racial integration in 1962.

Children, who are just figuring out what it means to be a person, not to mention what it means to be male or female, are watching us and are listening to the stories we tell them and paying attention to the images they see. Of course, they're *not* listening to a lot of things, too—which is why I hope she hasn't pieced together how frequently, say, teen or extramarital pregnancy is a plot point in some of our familial favorites (for example: *Once upon a Mattress, Hairspray,* and *Seven Brides for Seven Brothers,* which has wonderful choreography and a plotline junior feminists had best ignore). But this amazing and idiosyncratic pattern of honing in on the details of plot or theme is why she won't be introduced to *Miss Saigon* or *Rent* for a good long while (though I failed to anticipate how I'd explain the scene in *Joseph and the Amazing Technicolor Dreamcoat* where Mrs. Potiphar tries to seduce Donny Osmond before accusing him of rape—yet another reminder that the Bible often fails to be G-rated). Kids are trying to figure out our stories and to figure out where they fit in, what their place is in the world, and what their identity is going to entail.

Over time, I want my girls to feel that their options are nearly unlimited and that the rare limitations they may encounter have little to do with gender. To accomplish this, I make sure *Free to Be . . . You and Me*, that great '70s-era refutation of gender stereotypes for young children, is as much a part of our car-ride CD collection as *Disney Princesses Greatest Hits*. I put songs like "Parents Are People" on repeat. That song lists all the things mothers and fathers can be—doctors and taxi drivers are on the mommies' list; daddies can sell groceries or play cello. These parents are people, *people with children*, and the only thing a mommy can't be is a daddy, and the only thing a daddy can't be is a mommy. I want these songs ingrained in my daughters so they will know as surely as I did that the only limitations on their lives are individual ones and not a result of their gender. I want them to know and understand that the grammatical tautologies "Parents are People" alludes to are simply statements of fact about English—male parents are called daddies, female parents are called mommies (or, in our house, Mommy-o)—not about gender or humanity.

Are there gender differences that are larger or more meaningful than biological and grammatical categories? Other than shoving *Free to Be . . .* down their throats, how can I help Fiona and Calliope, and all the girls I work with, navigate the cloudy waters of gender difference? In *Cinderella Ate My Daughter,* Peggy Orenstein offers the reminder that boys and girls don't really have a sense of their gender until somewhere between age two and three, and even then they're not really sure what it entails. She tells this great story that apparently resides within the apocrypha of academic psychology:

A four-year-old boy named Jeremy . . . wore his favorite barrettes to school one day. "You're a *girl*," one of his classmates said accusingly, but the boy stood firm. No, he explained, he was a boy because he had a penis and testicles. The other child continued to taunt him. Finally, exasperated, Jeremy pulled down his pants to prove his point. His tormentor merely shrugged. "*Everyone* has a penis," he said. "Only girls wear barrettes."[8]

While we may giggle about the misplaced convictions of this junior bully, Orenstein shares this tale as an illustration of the work of neuroscientists who study gender, such as Lisa Eliot. Eliot suggests that part of the reason young children get confused about the concept of gender is because for a good long while, kids' brains are not developed to the point where they can fully grasp permanence. They may begin to understand that boys have penises and girls have vaginas, but they're not clear that they will *always* be the gender they are now and that their gender is, most likely, pretty fixed. It makes sense, then," Orenstein comments, "that to ensure you will stay the sex you were born you'd adhere rigidly to the rules as you see them and hope for the best. That's why four-year-olds, who are in what is called 'the inflexible stage,' become the self-appointed chiefs of the gender police."[9]

This comforts me, a bit, since a little part of my Christian feminist heart dies whenever Fiona tells me boys can't play with pink things and girls don't like basketball. But it doesn't comfort me much. Part of being human, we've noted, lies in our desire to make meaning, to assign meaning to various facts of life. Children, even if they don't fully grasp the facts of life, see and notice difference, and they, being tiny humans, are bound to assign meaning to those differences. It's a parental responsibility to help shape those meanings.

Fiona knows there are such things as boy and girl parts. (She will not resemble Jeremy's anecdotal protagonist so long as she has a baby boy cousin around or attends a day care where the rules of the Department of Children and Family Services require that the door to the classroom bathroom always remains open.) But it's up to us to help her understand what, if anything, the differences between the two mean.

For many parents, this responsibility is a daunting one—daunting enough to intimidate the indomitable Orenstein, as well as more easily cowed me—given the way women still struggle for equality in so many sectors of society. While the early years of my childhood seemed to still be riding the waves of *Free to Be . . . You and Me* gender neutrality, our kids were born in a time characterized by a resurgence in rhetoric about the complementary relationship between men and women and the essential differences between the two. Such rhetoric was particularly loud in certain Christian and other conservative religious circles (and most likely reemerged as an ongoing and unfolding reaction to the perceived successes of "women's lib" and the changing makeup of the average American family). The resurgence is also probably about gay marriage. Terrible antigay arguments that boil down to "It's Adam and Eve, not Adam and Steve" make even less sense if no one much believes gender is determinative of important traits. (My husband now playfully refers to the night before Christmas as "Christmas Steve.")

The assertion of rigid gender roles and the theological justification of women's secondary status recalls another throwback movement, the time in the late nineteenth century that the book *Ungodly Women: Gender and the First Wave of American Fundamentalism* describes. Women were starting to push for suffrage, to ask for recognition, to make headway; in response, "traditionalists" pushed back and began to define the boundaries of what scholars call "the cult of true womanhood."[10] Women who wanted to leave the house, to work, to have a vocation, to vote—these were women who (according to their opposition) eschewed their very identity as women, who cast off their responsibilities as wives and mothers and went against nature by demanding a voice in the public sphere.

Given the aspirations of earlier feminists, I have had no difficulty defining myself as a feminist and setting aside the views of traditionalists. First-wave feminists were concerned with equal participation in public, civic life, and second-wave feminists were concerned with equality in the private sectors of employment and the home. Today's third-wave feminists are harder to track; there are so many voices at the table now. But part of that wave has been focused on empowering women to be sexual beings, free to have "sex like men" (in other words, promiscuously, for pleasure, and with little attention to emotion or romance). I'm a little more ambivalent about that than I am about Betty Friedan's then-radical supposition in *The Feminine Mystique* that frustrated women should go to grad school. A good part of me—my own traditionalist streak, I guess you could call it—would rather my girls grow up to be second-wave feminists, seeking freedom in their vocations, if sexual freedom (and assumed promiscuity, with its attendant health risks) is the only criterion third-wave feminism has to recommend it.

I don't really mean that, though. I want my daughters—and sons, if I should ever have them—to grow up to claim the part of their identity that is gendered, that is sexual. Given my own ambivalence about third-wave feminism, I'm not surprised that many modern conservative Christians express real concern about the aims of this wave and have ramped up their efforts to "train up" the kind of girls who would never, ever, ever consider attempting to have "sex like men." Inculcating values of self-respect and a certain modesty is a noble goal, as is emphasizing having a beautiful spirit instead of a beautiful face or beautiful body. But these values are so often couched in a movement to reclaim girlie-girl culture, to raise modern-day Christian princesses ("daughters of the King"), a movement that seems decidedly less noble. The dichotomy that emerges in countless books for teenagers and their parents describes girls as guileless, witless potential victims who must rely entirely on the protection of Jesus, their daddies, and their future husbands, and boys as would-be sexual predators fighting a can't-win battle for their chastity against Satan himself. Nobody wins.

Yes, if seen in a generous light, this model (which I am carica-turing only slightly)[11] is an attempt to make sense of gender differ-ence, to afford everyone a special place and role in God's plan. Men are the leaders—holy protectors and providers; women are the nurturers—innocent, pure, and submissive. But I'm not inter-ested in this "special" role for women. Maybe it's because I spent too many of my formative years reading too many biographies.

The historical record on "separate but equal" speaks pretty clearly: There's no such thing.

What then does it mean that we are created male and female? Fundamentalist Christians like to refer to Genesis 2 when looking for the origin of inequality and strife between the sexes. The woman was created out of the man, from his rib. Then she sins, and leads him into sin, and we are forever lost; as punishment for her disobedience, the woman is rendered subservient. But Genesis 1 (which, in a wonderful example of the unclear chronology of the biblical witness, is actually the later rendering of the two creation accounts) suggests that man and woman are created not in sequence but simultaneously: "Then God said, 'Let us make humankind in our image, according to our likeness. . . .' So God created humankind in his image, in the image of God he created them; male and female he created them" (Gen. 1:26–27).

Biblical scholar Phyllis Trible was among the first to note (in the 1970s) that the Genesis 1 account demonstrates that in God's vision, men and women are a part of one another, in relationship, and it is in relationship that human beings reflect the image and likeness of God. But this view is not just in Genesis 1. Trible states that Genesis 2 and 3 reveal not only that men and women are bound to one another in relationship, but also that "in the garden" that relationship was one of equals.[12]

All that childhood reading about civil rights has convinced me that the "separate but equal" spheres offered by complementarians, conservative and otherwise, don't really exist. But it was my experiences of gender roles in my own family—and learning about the roles in Josh's home while he was growing up—that convinced me that the clear and unchanging separation of these roles are far from God-given. Josh and I both emerged from families that were—in their own very "vanilla," straight, white way—transgressors of strict and expected societal gender norms.

My dad was the cuddly one, the one who gave kisses and hugs, the one who cooked and packed lunches. Mom was always there when we needed her, supervising homework and helping to build the most awesome art projects for our classes, but she worked, too, and was never raised to be domestic. She trained in the theater, in tech and costuming; her favorite memories of early adulthood were of living and working in a terrible New York City walk-up with her best friend, subsisting on cans of baked beans and Entenmann's chocolate cake. My sisters and I grew up in a family that avoided rigidly maintained gender roles; our parents were clearly different from one another—in some ways that men and women are sometimes stereotypically different, and in others that simply reflected who they were and are as individuals. We grew up believing a marriage wasn't about one person providing and one person submitting, but about both people pitching in, because they're on the same team.

Josh's mother left their family when he was a toddler, leaving his dad with full custody of both Josh and his younger brother. John did an incredible job raising them as a single dad in a time when neither society nor the family courts thought much of fathers as nurturers. I stand in awe of those who single-parent—out of choice or necessity—who have the patience and the skill and the love to do it. John was everything to the boys: disciplinarian and nurturer, cook and provider, cheerleader and moral guide. He wasn't a perfect parent—but only because there is no such thing.

All this is to say that Josh and I are not particularly convinced by arguments that men naturally exhibit characteristics a, b, and c, and women are the opposite. Our parents weren't like that, and neither are we. In fact, I shudder whenever I see us conforming to any gender stereotypes. (Josh is a football fanatic who has an incredible propensity to ignore dirty dishes. I am a careless and easily distracted driver, and I sulk and wash those dishes instead of asking him to help.) But I want my girls to know that the different ways their grandparents and parents inhabit the world are fine—and not just fine, but of God. This is the better side of third-wave Christian feminism: We are empowered to live as we were created to be, as individuals, and in relationships.

Even so, I continue to be convinced that men and women are different in some inarguable ways. Physiology is the main one. It may be the only innate one. But our biological differences are, in most cases, the easiest ones to point to, easy to name and relatively easy to articulate when asked by our kids—even if we debate what vocabulary we want to teach them and at what ages. (Fiona was apparently paying attention to the discussion Josh and I were having one day as we drove the girls somewhere, and, in the middle of it, chimed in with a clarifying question: "What's *ovulating?*")

Children can see difference; they have an eye for it. It's part of their cognitive development to learn how to categorize things in "not like the other" sorts of ways. They know boys and girls are not the same and can see that men and women are not the same; if we tell them otherwise, they'll come to imagine we're lying to them. (A similar phenomenon is true of race: see "Why White Parents Don't Talk about Race" in *Nurture Shock*.) Another perhaps unsurprising bit of research in child psychology demonstrates that kids prefer to play with those who are like them, so they self-select by gender pretty early on. As one who cherishes her men friends, and who regrets mightily the many years I shyly feared the male of the species as one who might misread overtures of friendship as romantic interest, I would love to do what I can to help Fiona foster friendships with boys and to help her be as comfortable with them as, well, other human beings. I don't want to be heavy handed about it; I want to encourage her to make and maintain friendships with girls as well. But when she says something about how James is mean and boys are mean, we point out that she has lots of friends who are boys, including but not limited to Soren, Connor, and James, and that Dad and her Grandpas and Uncle Mike and (nearly-uncle-when-eventually-he-marries-Aunt-Tay)   Nathaniel

were all boys, and they're not mean. I don't want to fight; I just
want to offer counterexamples.

In addition to offering real world examples of awesome boys,
I seek out stories and songs and movies with boys and girls playing
together, being friends. Ramona and Howie, in Beverly Cleary's
books, are good examples, as are Nickelodeon's *Backyardigans* (if I
can be vigilant enough to make sure I fast forward through all the
commercials); I giddily await the day I can introduce her the friendship powerhouse of Ron, Harry, and Hermione in J. K. Rowling's
Harry Potter series. The aforementioned *Free to Be . . . You and Me*
is rife with illustrations: the song "When We Grow Up" is a duet
between a boy and a girl, and the lyrics have each child imagining
what he or she will be like as an adult. Questions about clothing
and career, about height and appearance—these kids are dreaming. I
love this song, although I object in some ways to the chorus, which
posits, "We don't have to change at all."[13] This is, of course, patently
false. Boys and girls change into men and women; life in this world
is all about change. Things that remain static are, quite simply, not
alive: they are dead. And while change may sometimes be fearsome
and fraught, it can also bring everything we ever dreamed of and
more: the chance to explore a vocation, the chance to fall in love,
the chance to grow and learn. Of course, what lyricist Shelley Miller
is getting at is that we don't have to change in predetermined ways,
to match what society expects of us, to live up to the modeled
gender roles offered by others. I never want Fiona and Callie to feel
limited by their gender, but I want them to know that being a girl is
wonderful and special, and becoming a woman is awesome (most of
the time), especially for the ways we change that are different from
men (who will experience their own awesome transformations).

My friend and colleague Ann has a two-and-a-half-year-old
daughter who apparently delights in being a girl. The other
morning, Claire said to Ann, "Mommy, when I grow up, I want to
be a girl."

Her mother replied, "Okay, sweetie. You can be lots of things plus a girl, too."

Claire was extremely excited by this news: "Like a monster! Or a dragon! Roar!"

I love this story: I giggled when Ann posted it on Facebook, and I wrote it down because I am charmed by Claire's gleeful lack of understanding. To be a girl is a privilege, a joy, and it's one that doesn't (apparently) preclude her from pursuing any of her other goals in life—which at this point, appear to include becoming a monster or a dragon. (Good choices, I think.)

Just as Orenstein reminded us that little kids don't really understand the permanence of biological sex, the kids on *Free to Be . . . You and Me* (voiced by adults) seem to imagine an androgyny that will continue on into the future, an androgyny I don't really see, and I know my pink-loving eldest daughter can't see. I wonder how to make sense of all this for my girls, and for myself. Phyllis Trible provides a helpful starting point in her analysis of Genesis 2 and 3. She notes that the first divine act of creation in Genesis 2 is one of androgyny, and the final act of the chapter is one of sexuality. The Hebrew word we tend to translate as *Adam* is really just *human*. Before Eve, Adam is no more male than female. Adam is a creature for whom gender not only does not matter but does not exist. It's in the creation of the woman, in Adam's responding to this new creature, that he recognizes himself as male, and she herself as female. It's the differentiation in relationship that's special, not the gender itself.[14]

In both Trible and *Free to Be . . . You and Me,* in this vision of boys and girls, male and female, as one—as partners and friends, living out their callings in freedom, working to change that which is oppressive or unjust—I see the reign of God. That's gospel as far as I can tell.

My favorite, and Fee's second most requested, song from *Free to Be* concludes:

When I grow up I'm going to be happy
And do what I like to do,
Like making noise and making faces
And making friends like you.
And when we grow up do you think we'll see
That I'm still like you
And you're still like me?[15]

The Christian hope isn't that we don't have to change at all; in fact, it's that we *will* be changed. We will not remain androgynous and alone; we will be differentiated and in relationship. The change we hope and long for is not that we each go off to our own little spheres, however. It's that we'll all be made one. "For all are one in Christ Jesus"—boys and girls and everybody in between.

CHAPTER 13

Move, Mommy, Move

On sharing, and life in a family, and making room without getting crowded out

THE CLOCK ON MY BEDSIDE TABLE SAYS 12:28 A.M., AND I HAVE no choice but to believe it. Jonathan is just a few weeks old and still sleeps in the bassinet in the corner of our room. I've been up with him so many times since we went to bed an hour and a half ago that I've completely lost track of what time it is. It could just as easily be 3:00 a.m.—and I'd be hard pressed to tell you the day.

We finally get settled again, Jonathan in a clean diaper, swaddled and happy (for the moment), sucking on a pacifier, the Sleep Sheep tuned to whale noises. I climb back into bed, one part of me longing to sink deep into my pillow and back into sleep, the other part of me listening to the gurgling and breathing in the corner, half expecting him to wake back up and cry again.

I'm not quite asleep when I hear footsteps in the hallway, and Rob and I realize in the same instant that Harper is awake. We both sigh: *This is what it's like to have two.* She doesn't say anything for a moment and doesn't come into our room, so I call out to her: "Harper? What do you need?"

"A drink," she says, sleepy but awake. We hear her in the bathroom, opening the cabinet where her cup is kept, turning on the water.

"Are you getting it yourself?" I ask, needlessly, but it is unusual for her to be up in the middle of the night, much less taking care of things herself.

"Yes," she calls back, and Rob and I look at each other.

"What a big kid," he whispers to me. It's true; since she turned four in July and became a big sister, she has matured by leaps and bounds.

I hear her pad back to her room and I have a fleeting hope that that's it, and we'll all be back asleep again in a moment. But my hope is short lived. She appears a moment later next to my bed, elephant in hand.

"I want to snuggle with you," she says.

"No, sweetheart, you need to be in your own bed." I start to get up. "I'll walk you back to your room."

"No!" She is instantly in tears. "No, Mama! I want to snuggle with you! In here!"

I look at her for a moment, weighing my options. Her pleading eyes convince me we'll be in for a long fight if I try to get her back into her own bed. "Okay," I sigh, and start to scoot over to make room for her.

"No, in the middle." She climbs over me and burrows down into the pillows between Rob and me. She's asleep a moment later.

When Jonathan's hungry cry wakes me again a few hours later, I take him into the den to nurse, because I don't want to risk waking Harper. By the time I get back and settle Jonathan back into the bassinet, she has stretched out onto my pillow, taking up my entire side of the bed with her gangly limbs (she's tall for her age anyway, and now, compared to Jonathan's newborn baby legs, hers are gigantic).

I shove her over—she doesn't wake—and climb back in myself, listening to the sounds of my sleeping family.

It's kind of sweet, I think, all four of us, together in this one room.

It's kind of peaceful, I think, the way Jonathan's newborn gurgles mix with Rob's deep breathing and Harper's shallow inhalations.

But mostly, I think, it's kind of crowded.

When I was about six months pregnant with Harper, I ran into an acquaintance I hadn't seen in a while who didn't know I was expecting. After we said hello, he pointed at my growing tummy. "You are two," he said. I laughed and agreed.

You are two.

I've found myself coming back to those words often in the years since I first heard them, as I try to remember what it was like before I was two—before I shared my body with a batch of cells that became a human life; before I was responsible for feeding, clothing, and protecting first one and now two little bodies; before there were four people sleeping in my bedroom. There was a time, I remember vaguely, when it was just me. Or at least it was just Rob and me—and even after we married we were independent from each other in a way we aren't now. In the years before we had kids, we had our own schedules, made our own plans. Then I was two, and then Harper was born, and there were three of us. And now that Jonathan is here, there are four.

It's gotten crowded around here.

It started early, this baby-induced crowding, as the dividing cells of pregnancy crowded out my internal organs, shoving my stomach up under my ribs and pressing down on my bladder so I was constantly running to the bathroom. The sense that my body is not my own didn't end with birth, either. Right now, my nursing breasts belong to Jonathan, and my body is still so intimately tied to his that I can't be away from him for more than three hours without taking along my breast pump. I know from experience that even after I stop nursing it'll be a long time before this body is my own again. When Harper was about two, we met up with some childless friends at a restaurant for lunch. They watched, grinning (and not one bit enviously), as Harper climbed back and forth over me, into my lap and out, sticky hands on my head and shoulders, grabbing at my hair and taking food off my plate. "It's like you're a jungle gym!" one friend declared.

And then there's all the ways that children fill up our lives with their things, their personalities, their need for attention—in a way that seems to crowd out the very stuff of the people we were before. When Callie was born, Bromleigh gave up her beloved writing spot so their guest room/office could be turned into the nursery. Now, she writes hunched over her laptop while sitting on her bed. Rob and I have some camping gear we haven't used since before Harper was born; it's buried in the back of the garage, behind strollers and a Whiffle Ball bat and Harper's new bike. We've given over one whole corner of our living room to Harper's "art station," with bins overflowing with crayons and markers, and scraps of paper constantly littering the floor. After noticing recently that the wall behind her easel is completely covered with paint splatters, I gave thanks that we're not planning to sell the house any time soon.

The car has gotten crowded, too, now that we have two car seats in the back. To this point, we've resisted a minivan, insisting there's plenty of room in our hatchback, proud of our commitment to small, energy-efficient cars. But when my in-laws were visiting recently and we had to take two cars to dinner, and when I think about packing for an upcoming road trip, I start to wonder if we are simply postponing the inevitable. Bromleigh and Josh succumbed recently, and she calls me now from her Bluetooth-equipped Swagger Wagon,[1] and I find myself envious of her seating capacity.

There's this song I keep thinking of as I contemplate our crowded car, our crowded bed, our crowded life. I can't remember where I learned it; it's been in my head since before Harper was born, so maybe it's something I sang as a kid. It's a counting song that counts backwards from five to one and repeats incessantly, with a sing-songy melody:

Five bears in the bed and the little one said, "I'm crowded! Roll
     over!"
So they all rolled over and one fell out.
Four bears in the bed and the little one said, "I'm crowded! Roll
     over!"
So they all . . .

Most parents, I imagine, have at some point made a list of
things they gave up when children appeared in their lives: sleeping
in, freedom, money, travel, uninterrupted time in the bathroom,
movies in theaters, meals in restaurants, intelligent conversation
with other adults, and so on. On some level, this is just what parents
do. We move over. We let our children crawl all over us and eat food
off our plates. We make room in our beds, our houses, and our lives
for these little people and all their stuff and all their needs.

But what if we move over so far that we roll right off the bed?

Among the many, many children's books that line our shelves
are five copies of Shel Silverstein's *The Giving Tree*. We already had
two copies, and then we were given three more at the baby shower
the church threw us before Jonathan was born. (We'll donate most
of them somewhere, I promise; we don't need five copies.) I like
Silverstein's poetry. And I understand why *The Giving Tree* is a
classic, I do. It's a sweet story about a tree that loves a boy so much
that she gives everything she has for him and is there for him at
every major point in his life. I can see why it's a popular gift at baby
showers. On the surface, isn't that what parenthood is? Aren't we
supposed to give everything we have for our kids?

But Bonnie Miller-McLemore, in *In the Midst of Chaos,*
critiques *The Giving Tree* as a model for parenting, suggesting that
complete self-sacrifice may not be such a helpful ideal.[2] After all,
the tree's relationship with the boy robs the tree of everything that
makes her a tree: leaves, branches, trunk. At the end of the book
she is nothing more than a chopped-down stump. This is a lousy

metaphor for any healthy relationship, I think, and it certainly isn't how I want to love my children. I don't want there to be nothing left of me when my children are grown.

I'm pretty sure this desire to have a life beyond my children—to avoid being completely crowded out—doesn't make me a bad mom. Miller-McLemore seems to agree. In *Also a Mother: Work and Family as Theological Dilemma,* Miller-McLemore calls for a new understanding of motherhood, one that allows space for mothers to care for their children and also participate in creative, productive work beyond the family. The Christian tradition, she asserts—fueled by texts like 1 Timothy that force women into silence and claim salvation for women only through childbearing—has perpetuated the ideal that women find their true selves only through the act of mothering. She argues that for women to embrace their full humanity, we must also nurture other aspects of our lives.

This is true for fathers, too, I think. Certainly, men don't find their internal organs rearranged by growing babies; their bodies are not as intimately tied to their children's, at least at first. But Rob gets used as a jungle gym at least as much as I do. Harper eats off his plate just as often as mine (maybe more; he's more generous than I am). He has little room in his life anymore for hobbies or friends—especially of the kid-free variety. And he also has to roll over when Harper climbs into bed with us.

"Most children," writes Miller-McLemore, "do not need or benefit from the kind of unconditional self-sacrificial love that Christianity often esteems as the ideal."[3] She continues:

> While critical moments call for self-giving love, . . . this should not be the ideal that is hung over the heads of parents struggling to love their children. The ideal of sacrifice creates virtues impossible to emulate, distorting relationships between parent and child, and between mother and father. It exaggerates the amount of energy a single person can or should bestow upon children, and it misjudges the possible damage done by the absence of a

father's matching self-giving love. Not only is loving sacrifice impossible as a goal, it denies women the complex realities of maternal labor—that a good mother can sometimes hate her children, that a mother may love her children, but hate mothering, that vesting one person with full responsibility for mothering may not be wise, or even possible. The ideal harms persons, particularly women, who already are overprogrammed to give endlessly, leaving them ashamed of the self-interest that naturally accompanies their love.[4]

Both mothers and fathers need some sort of balance in our lives, lest we give ourselves over entirely and find ourselves left with nothing but a lifeless stump. I'm not willing to give my entire life to my children. There are some things that are still mine—time with friends, my work, dinner with my husband, at least a little space in my bed, a whole pillow to myself.

Of course, I'm grateful for these people with whom I share my life, even if it gets crowded sometimes. I wouldn't wish them away for anything. At the end of that song about the crowded, rolling bears, there's just one bear left, the little one, who had been complaining all along about how crowded he was. But once all the other bears have rolled over and fallen right out of the bed, the little bear concludes the song by himself, mournfully declaring, "I'm lonely."

I remember another night in our crowded bed, a couple of months before Jonathan was born. After awakening from a bad dream she couldn't remember, Harper had come in and made her way to the middle of our bed, where she fell asleep again almost instantly, safe from whatever demons had tormented her in the other room. Despite the crowding, I like sleeping next to her. After almost four years, her body had not forgotten that it once was part of me, and she instinctively curled into the space between my chest and my knees, her feet resting on the tops of my bent thighs. I stretched my own feet down to touch Rob's much bigger ones at the end of the bed. Inside me, the newly forming feet of the baby we didn't yet know fluttered, as if to remind me that there were more than three of us in this bed. It is good—if not always restful—to share a bed with people whose bodies you love.

So what to do? How do we make room without losing ourselves?

Sure, we find good child care, and take people up on offers to help. We read grown-up books occasionally. We make time for work that fulfills us and maybe even makes the world a better place. We plan date nights with our spouses. We declare that some parts of the house are off limits to little paint-covered hands. But maybe, also, we accept the fact that life in a family is messy and crowded and requires a great deal of negotiation—that being part of a family means sharing the whole of our lives with other people. In fact, maybe a better ideal than sacrifice—giving everything we've got—is *sharing:* Everybody gives something and there's enough to go around.[5]

At the top of Robert Fulghum's famous list of things he learned in kindergarten—all he ever needed to know—is this: "Share everything." Our kids aren't in kindergarten quite yet, but they're learning this lesson. When Bromleigh's family visited us recently, Harper and Fiona fought over a pink toy cell phone. Never mind that there were actually three toy cell phones—even one for Callie to toddle around with. (Thankfully, Jonathan was content to suck on his hands, oblivious to the negotiations among the girls.) It was the pink one that caused all the trouble. We were never sure if it was the phone's color or the fact that it made the most inter-esting beeping sounds, but we grown-ups spent no small amount of time encouraging them to take turns. Eventually, they managed to share pretty well, coming to an understanding that there would be enough time for each of them to have a turn with the pink phone.

Harper has had to share a lot lately, especially since Jonathan's birth has given her not just a brother but also a roommate. As we awaited his arrival and dug all our baby gear out of storage, we also transformed "her" room to "their" room. We moved her bed over to one corner, bought a new dresser so the one she'd been using could return to its original purpose as a changing table, and set up the crib on the other side of the room. We reorganized the closet, sorted through toys and books, and got rid of a toddler desk she never really used. "When the baby comes, he'll sleep right here," we told her. She was thrilled.

When he arrived, we kept him in our room for the first few weeks, much to Harper's dismay. "When will Jonathan sleep in my room?" she asked, nearly every night. Now that he does, the arrangement seems to be working out well. She's a sound sleeper and only occasionally stirs when he wakes up for his middle-of-the-night feedings. He, so far, has been content to sit with us for story time and then drift off in his crib while she sits on her bed and talks herself to sleep.

I am not naïve enough to think both of them will always be so agreeable. It will soon dawn on her, I suspect, that he is not simply a guest but a permanent addition. There will be arguments over toys; she won't always sleep so peacefully; he'll want to be part of everything she does. It won't always be so fun.

She'll soon learn that she has to share her grandparents, too. For more than three years, she was the only grandchild to four doting grandparents, and now, within the space of a year, she has gained a sibling and two cousins. Now, she's one of four. Granted, she'll always be the oldest, and judging by her personality, she'll likely be the ringleader at years of family gatherings. But the focus will no longer be all on her. She's quickly learning that the universe does not revolve around her. She is learning (remarkably gracefully, I should add) that being in a family requires sharing.

During the last couple of months of my pregnancy, I noticed that Harper was climbing onto my lap more often than usual. We'd be sitting at dinner, and out of the blue, she'd worm her way under my arm and up onto my knees. There wasn't much lap left at that point, and there was even less as the weeks wore on, but still she found a way to wrap herself around me, to make room for herself in the circle of my arms. It was as if she knew she'd have to begin sharing that space soon; my lap would no longer be her domain alone. I felt the shift, too. As the new baby grew, as my body took on the task of sustaining another life, Harper was growing as well and needed me less and less. I found myself inventing reasons to pick her up and hold her.

Since Jonathan's birth, I think Harper and I have both been pleasantly surprised to find there is plenty of lap again. There's space now for her to climb up and get her whole body up against mine, arms around my neck and legs around my waist. And now that I'm no longer pregnant, I can run and play more than I've been able to for a long time. She squealed with delight as I chased her around the playground the other night.

She hadn't lost me. I didn't get swallowed up by my pregnant belly. The new baby hasn't crowded her out. Even with Jonathan here, there is enough of me to go around.

I can't quite explain how that happens. Writer and pastor Heidi Neumark, in her lovely and inspiring book *Breathing Space,* tells of her work at a church in a tough neighborhood in the South Bronx. She poured her heart and soul into that congregation, helping it transform from an older, dying church to a living, vital one doing ministry with the people in the community. It was all-consuming work, and Neumark often worried about the affect it had on her young children, Hans and Ana. But she discovered that even then, there was enough:

> So often love and energy feel divided, but even more often they are multiplied. For years, Hans had a recurrent bedtime question after I'd tell him that I loved him:
>
> "Mommy, are you sure that you love me?"
>
> "Of course, Hans, you know I love you. I love you with all my heart."
>
> "With all your heart?"

"Yes, with all my heart."

"How many hearts do you have, Mommy?"

"Just one."

"But how can you love me with *all* your heart if you love Ana, too?"

The answer was always the same: "Because love is a miracle. Because I can. Because I do."[6]

Love is a miracle.

There's a miracle story in the Bible that's so important that it shows up in all four Gospels.[7] It takes place on a crowded hillside where thousands of people have gathered to hear Jesus preach. It gets to be late in the day, and the people are getting hungry. Someone starts passing around a basket of bread and fish. It's barely enough for one family, but somehow everyone gets fed with plenty left over. There's enough to go around.

Love is like that, somehow. Even when it seems like there can't possibly be enough, there is.

I want my kids to know they are loved, fully and equally. I want them to know there will always be enough of me to go around. I want our family to be a place where we practice that sort of miracle, knowing there will be times we don't do it very well. I want our family to be a place where even when it feels like we're giving up everything, we're finding ourselves again. I want our family to share.

Sharing is risky business, of course. The other kid at the sandbox could break the shovel if you let him play with it. You might not get your doll back. Sharing my body with these two children means I may never again fit into that cute brown dress I bought pre-pregnancy. Sharing my life with these three other people means I don't get much quiet time to read; it means the house is almost always a little more cluttered (and sometimes a lot more cluttered) than I'd like. Rob and I are tied to each other's schedules, our lives are intertwined in a way they never were before. Sometimes we step on one another's toes—literally and metaphorically. Sometimes the thing we're sharing is a case of pinkeye that sends us all to the doctor for eyedrops.

But the great thing about sharing is that it goes both ways. Never, in *The Giving Tree,* does the boy bring water or fertilizer to the tree; the giving is completely one-sided. Sharing, almost by definition, demands reciprocity. "Pregnancy and care of children," writes Miller-McLemore, "present an opportunity to realize, perhaps for the first time, that sacrifice—responsiveness to others, and autonomy—responsiveness to oneself—are not mutually exclusive."[8] Sharing *is* giving, and sometimes it's sacrifice. But it's not an all-consuming sacrifice that leaves us with nothing. Instead, it's the kind of giving that comes right back to us, sometimes in unexpected ways.

Being in a family doesn't mean giving up who you are. It means sharing who you are. It's not without risk. Our toys, our bodies, our beds, our homes might come back a little worse for the wear. But living faithfully requires a trust that there will be enough to go around. There's enough room in the bedroom for both Harper and Jonathan. There's enough room on my lap for both of them. The hope, here, on those days when I feel stretched to the limit and there are too many people in my bed, is the assurance that there is enough.

This morning, Harper came into the bathroom while I was in the shower. Though we're working on privacy, we still pretty much have an open-door policy in our bathroom, and there are often moments in the morning rush when all four of us are in there. (Why yes, I *am* dreading the teenage years.) But this morning Rob was off at the gym, and Jonathan was still in his crib, so it was just the two of us. She was in a good mood and dressed already—something of a miracle in itself—and though I don't think she had anything she needed to do in the bathroom, she gravitates toward people and doesn't like to be alone.

"Hi, Mom," she said, from the other side of the shower curtain. "I love you."

I smiled and said I loved her too, and went back to washing my hair.

"What comes after L in *love,* Mom?" she asked a minute later.

"O," I said, and vaguely wondered what she was doing. She's just on the verge of reading these days, and often sounds out words or wants to know how to spell something.

When I turned off the water and reached for my towel, she was standing next to the tub, grinning at me. "Look what I did, Mom. See?" In the fog on the mirror above the sink, she had written the words *Mom* and *Love* and had drawn a lopsided smiley face. "Because I couldn't get in the shower to hug you."

Love is a miracle.

Dancing with Her Daddy on a Saturday Morning

On vocation, and praise, and becoming who we are

One Saturday morning, two months before Fiona's second birthday, our family was preparing to move. House-cleaning needs always escalate before a move, as boxes accumulate, accent pieces are packed away, and dusty surfaces and disorganized drawers emerge in the void. Nature abhors a vacuum.

The day's work included hours' worth of cleaning and packing. I'd drawn kitchen duty for the first shift and was unloading the dishwasher while Josh and Fee were in the living room dusting and picking up toddler toys. Fee, like many her age, liked to "clean" and never minded much when we did it, as long as we allowed her to "help." That's all well and good, a habit encouraged by Montessori catalogues full of tiny working carpet sweepers, and one we can indulge, so long as the house is already mostly clean: untidy but not dirty. In those times, we hand her a dust cloth for the coffee table and let her have at it. On this particular morning, however, the work required cleaning products not suitable for toddler use, and Josh's ability to proceed was considerably hampered by her desire to eat the furniture-waxing foam and his need to prevent her from doing so.

Perhaps, then, it is not surprising that only about five minutes after starting, Josh and Fiona were taking a dance break. The stereo was cranked up loud (all the way to eleven), playing a great song called "In the Aeroplane over the Sea" by the brilliantly and oddly named group Neutral Milk Hotel. It features a nice vocal, a strumming guitar, horns, and a saw. I'm not a musician, but to me it sounds like a waltz—melodic and moving.

A few moments after the song began, I heard our (very verbal) girl yelling, "No, Daddy! No dancing like that! Like *this!*"

Glass in hand, I left my kitchen duties to investigate. Josh was standing in the living room, suggesting a variety of cheesy dance moves to the little critic. You've seen them all before—at weddings, at some of the lamer clubs: the school bus, the lawn mower, the sprinkler, the shopping cart. Hipsters perform them ironically; Josh was being silly.

Fiona was not having any of it. She loves to be silly, but every now and again she takes a turn for the earnest. "No, Daddy! Like this!" She lifted her arms and swayed back and forth, and then began to spin.

We try not to laugh at her, because that's mean. But there are times when she is so impossibly cute, so very committed to the appropriateness of something, that we cannot but marvel at her force of will, the particularities of her personality. Wasn't it just yesterday that she was just a tiny, mostly inanimate being? When did she get an opinion?

As amused as I was by her insistence in that moment, the thing that struck me, watching her dance, was how absolutely right she was in chastising her daddy. Of course, she shouldn't have yelled at him . . . but he wasn't moving to the beat. He was dancing, but not to the music. She was swaying back and forth in time; she was listening and feeling the rhythm, and she was so confident she was doing it the right way that she would defend it over another.

As a very small child, I was, by all accounts, a lot like Fiona—willful and chatty and a fierce opponent of naps. My parents celebrate the universe's justice, nearly thirty years in the making. She's a handful. But this was the first time I had realized our shared affinity around dancing. For years my favorite thing had been to put on music and dance around our living room, singing, forcing friends and family to watch "performances." At age six, I dreamed of starring on Broadway; I was convinced I would one day dance with Gene Kelly in a Hollywood musical. (How my heart ached when I saw *That's Entertainment* and realized my dashing would-be co-star was roughly seventy years my senior!)

But eventually that love, and the joy I knew in my living room performances, faded away. I forgot it. It was pushed out of my heart and life by the introduction of actual dance classes—and by fear. And then I stopped dancing. I stopped hearing the beat and listening to music and choreographing my own routines. I ceased dancing for pleasure.

The problem was that when I got to dance classes—ballet and tap at Lynette's School of Dance—I found that it was hard. Hard to coordinate the steps and arm movements, hard to move in time with my fellow dancers and with the music. My feet always seemed too slow, too heavy. And because it was hard, I got frustrated. I was one of those kids who had a hard time sticking with things I wasn't immediately good at; I am what the experts call "lazy." So rather than struggle with dancing, I turned to something I was good at—reading—and retreated into books.

My dance "career" was thus pretty much over by the time I reached upper-elementary school, and as the years of early adolescence arrived, I was resigned to a stereotypical identity as a klutzy, slow, smart girl. Afraid of feeling embarrassed or calling attention to myself, I avoided dancing, and I rarely sang loud enough to be heard in choir. Convinced I was clumsy, I did not trust myself to find and move to the beat. I spent a lot of time at the Springman Junior High Action Dances congregating by the radiators with similarly intimidated girls.

In those years I was routinely told I was smart; everyone believed in me; I was praised and given mountains of incredible academic (and other) opportunities for success. So where did the rampant insecurity come from? Po Bronson and Ashley Merryman, authors of the best-selling book *NurtureShock,* consider the subject of praise and achievement in a chapter called "The Inverse Power of Praise." They explain that kids who are told they're smart are less willing to take risks to try something challenging that might threaten the perception of themselves as smart; kids whose *efforts* and perseverance are rewarded continue to exert effort and achieve more. Apparently, kids are also extremely good at determining when adults are being disingenuous in their praise. They tend to know when they're being patronized and often assume it's because adults think they can't handle the truth. They then begin to fear failure even more, because they believe it's taboo—something that can't even be named.[1]

The responses of kids to the different types of praise that Bronson describes in this chapter (he and Merryman alternate chapters, like Lee and I have done in this book) are consistent with some of my experiences. I was always told I was smart and was generally unwilling to do things for which I lacked an innate talent.

These memories flooded my mind as I watched Fiona sway her arms back and forth. I want to praise her, to honor who she is. I try hard to praise her in the ways Bronson prescribes, because I don't want to exert that "inverse power of praise." But it's a hard speech pattern to set, not least because I want her to know that I love her and delight in her because of *who she is,* not because of *what she does.* Though my parents were raising my sisters and me years before *NurtureShock* hit the shelves, they probably experienced the same qualms about how to encourage my sisters and me without spoiling us or implying that their love was dependent on our achievements. I may have been scared to try new things and to fail; however, it certainly wasn't because I feared *my parents'* judgment or disapproval. Their unconditional love for us was made abundantly clear.

My dad's insistence on the gentle and constant reminder of their love probably came about in part because of his childhood experiences in an affluent, achievement-oriented Chicago suburb in the 1950s. Both my parents were raised, like so many of their peers, to be joiners—to do Scouts and music lessons and sports and to participate in church groups and clubs at school. They were well rounded, exposed to a host of opportunities, and developed some considerable skills before they reached adulthood. My dad sings and plays both bass and guitar (he might have ended up a musician instead of a pastor if it weren't for 8:00 a.m. music theory courses in college), and my mother can build and create things with fabric that you wouldn't believe. They started learning how to do these incredible, life-giving, career-shaping things when they were very young.

In spite of their own early successes, my parents were hugely turned off by the achievement-oriented, push-your-kids-till-they-drop mentality they saw among many parents in the North Shore Chicago communities in which I was raised. They didn't think the greatest virtue a kid could achieve was competitiveness; they were not convinced that a child's worth was best reflected in straight As or MVP status on the traveling soccer team.

That's not to say that we weren't encouraged to do well in school or that we weren't signed up for a variety of classes and opportunities. My sisters and I are joiners, and we value our achievements. I made it into Lynette's School of Dance, after all. But we were allowed to quit. If we decided we didn't want to do something anymore, we weren't made to stick with it. I am, thus, a former dancer, a former trumpet player, and a former runner. I can sew, sort of, if my mother helps me. I can sing and have decent pitch, but I never made it to a music theory class and have trouble reading music. I am able to lead hymns, but my Broadway dreams are not going to be realized in this lifetime. For a long time I told my parents, with falsely inflated indignation, and the assurance of pop-culture psychology that encourages us to blame our parents for everything, that it is their fault I'm not good at anything.

Watching Fiona dance, reflecting on *how* I convey my love, I also recalled something my dad would often say in the midst of conciliatory talks we'd share after an argument about my curfew or my boyfriend or the relationship between the two. He claimed my biggest liability growing up was his childhood and adolescence; he regularly admitted that he parented in response to his own joys and risk-seeking behaviors more than my own. I absolutely don't want to parent Fiona *that way* . . . except for sometimes.

Do you know what I mean? My primary objection to my dad's claim all those years ago was that I believed I needed to experience things for myself. I needed to go through heartbreak and struggle and feel the consequences of my choices. I was irritated beyond measure that he would assume he could or should protect me from them. And yet here I sit, a scant fifteen years later, plotting to parent my kid the same way.

Parenting well seems to require a certain amount of self-reflection. We're supposed to be aware of how we were raised so that we can avoid the particular pitfalls of our upbringing. But we also need to note the wonderful, generative things our parents did so that we can make a point to repeat them. That approach makes sense, to a point. But the world has changed in some ways, and our kids are *not us.* They are their own people. This is something I really struggle with, given the myriad similarities between my daughters and me.

Watching Fiona dance that morning, seeing her concentration and her commitment to the task at hand—dancing to the music—I wanted things to be different for her from the way they were for me. I longed for the sure knowledge that I could help her sustain her joy, her ease, and her trust in herself. I wanted a failsafe way to protect her from the fear of failure that kept me, for so long, from trying new things, from spending time trying to gain skills in areas that challenged me. I wanted her to know grace.

I know, let me assure you, that all this "angsting" about her future was far too much to put on a toddler who was just dancing with her daddy on a Saturday morning. But this reflection is not all about angst; I wonder about Fiona's future in moments of amusement and joy as well. As I consider my responsibilities as a parent, I find myself pondering heavy questions. *Who is this small person? Who will she be?*

I love Fiona now and have since before she was born, before she was herself. I will always love her, and I want her to know the unconditional nature of my love. I want her to be assured that I will love her, whoever she turns out to be. Still, I wonder about who she will be, because, as her mother, I have some responsibilities toward her—to keep her safe and fed and loved, but also to help her to discover her vocation. *How can I help her become the person God has called and created her to be?*

In Christian tradition, this question of who each of us will be is a question not just of identity but of "vocation." *Who am I?* is related to *Who does God want me to be, and what does God call me to do with this life?* The word *vocation* comes from the Latin word *vocare*, which is "to call." My high school language was German, so my first association with the notion of calling was *beruf* (because the churches I grew up in hadn't given me any familiarity with it in a Christian context), which is usually defined as either "calling" or "profession." *Berufen*, the verb, though, isn't the word you'd use if you were going to call out to a person or call someone on the phone; it's meaning is closer to "appoint." Vocation, then, is about what God appoints us to do.

Everybody has a vocation—at least one—which is to say that everybody has gifts and graces and can do something with them in the world, and that those gifts and graces, and the vocations they point to, will carve out and pave the particular paths our discipleship will take. If we're lucky, our vocational lives will play a part in our professional lives. (Like many in the church, I have often thought of *calling* as a synonym for *profession*). But Martin Luther and John

Calvin, among others, say that we also have vocations as spouses and parents and church members and citizens. The wonderful Christian writer and pastor Frederick Buechner acknowledges that discerning our primary vocation is hard. A lot of voices—of success and status, parental and societal expectations—can make it hard for us to hear what God is calling us to do.[2] (I had a friend whose parents would support her to the ends of the earth but who believed the only two acceptable professions for her to pursue were law or medicine. Their expectations caused her no small amount of stress in college as she discovered her great love of American studies classes and her great loathing of organic chemistry. She's a doctor now, and I think she still wonders if it's because medicine is her true calling or because it was her parents' hope for her.)

Buechner offers us a rule of thumb for honing in on the voice of God through all the distortion: "By and large a good rule for finding out [your vocation] is this: The kind of work God usually calls you to is the kind of work (a) that you need most to do and (b) that the world most needs to have done." He vetoes serving as a doctor in a leper colony, even though that's an incredibly noble thing, if you discover that such work saps your will to live. But he also rejects writing cigarette ads as a vocation, even if you really enjoy it. "Neither the hair shirt nor the soft berth will do. The place God calls you to is the place where your deep gladness and the world's deep hunger meet."[3]

Sometimes finding one's deep gladness is harder than it sounds. I have two master's degrees and have worked in churches for nearly a decade, and I still ask myself most days what I am going to be when I grow up. (Josh just *adores* this, because I prefer to entertain these questions aloud as he is trying to fall asleep beside me. When I point out that this is often the only time we have together to talk, he, in turn, reminds me of his 5:00 a.m. alarm and my tendency to work myself into insomnia.) I am pretty clear, though, that whatever I do, I'll be in ministry somehow, and I'll be writing. I'm also remarkably clear about my vocation as a mother and as

Josh's partner in crime. I have the gifts and graces, the passion and commitment (most days at any rate) to parent *these* girls and to be married to *this* man.

In the long run, it hasn't been all that terrible that I left dancing behind. It was neither my heart's great passion nor the world's great need from me. That's not to say that it isn't the vocation for some; my friend Jaime danced and danced and finally decided not to finish college so she would have more time to teach dancing. And she's a wonderful dance teacher, helping kids and adults express themselves, stay fit, and have fun through dance classes at a local park district.

Finding one's vocation is a tricky thing, because vocation isn't synonymous with talent or affinity or even passion. We keep changing throughout our lives, and the world's needs keep changing. But that dynamic reality is exciting, too. My mother, who sewed and worked in the theater, claimed she never had the patience for kids. But eventually she started teaching drama in a high school, and found she loved it. As it happens, the school district in which she works has attracted a lot of families with autistic kids. She's found that drama classes can help autistic kids gain skills in communication and practicing empathy. So she and a special ed teacher designed a first-of-its-kind course in which autistic and gen ed students work together—the gen ed kids learn about teaching drama and special ed, and the autistic kids practice those much-needed skills according to their individually tailored learning goals. It's not like her Drama 4 class, where everybody's trying to be a star, nor is it a self-contained special ed class. Watching the students learn to work together, and to hurdle barriers of development and experience, is incredible and awe-inspiring and heartbreaking, and if you'd asked her twenty years ago if this would be her work, she would have called you crazy.

Vocation requires us to make a difference in the world, and to that end, we need not only to figure out *the means* by which we might make that difference, we must also acquire the skills to do it. The burden of equipping our kids for a changing world and a changing economy can be downright unbearable for parents who want to prepare their kids for anything and everything that might come their way. But we also don't want to limit our kids by forcing them into choosing a vocation or focusing on one of their gifts at too early an age. A friend of mine, mother to triplets, is nearly moved to violence when someone asks her (in front of her kids! What is it with people?) which one is the pretty one, and which one is the smart one, and which one is the athletic one. Stacy wants to affirm the differences between her girls, but she also wants to avoid at all costs typecasting them in their own lives.

Stacy's recognition that her daughters are uniquely gifted individuals, despite their threesomeness, is taken to an extreme by many U.S. parents, who want their children to believe they can do anything, be anything. This vision of limitless success is our national dream and the way so many parents translate their love for their kids into hope for their future. An astronaut, the president, a surgeon, a star—*whatever you want to be, darling.* Po Bronson, author of the chapter on praise in *NurtureShock,* recognizes that navigating the murky waters between unconditional love and equipping kids to meet high expectations (and the demands of our economy) can be an incredibly difficult task and posits that many parents resolve it by taking up the tenets of "self-esteem culture." Bronson illustrates the hazards of this approach by citing an interview with a teacher, who reported, "I had a mother say, 'You are destroying my child's self-esteem,' because I'd given her son a C. I told her, 'Your child is capable of better work.' I'm not there to make them *feel* better. I'm there to make them *do* better."[4]

We parents are our children's first teachers, of course, but we're called to nurture and love them in ways teachers aren't. We *are* called to help our kids feel better, to help them grow into a sense of self. But, my educator husband reminds me, it's neither loving nor nurturing to lie to kids about their abilities, to leave them to be taught about their limitations by the big, cold world.

In 2011, *The Wall Street Journal* sparked a national conversation about expectations, praise, and parental styles when the paper published "Why Chinese Mothers Are Superior," an article excerpted from legal scholar Amy Chua's memoir, *Battle Hymn of the Tiger Mother.* Chua, who has written several other books, got a lot of flack (and publicity) for taking aim at (admittedly, an intentionally straw-man version of) what she called "Western parents," who are, she argued, infinitely inferior at raising successful children than Chinese parents. The book seems to suggest that being a strict parent with incredibly high, even unreachable expectations and forbidding most beloved and time-consuming childhood pursuits is a surefire way to get your kid performing at Carnegie Hall before reaching the age of majority. Chua has done a lot of backpeddling in the face of the flack, reminding critics that the book is memoir, not manual, and that it's largely a story of self-parody in which her kids get all the best lines.

I bought the book, albeit at deep discount at a closing bookstore, because despite all the inflated controversy, Chua spoke to my regrets about my childhood reluctance to stick with difficult projects. Chua writes:

> What Chinese parents understand is that nothing is fun until you're good at it. To get good at anything you have to work, and children on their own never want to work, which is why it is crucial to override their preferences. Tenacious practice, practice, practice is crucial for excellence; rote repetition is underrated in America. Once a child starts to excel at something—whether it's math, piano, pitching, or ballet—he or she gets praise, admiration, and satisfaction. This builds confidence and makes the once not-fun activity fun.[5]

Chua points out that both types of parents in the strict ideological dichotomy she's constructed, *both* Western and Chinese parents, love their children. But she contends that Western parents err by worrying so much about developing children's self-esteem that they praise them at every turn, refrain from criticism, and allow them to set their own limits. Chinese parents, on the other hand, believe their children can do anything they put their minds to, as long as they're willing to work hard enough. The children will be confident and proud as they see their skills grow. If you love your kids, you work them until they develop skills and mastery.

I think there's something to this: Parents should help their children develop skills and learn to stretch themselves, as their kids discover and develop the gifts that will point them to their vocations. Maybe if my parents had kept at me with the trumpet, I might have acquired some discipline that would have helped me as a student and a writer, or developed the confidence that mastery of a difficult endeavor brings.

These days, Fiona doesn't seem to be lacking confidence. But wherever this confidence came from, she didn't develop it in response to any particular mastery. When we got a piano shortly after her fourth birthday, Miss Confident climbed up on the bench and began banging *(Gently, please!)* on the keys. Beyond excited to own a piano, about all that represented in my mind, I enthusiastically asked my big girl, "Would you like to have lessons, to learn how to play?"

"I don't need lessons! I'm an expert!" she retorted.

Despite her declaration, I do intend to get Fiona some piano lessons. After all, without mastery, her confidence is a false one, and I want her deep gladness to have a sturdy foundation. I regret that I never learned to play the piano; I have to rely on the cyber-hymnal (www.hymntime.com) to help me pick out hymn tunes. Lee credits her early piano lessons with leading her to play the flute, which helped her grow into a love of music and gave her an ability to read music that very much facilitates the communal singing we both so love in Christian worship. Because the world's hunger seems to grow ever deeper, it's important for all of us to have a wide variety of skills at our disposal, even if their usefulness isn't immediately obvious.

What was interesting to me about Amy Chua's book was her general lack of concern about the usefulness of the skills her kids acquired as musicians. She definitely did not intend for them to become musicians. She wanted them to learn discipline, and she knows music helps with math, and she made some claims about aesthetics.

I admire the way Chua dedicated so much time to helping her girls become excellent musicians and students. But two things in particular troubled me deeply, and I hope to avoid them as we begin to introduce Fiona to lessons and skills and hobbies: the way she often spoke harshly to her children and the bar she set for measuring their achievements. Although she writes, "If I could push a magic button and choose either happiness or success for my children, I'd choose happiness in a second,"[6] her account belies this choice. We can't repeatedly sacrifice the short-term joy and play and self-discovery of our kids and still expect them to be happy in the long run any more than we can continually give in to their every whim and imagine they'll grow up to be anything other than unsocialized, undisciplined, spoiled monsters (with an overestimation of their self-worth).

There are—there must be—ways to parent kids that help them find joy and success in their vocations and yet don't emphasize the constant need for ever more elaborate forms of outside affirmation (for kid or Tiger Mother). I grew up, as I mentioned, in affluent towns, blessed with excellent public schools and abundant resources. Friends of mine grew up to get MBAs from Wharton, become Rhodes Scholars, and earn PhDs. (They also work for the marginalized, serve on the boards of philanthropies, and take their poorer friends like me out to dinner.) One of my friends played with the Chicago Symphony Orchestra while we were still in high school. I am now quite accustomed to *not* being the smartest kid in the room, and I am A-okay with that. Some of my college friends had been valedictorians at their high schools, and they were temporarily undone when they got to a bigger pond and discovered there were a lot more fish swimming around. If they weren't the biggest fish, the best student, they didn't quite know who they were supposed to be.

What made me mostly okay with being less impressive than my friends, with having a good, even periodically great, GPA but never being the valedictorian, is, I think, the fact that my parents never expected me to be "the best." And not because of low expectations, but because they seem to believe that, when it comes to things of value, there's no such thing as "the best." Their work—in theater, in ministry, in music—is highly collaborative. In their worlds it takes a lot of skilled people working together to accomplish what needs doing, but the primary accomplishment is measured through not competition but collaboration. What's required, in the body of Christ and beyond, is creativity, not rivalry.

The lessons of creative collaboration my parents modeled are at odds with our culture in a number of ways. While Christian theological anthropology traditionally posits that humans are sinners, even more dominant in U.S. culture is the influence of the anthropology underlying capitalist economic theory, which posits that we're all self-interested and inherently lazy, and competition is the only way to motivate people to act otherwise. My parents and I share some slightly different assumptions; we think humans can be motivated by other things.

When we've found our vocations, or when we're beginning to glimpse what they might be, we may find ourselves motivated by the desire to do our work better, to become more fully in command of our gifts. The writer L. L. Barkat describes how her daughter has stolen her mother's copy of Norton Anthology volume *The Making of a Poem* and has been using it to practice composing different types of poems. Given the stereotypes about the challenges of parenting eighth-grade girls, Barkat appears to be doing something right to have a kid obsessed with a Norton Anthology instead of, say, Justin Bieber or her weight. Barkat writes:

> My girl is a middle-schooler, and she is working harder than I am at the art of poetry.
>
> When we possess a little natural talent for writing, we might be tempted to coast along. Why try to master these things called words? Isn't writing an art? Doesn't that mean we can just let things pour out as they will? I know a lot of writers who don't work very hard, thinking this is no disaster. They set down the first thing that comes to mind, and they want that to be the end of it. I have sometimes been this kind of writer, especially when it comes to poetry.
>
> My girl is a middle schooler. I am not. She is working hard at poetry. I am not. So I steal away and work to change the situation.[7]

Human beings may well be prone to sin and shortsightedness, but we're also made in the image of God—which means, among other things, that we're creative. We're moved and motivated to make new things, to be co-creators with the Creator. We don't need to be "the best." This radically egalitarian understanding of humanity functions better if we're all engaged in life-giving, creative work that utilizes our particular gifts and meets the needs of the world.

While Amy Chua claims that her approach to parenting helps kids earn self-esteem, and that shaming and punishment are positive motivators that encourage growth, I read a lot of fear between the lines of her story and the stories of other parents I've known. Will my kid be able to compete? Will he spend his twenties living in my basement? Will she get a job and stay off drugs?

In both my experience and my theology, fear is generally understood to be a lousy motivator. It gets us moving sometimes but not often in the direction we ought to go. Much more powerful and productive is the willingness to take a chance, to take a risk, to open ourselves to the possibility of failure. And we're far more willing to take those risks, to take those chances, to try something new, if we know there's a net under us.

Po Bronson, trying to change the way he praised his son and equipped him for life, found that his son responded well to the emphasis on his efforts rather than his virtues. But Bronson discovered that he, as the dad, was the real "praise junkie" in the family. He missed offering universal praise and realized that "'You're great—I'm proud of you' was a way [he] expressed unconditional love."[8] Busy parents, especially those of us who don't feel we're able to spend enough quality time with our kids after long school and work days, want to cram words of affirmation in at every possible opportunity, to let our kids know "we are in your corner, we are here for you, we believe in you."[9]

Now, perhaps this is a pedestrian observation, but I can't help wondering if parents might convey that to their children by actually telling them, regularly, that they love them unconditionally. Josh and I do this all the time. We learned it from our parents, who cooed the words at us from infancy, and never quit, even when we were arguing, even when we rolled our eyes at them.

I don't know how or if that sort of assurance has a place in the *NurtureShock* or Tiger Mother worldview. But it's been a key part of how I was raised and how I hope to raise my girls: I want them to know they are loved beyond measure, beyond reason, simply because of who they are. They are beloved; I want that knowledge to one day give them the courage they need to go out and find their callings. In theological terms, we call this the assurance of grace. It comes from Romans 8, where the apostle Paul assures us that nothing in all creation can separate us from the love of God: not angels nor demons, not a B-, or even a C-.

What will Fiona be when she grows up? What will her service to the world be? I have no idea. Not yet. And I'm fairly certain she doesn't know yet, either. Very few of us know at such an early age enough about the needs of the world or the passions of our hearts to name our vocations. Parker Palmer, a Quaker writer of some renown, tells about how he always imagined that he would be a naval pilot when he grew up. He didn't follow that path, for a variety of reasons. But he looks back at his childhood obsessions with the military and the air, and can see his passion. The other thing he sees now, with the benefit of fifty years of hindsight, is that he kept meticulous little books, full of notes and drawings. Of planes, mostly. But he didn't become a pilot; he became a writer.[10]

I was fairly lousy at the trumpet and never felt comfortable on a dance floor until I got to college and could ease my fears with a drink or two. (I can dance now. Not well, but comfortably, sober. I consider this a sign that either I am finally a grown-up or I have lost of most of my capacity to be embarrassed.) But I have found a vocation, even several vocations, as a parent and a spouse and a minister and a writer. My parents and I fought constantly about how much time I spent on the phone with my friends. The only class I always excelled in was English. No matter what else I did, I always turned in my journal. I could produce pages of personal reflection. And guess what? I am a pastor and a writer, one who wishes she could play the piano or enjoyed working out, but who spends the bulk of her professional life talking with people—on the phone, in person—and writing about her reflections on life, God, and Scripture. Go figure.

It is such fun to wonder about who Fiona—and now, who Miss Callie—will become. I delight in getting to know them in their particularity and in seeing their joy in discovering themselves. Of course, parents play an incredible role in shaping their children's lives and the people they grow to be. Josh and I note that Fiona is a petite person. We wonder if she might want to be a gymnast or a dancer or a jockey. We speculate about what we might do if she found a talent and a passion for one of those pursuits. Would we take her to lessons and workouts at six in the morning? Would we shell out for coaches and equipment? Would we let her miss church for competitions? C. S. Lewis once wrote that a book cannot be something its writer is not;[11] I sometimes wonder if a kid can be something his or her parent is not. Is Fiona out of the running for the Olympics simply because I am her mother?

I don't want to limit my girls. What I want for my kids is nothing short of the abundant life Jesus describes, a life full of opportunities to love and flourish. I do believe, though—and I have seen this in my ministry and among family and friends—that contentment and joy come in finding your place in the world, in doing something you love. If you can find those things, or start to name them, the rest begins to fall into place.

As Fiona grows in self-knowledge, I hope and pray her experience of her own limitations will be enlightening and not too devastating. *(Dear Lord, please do not let her deep gladness be in basketball, as there is no way she will ever be tall enough.)* I want her, in whatever she pursues in this life, in whatever her calling turns out to be, to find a way to be her truest self, to grow into the person God has called and created and gifted her to be.

In the early 1970s the prolific church historian Martin Marty wrote a slim volume on vocation called *You Are Promise.* (It features some awesomely terrible, circa-1973 psychedelic drawings.) The book is a charming entry to a range of philosophical and theological discussions about the nature of human life and our sense of identity in the modern world. But the title pretty much says it all.

You are promise, my darling.

You are my beloved, with whom I am well pleased.

May the Holy Spirit guide you in the way that leads to life eternal. And if you discern that your heart's deep gladness really requires toe shoes or 6:00 a.m. practices, know that I will do my best to honor God's call on your life.

Of All the Years

*On change, and the passage of time,
and the assurance of grace*

Time, like an ever-rolling stream, soon bears us all away.
—Isaac Watts, "O God, Our Help in Ages Past"

Lord, you have been our dwelling place in all generations.
Before the mountains were brought forth,
or ever you had formed the earth and the world,
from everlasting to everlasting you are God.

—Psalm 90:1-2

IT IS THE WEEK OF THANKSGIVING, AND JOSH AND BROMLEIGH AND
their girls are visiting, making their annual trek east to visit family
for the holiday. It's been almost exactly five years since that visit to
the microbrewery where Bromleigh had her telltale cup of decaf
coffee. That night, there were just the four of us, and we didn't have
to worry about high chairs or bedtimes. Now, our families have
doubled in size. There are eight of us, and our house is filled with
the sounds of giggling preschoolers, a not-quite-talking toddler, a
wailing baby, and four grown-ups eager to catch up on one another's lives.

Before dinner, Fiona and Harper invade the dress-up bin and develop some kind of game, the details of which we adults aren't privy to. Though it's been two years since the last time they'd played together, they seem to be enjoying each other.

"I'm so pleased," Bromleigh says to me, after they have paraded through the kitchen, Harper wearing high heels and a princess dress; Fiona, gold slippers and a ballet outfit.

"I know! We'd be so sad if they didn't get along."

The princess and the ballerina have to contend with Callie, who, at eighteen months, follows them around the house. "Let her play with you," Bromleigh reminds them, and the older girls do a decent job of including her. Later, at bedtime, we take a picture of the four of them in their pajamas, everybody in pink except Jonathan, barely eight weeks old, who lies gamely on his sister's lap. We can't get all of them to look at the camera at the same time, but it doesn't matter. The picture is cute anyway.

It occurs to me that the next time the four of them are all together, Callie and Jonathan will be entirely different people. Callie will have mastered the words she is working so hard on now. Jonathan will be the one toddling behind the bigger kids and wanting to play. Harper and Fiona will start kindergarten this fall; the next time they play together, they won't be preschoolers anymore.

Time, like an ever-rolling stream, soon bears us all away.

In the early weeks after Jonathan was born, my regular nursing spot was a couch in our den, near a big window that overlooks our backyard. He was born in late September, which in North Carolina is still essentially summer, and the leaves on the tree outside our den window were full and green. Because I had to sit still during those weeks of nursing (what a gift it is to feed a baby: You literally have to sit still to do it), I noticed the leaves falling in a way I hadn't before. Gradually they'd fall, one at a time, or sometimes many would come down in a big flurry with a gust of wind. Every day there were fewer and fewer on the tree, and by the time I went back to work and stopped sitting there quite so regularly, the tree was nearly bare. The squirrels had to scurry up to the highest flimsy branches to get the acorns still lingering there.

That tree has become an anchor for me as I've nearly come unmoored at the thought of how quickly Jonathan's babyhood is slipping away. Going back to the doctor for my six-week post-partum checkup, a wave of sadness hit me. I found myself missing those last weeks of being pregnant. Maybe not the swollen ankles, but the anticipation, the nesting, the closeness of our family, the sense of excitement that came in knowing everything was about to change. I won't have that again, I don't think. I don't expect we'll have another newborn sleeping in the corner of our room. Gone are the days when I would spend hours doing nothing more than eating lunch and holding a baby. That season is over.

It's okay. It's sad, and I miss it—but it's okay. I won't be in college again either, or a newlywed. Seasons change. I miss the newborn that Jonathan was, but I love the roly-poly ball of smiles he is becoming. I miss the toddler that Harper was, seemingly just an instant ago, but I love the inquisitive, imaginative, creative kid she is now. I miss that other season, but this season is good, too.

It won't be long, I know, before that tree in the back yard is budding, before its leaves are green again. Jonathan will be crawling by then, I suspect, and I'll be chasing him instead of sitting in the den and watching the seasons change. But there's something comforting about the cyclical nature of the seasons: The leaves always come back.

From everlasting to everlasting, you are God.

My mother saved a number of books from my childhood to give to her grandchildren. They show up, occasionally, tucked into birthday packages or left behind after she visits. A recent favorite is a slim little paperback called *Little Raccoon and the Thing in the Pool.* It's falling apart, now, but we still love the story contained on the tattered pages.

Little Raccoon's mother sends Little Raccoon fishing for crayfish to bring home for supper. He's never gone by himself, and the best place to catch crayfish is at the running stream, on the far side of the big pool. When he gets there, Little Raccoon peers into the water and sees a threatening face. Frightened, he turns and runs all the way home, where his mother convinces him to try again:

> "Just smile," said Mother Raccoon.
> "Is that all?" asked Little Raccoon. "Are you sure?"
> "That is all," said his mother. "I am sure."
> Little Raccoon was brave and his mother was sure. So he went all the way back to the pool again.[1]

It turns out, of course, that the thing in the pool is Little Raccoon's reflection, and once he smiles at it, it stops being frightening. "Little Raccoon was brave, and his mother was sure." His mother's assurance that all will be well gives Little Raccoon the confidence to go out into the big, scary world.

Once, at a swim lesson when Harper was about three and a half, she did not want to get into the water. She'd been taking lessons for quite a while by then, and there was nothing new about what the kids were learning on this particular day. But something had set her off, and she did not want to go. She stood next to the swimming pool holding on to my hand, and no amount of encouragement or demand on my part would convince her to change her mind. I finally realized: *I have to let go first.* So I squirmed my hand out of hers, gave her a kiss on the head, and went to sit down on the bleachers to watch. She looked at me for a minute and then turned to join her class in the water. I don't know exactly what was going through her mind that day, whether she was scared or just feeling ornery. But what I hope is that she felt safe. I want her to trust in my confidence. Not that everything will always go well, but that everything will be *all right.*

I don't always feel sure, of course (and I suspect that Mother Raccoon didn't either). It's unnerving the way time flies, the way these seasons change so fast. I don't know what life will be like when Harper heads to kindergarten next year. I don't know what to expect or what scary things await us. But I am *sure*: of my love for her, of God's love for her, of God's faithfulness to all of us.

These lives of ours are fleeting. The seasons keep changing. We are grateful for the everlasting, unchanging, abiding love of God.

Notes

Foreword
1. David James Duncan, *The Brothers K* (New York: Bantam, 1992).

Introduction: The Hopes and Fears
1. Glennon Melton, "Happy Birthday, Precious Monkees!" Momastery. com, July 25, 2010.

Chapter 1: Leap of Faith
1. Lori Leibovich, ed., *Maybe Baby* (New York: Salon Media Group, 2006), xvi.
2. Frank Rogers Jr., "Discernment," *Practicing Our Faith: A Way of Life for a Searching People,* ed. Dorothy C. Bass (San Francisco: Jossey-Bass, 1997), 107.
3. Ibid., 106.
4. "Way open" and "letting your life speak" are traditional Quaker notions. I found Parker Palmer's book *Let Your Life Speak: Listening for the Voice of Vocation* (San Francisco: Jossey-Bass, 2000) to be particularly helpful.

Chapter 2: My Body, My Fault
1. Harold S. Kushner, *When Bad Things Happen to Good People* (New York: Schocken Books, 2001).
2. Ibid., 65–66.
3. H. Richard Niebuhr, *The Responsible Self: An Essay in Christian Moral Philosophy* (Louisville: Westminster John Knox, 1999), 177.

Chapter 3: Called by Name
1. We conceded this point, slightly, with our second child; Jonathan is, in fact, a biblical name.

2. Lois Lane is, of course, Superman's longtime girlfriend.

3. Kahlil Gibran, *The Prophet* (New York: Knopf, 1997), 17.

4. The biblical tradition is full of meaning-laden names. The Hebrew people are called Israel because they are descendants of Jacob, whose name was changed to Israel—meaning "one who strives with God"—after he wrestled with an angel on the banks of the Jabbok (Gen. 32). Abram becomes Abraham—"ancestor of a multitude"—when God makes the covenant with him (Gen. 17). Jesus is the Greek form of the Hebrew name Joshua, which means "The Lord saves." The book of Ruth is particularly fun: All the main characters have significant names, including my two favorites, Naomi's sons. Their names mean something like "Sickness" and "Spent," appropriate for characters who die a mere five verses into the story. Even the name of God reminds us that our names are intimately tied up with who we are: When Moses, at the burning bush, asks about God's name, God replies: "I am who I am" (Exod. 3). And many more . . .

5. Mark G. Toulouse, *Joined in Discipleship: The Shaping of Contemporary Disciples Identity* (St. Louis: Chalice Press, 1997), 142–43.

6. http://www.disciples.org/AboutTheDisciples/TheDesignofthe ChristianChurch/tabid/228/Default.aspx

CHAPTER 4: BEDTIME

1. Madeleine L'Engle, *The Irrational Season* (San Francisco: Harper SanFrancisco, 1977), 44.

2. Meredith F. Small, *Our Babies, Ourselves* (New York: Doubleday Books, 1998).

3. Peter Berger, *A Rumor of Angels: Modern Society and the Rediscovery of the Supernatural* (New York: Doubleday & Co., 1969), 68.

4. Ibid., 70–71, emphasis mine.

5. Julian of Norwich, *Revelations of Divine Love* (London: Penguin Classics, 1998), 85–86.

CHAPTER 5: GOOD WORK

1. Abraham Joshua Heschel, *The Sabbath* (New York: Farrar, Straus and Giroux, 1951), 13.

2. Ibid., 22–23.

3. Thich Nhat Hanh, *The Miracle of Mindfulness: An Introduction to the Practice of Meditation* (Boston: Beacon Press, 1975), 4.

4. I'm dearly looking forward to reading MaryAnn McKibben Dana's forthcoming book *Sabbath in the Suburbs* (St. Louis: Chalice Press,

2012), which chronicles her family's attempt to practice sabbath in the midst of their busy lives.

Chapter 6: Cuddling, and Other Not-So-Precious Things about Incarnation

1. http://www.sortacrunchy.net/sortacrunchy/. I don't read this blog, but my friend, the writer and pastor Katherine Willis Pershey, does, and she introduced the phrase to my personal lexicon.
2. "A Service of Word and Table I," *The United Methodist Hymnal* (Nashville: The United Methodist Publishing House, 1989), 10.
3. Reinhold Niebuhr, *The Children of Light and the Children of Darkness* (Upper Saddle River, NJ: Prentice Hall, 1974).
4. Serene Jones, "What's Wrong with Us?" in *Essentials of Christian Theology,* ed. William Placher (Louisville: Westminster John Knox Press, 2003).
5. Kim Barker, Linda de Meillon, and Leigh Harrison, *Birthed in Prayer: Pregnancy as Spiritual Journey* (Nashville: Upper Room Books, 2008), 146.
6. Ibid., 147.
7. Kristine A. Culp, *Vulnerability and Glory: A Theological Account* (Louisville: Westminster John Knox, 2010).

Chapter 7: Saying Grace

1. Marcus J. Borg, *The Heart of Christianity: Rediscovering a Life of Faith* (New York: HarperCollins, 2003), 114.
2. I now give this book away at baby dedications, because I love it so much: Desmond M. Tutu, *Children of God Storybook Bible* (Grand Rapids: Zondervan, 2010).

Chapter 8: I'm the Mommy, That's Why

1. Tina Fey, *Bossypants* (New York: Little, Brown and Company, 2011), 240.
2. Immanuel Kant, "Grounding for the Metaphysics of Morals," in *Classics of Moral and Political Theory, Second Edition,* ed. Michael L. Morgan (Indianapolis: Hackett Publishing Company, 1996), 1004. *Act as if the maxim of your action were to become through your will a universal law of nature.*
3. http://archives.umc.org/interior.asp?ptid=1&mid=1649
4. W. Stephen Gunter, et al., *Wesley and the Quadrilateral: Renewing the Conversation* (Nashville: Abingdon Press, 1997).

5. Ayelet Waldman, *Bad Mother: A Chronicle of Maternal Crimes, Minor Calamities, and Occasional Moments of Grace* (New York: Doubleday, 2009), 122–136.

6. Marybeth Hicks, *Bringing Up Geeks* (New York: Berkley Trade, 2008).

7. So wonderful. You really must have it for your collection. Marie-Hélène Delval, *Images of God for Young Children* (Grand Rapids, MI: Eerdmans Books for Young Readers, 2011).

8. Ibid., 82.

CHAPTER 9: WASHING THE DIAPERS

1. http://lens.blogs.nytimes.com/2011/08/04/where-children-sleep/

2. Bonnie Miller-McLemore, *In the Midst of Chaos: Caring for Children as Spiritual Practice* (San Francisco: Jossey-Bass, 2007), 104.

3. Bromleigh McCleneghan, http://www.ministrymatters.com/all/article/entry/1087/talking-to-kids-about-bin-laden

4. http://www.weekofcompassion.org/storage/pdf/SharingCalendar12.pdf

CHAPTER 10: THE RAGE

1. Nick Hornby, *The Polysyllabic Spree* (San Francisco: Believer Books, 2004), 125.

2. Gary Chapman, *Anger: Handling a Powerful Emotion in a Healthy Way* (Chicago: Northfield Publishing), 61.

3. Ibid., 63.

4. The National Center on Shaken Baby Syndrome, http://www.dont-shake.org/sbs.php?topNavID=3&subNavID=21&navID=21#8

5. Alice Park, "Study: Shaken-Baby Cases Rose During the Recession," *Time,* May 3, 2010.

6. Harvey Karp, *The Happiest Baby on the Block: The New Way to Calm Crying and Help Your Newborn Baby Sleep Longer* (New York: Bantam Books, 2003), 62.

7. Paul Tillich, *Systematic Theology, Volume II: Existence and the Christ* (Chicago: The University of Chicago, 1957), 76–77.

8. Lisa Belkin, "When Mom and Dad Share It All," *New York Times Magazine,* June 15, 2008. Online at http://www.nytimes.com/2008/06/15/magazine/15parenting-t.html?pagewanted=all

9. "A Satellite Stars and an Ocean Behind You," words and music by John Dragonetti and Blake Hazard, on *Love Notes, LetterBombs,* released April 2011.

10. Madeleine L'Engle, *Two-Part Invention: The Story of a Marriage* (New York: Harper One: 1988), 89.

CHAPTER 11: BIRTHDAYS AND BABY BOOKS

1. Carleen Healy, http://www.nickandcarleen.blogspot.com/2012/02/memory-keeping.html

2. Bonnie Miller-McLemore explores the holiness of everyday life in a family in her chapter "Sanctifying the Ordinary," in *In the Midst of Chaos: Caring for Children as Spiritual Practice* (San Francisco: Jossey-Bass, 2007), 21ff.

3. Barbara Brown Taylor, *An Altar in the World* (New York: Harper Collins, 2009), xix.

4. Ibid., 23.

5. Quoted in Marcus Borg, *Heart of Christianity: Rediscovering a Life of Faith* (San Francisco: HarperSanFrancisco, 2004), 155, from an audiotape provided by Rev. David McConnell, a United Methodist pastor in Montana.

6. MaryAnn McKibben Dana, *The Blue Room* blog: http://theblue-roomblog.org/2011/10/03/what-it-means-to-be-attentive/

7. MaryAnn McKibben Dana, http://theblueroomblog.org/2011/09/08/the-memory-project//. Dana also links to http://www.happiness-project.com/happiness_project/2007/08/why-i-started-k.html, where Gretchen Rubin talks about one-sentence journals.

8. MaryAnn McKibben Dana, http://theblueroomblog.org/2012/02/22/update-on-the-memory-project/

9. There's some debate in my family as to where this song came from. Our best guess is that we learned it from a Mennonite congregation we spent some time with when my sister and I were little.

CHAPTER 12: WHEN CHRISTIAN FEMINISTS GIVE BIRTH TO PRINCESSES

1. Peggy Orenstein, *Cinderella Ate My Daughter: Dispatches from the Front Lines of the New Girlie-Girl Culture* (New York: HarperCollins, 2011), 2.

2. Check out the Intersex Society of North America at http://www.isna.org/ for more information.

3. Bromleigh McCleneghan, "Of Feminism and Pink Things," Fidelia's Sisters, February 2012, www.youngclergywomen.org/the_young_clergy_women_pr/2012/02/of-feminism-and-pink-things.html

4. Betty A. DeBerg, *Ungodly Women: Gender and the First Wave of American Fundamentalism* (Minneapolis: Augsburg Fortress, 1990).
5. Margaret Atwood, *The Handmaid's Tale* (New York: Anchor Books, 1986).
6. Nancy Leigh DeMoss and Dannah Gresh, *Lies Young Women Believe and the Truth that Sets Them Free* (Chicago: Moody Press, 2008).
7. Orenstein, *Cinderella Ate My Daughter*, 13.
8. Ibid., 60.
9. Ibid., 61.
10. DeBerg, *Ungodly Women*.
11. Examples of such titles include James Dobson, *Bringing Up Boys: Practical Advice and Encouragement for Those Shaping the Next Generation of Men* (Carol Stream, IL: Tyndale House, 2001) and *Bringing Up Girls: Practical Advice and Encouragement for Those Shaping the Next Generation of Women* (Carol Stream, IL: Tyndale House, 2010); Pam Farrel and Doreen Hanna, *Raising a Modern-Day Princess: Inspiring Purpose, Value, and Strength in Your Daughter* (Carol Stream, IL: Tyndale House, 2009); and Stephen Arterburn and Fred Stoeker with Mike Yorkey, *Every Young Man's Battle: Strategies for Victory in the Real World of Sexual Temptation* (Colorado Springs: WaterBrook Press, 2009).
12. Phyllis Trible, "Eve and Adam: Genesis 2–3 Reread," in *Womanspirit Rising: A Feminist Reader in Religion,* eds. Carol P. Christ and Judith Plaskow. (San Francisco: HarperSanFrancisco, 1992), 74–83.
13. "When We Grow Up," by Stephen Lawrence (music) and Shelley Miller (lyrics), *Free to Be . . . You and Me (35th Anniversary Edition),* conceived by Marlo Thomas; eds. Carole Hart, Letty Cottin Pogrebin, Mary Rodgers, and Marlo Thomas; original editor: Francine Klagsbrun (Philadelphia: Running Press Kids, 2008).
14. Trible, "Eve and Adam," 76–77.
15. "When We Grow Up."

Chapter 13: Move, Mommy, Move
1. You've seen those commercials, right? Where Toyota tries to convince us that owning a minivan is cool? http://toyotaswaggerwagon.com/
2. Bonnie Miller-McLemore, *In the Midst of Chaos: Caring for Children as Spiritual Practice* (San Francisco: Jossey-Bass, 2007), 80. The chapter "Giving unto Others . . . But What about Myself?" was helpful in my thinking about the role of sharing and sacrifice in family life.

3. Bonnie Miller-McLemore, *Also a Mother: Work and Family as Theological Dilemma* (Nashville: Abingdon Press, 1994), 162.

4. Ibid., 164.

5. Miller-McLemore uses the term *mutuality* as an alternative to self-sacrifice. *In the Midst of Chaos,* 86.

6. Heidi B. Neumark, *Breathing Space: A Spiritual Journey in the South Bronx* (Boston: Beacon Press, 2003), 85.

7. Matthew 14:13–21; Mark 6:31–44; Luke 9:10–17; John 6:5–15. See also Mark 8:1–9 and Matthew 15:32–39.

8. Miller-McLemore, *Also a Mother,* 124.

Chapter 14: Dancing with her Daddy on a Saturday Morning

1. Po Bronson and Ashley Merryman, *NurtureShock* (New York: Twelve, 2009), 11–26.

2. Frederick Buechner, *Wishful Thinking: A Theological ABC* (New York: Harper and Row, 1973).

3. Ibid., 95.

4. Bronson and Merryman, *NurtureShock,* 21.

5. Amy Chua, *Battle Hymn of the Tiger Mother* (New York: The Penguin Press, 2011), 29.

6. http://amychua.com/.

7. L. L. Barkat, *Rumors of Water: Thoughts on Creativity and Writing* (Ossining, NY: T. S. Poetry Press, 2011), 73–74.

8. Bronson and Merryman, *NurtureShock,* 25.

9. Ibid.

10. Parker Palmer, *Let Your Life Speak: Listening for the Voice of Vocation* (San Francisco: Jossey-Bass, 2000), 14–15.

11. Katherine Paterson, "Are You There, God?" *The Best American Spiritual Writing 2006,* ed. Peter J. Gomes (New York: Houghton Mifflin Company, 2006), 201.

Conclusion: Of All the Years

1. Lillian Moore, *Little Raccoon and the Thing in the Pool* (New York: Scholastic Book Services, 1963), 36–38.